WITCH COUNTRY

Seeking the Witch in the British Landscape

SARAH ROBINSON

Womancraft Publishing

Published by Womancraft Publishing, 2025
www.womancraftpublishing.com

ISBN 978-1-916672-04-8

Witch Country is also available in ebook format: ISBN 978-1-916672-05-5

Cover image 'Earth Magic. Primroses & Celandines, West Penwith.' © Sarah Vivian

Illustrations: Lucy H. Pearce

Womancraft Publishing is committed to sharing powerful new women's voices, through a collaborative publishing process. We are proud to midwife this work, however the story, the experiences and the words are the author's alone. A percentage of Womancraft Publishing profits are invested back into the environment reforesting the tropics (via TreeSisters) and forward into the community.

Also by Sarah Robinson

The Witch and the Wildwood: Folk Wisdom, Fairy Tale & Fantastic Lore

The Kitchen Witch Companion: Recipes, Rituals & Reflections (with Lucy H. Pearce)

Kitchen Witch: Food, Folklore & Fairy Tale

Enchanted Journeys: Guided Meditations for Magical Transformation

Yoga for Witches

Yin Magic: how to be still

Praise for *Witch Country*

Full of good stories, this is a thoughtful and warm meditative journey through the witchy locations and landscapes of Britain, drawing on folklore, history and nature writing to guide readers on their own walks and inspire them to appreciate the stories of accused witches.

Marion Gibson, professor of Renaissance and Magical Literatures, University of Exeter, author of *Witchcraft: A History in Thirteen Trials* and *The Witches of St Osyth*

Beautifully written, absorbing and strangely seductive, this book is a panacea; everyone should read it. Robinson's gentle yet powerful journey through the seasons is balm for the soul. It should be in schools, workplaces and the halls of government. Its grounding, healing message is what we all need right now. Robinson for Minister of Magic and Wonder!

Miriam Darlington, *The Times*, author of *Otter Country* and *Owl Sense*

Sarah Robinson takes us with her on an amazing journey of discovery, interweaving the history, legends and superstitions surrounding the much-maligned witches, healers and wisewomen of the past – their stories still preserved in old manuscripts, in old tales, in the landscape, in ancient sites, in caves and woods. This is a sensitive, well researched investigation. It is insightful, thought-provoking and sometimes shocking, as Sarah upturns the history of the witch in our land. She gathers her experiences and explores her relationship with what she discovers – draws from the spirits of place, the sense of 'Other', the wildlife and nature connection that she experiences along the way. Historical facts interweave with tales passed down through countless generations. This is a thoroughly enjoyable read, told with insight, good humour and a refreshing honesty. It is a great inspiration to us all to get out into our ancient landscape and experience our interconnectedness for ourselves.

Glennie Kindred, author of *Earth's Cycle of Celebration, Between the Worlds* and many more

A warm, witty and witchy tour of Britain, attentive to hidden voices, rich folklore and vital history.

Patrick Barkham, natural history writer for *The Guardian*, author of *Badgerlands, Islander* and *The Butterfly Isles*

CONTENTS

MAP

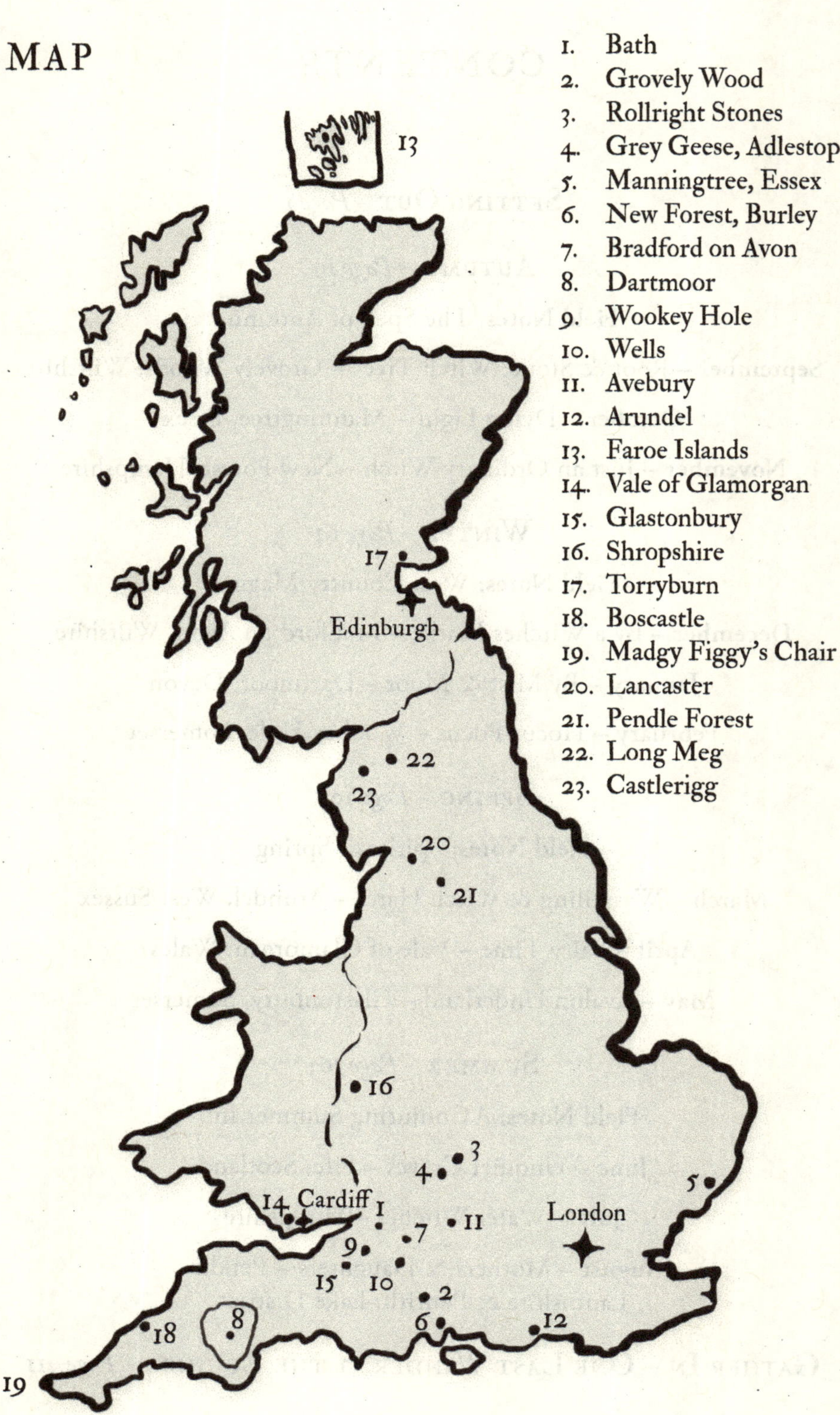

1. Bath
2. Grovely Wood
3. Rollright Stones
4. Grey Geese, Adlestop
5. Manningtree, Essex
6. New Forest, Burley
7. Bradford on Avon
8. Dartmoor
9. Wookey Hole
10. Wells
11. Avebury
12. Arundel
13. Faroe Islands
14. Vale of Glamorgan
15. Glastonbury
16. Shropshire
17. Torryburn
18. Boscastle
19. Madgy Figgy's Chair
20. Lancaster
21. Pendle Forest
22. Long Meg
23. Castlerigg
13
17
Edinburgh
22
23
20
21
16
3
4
5
14
Cardiff
1
11
London
7
9
15
10
2
6
12
8
18
19

Welcome, traveller, to a journey through both the enchanting and the eerie. Alongside tales of wonder and adventure lie narratives of prejudice and cruelty. So, as we navigate these realms, I will do my utmost to do so with reverence and sensitivity. Reader discretion may be advised as we venture into darker territories. My intention is to illuminate the complex stories woven into the fabric of the land alongside the beauty and wonder of the natural world, inviting you to explore with open minds and steady hearts…

SETTING OUT

THE LAND IS FULL OF WITCHES...
THEY ABOUND IN ALL PLACES...*

* Words of Judge Sir Edmund Anderson, given in his address to the jury at the London trial of Elisabeth Jackson, charged with bewitching Mary Glover in 1602. As cited in *A Mirror of Witchcraft*, Christina Hole (1957) and *Witchcraft and Hysteria in Elizabethan London*, Michael MacDonald (1991)

I met with a witch on my walk today, just metres from my front door. She did not have much to say. They often don't. History tells us that accused witches on trial rarely got the chance to speak to their innocence, and anything they did say was seldom considered of value. Or maybe they were too busy flying to all corners of the British Isles raising storms and mists to chat much. But meet a witch I did, which is very appropriate, or maybe somewhat predictable, as I walked from my home in the final days of September. The autumn equinox has passed, meaning we've tipped into the dark half of the year and that hallowed and witchy month of October is looming. Sadly, the witch I encountered was nothing more than a plastic decoration for the Halloween season ahead, a mere caricature of the magic that hangs from the image of the witch, but it is a place to start nonetheless. Maybe this decoration is my prompt to get out there and discover the true symbols of the hair-raising history of the witch – far beyond the fancy dress image of warts and pointed hats that are ubiquitous in our culture.

This is the beginning of a journey, one that will remind me and you, I hope, that we are surrounded by witches in the landscape of Britain. On any given day, on any given walk, you could encounter many. How you might encounter them is so varied and plentiful it does occasionally tip me into overwhelm. They might be in tree form, elder and juniper, for example. They might be as animals – I found stories of the witch transforming into hares, greyhounds, foxes and even bees. You might pass a great standing stone said to be a solidified witch or a woman who danced on a holy day. They may dwell in the mist (or be responsible for it), in foxgloves, or in green water pools. This, of course, is the rich realm of folklore, myth and fairy tale. But you could also just as likely pass a follower of the religion of Wicca* – who are called witches, as well as places of (in)justice where real people were accused and killed for practising witchcraft, or a person who has claimed the name witch for themselves or who, over their lifetime has had the title whispered about them.

* At the time of writing, according to census data of England and Wales 74,000 people identified as pagan and 13,000 as Wiccan, a religion whose roots lie in pre-Christian traditions, folklore, folk witchcraft and ritual magic. (ons.gov.uk Office for National Statistics)

Exploring the landscape

One might and can, explore the landscape in many ways: by visiting ancient sights, pathways and woodland groves, by tracking wildflowers, foraging for herbs and watching birds on migratory paths. I want to explore the landscape with the witch. Why witches? Well, for starters, they are woven into the stories of Britain – our history, religion and myth – the witches fly through them all. The witch figure exists around the world, with varying names and embodiments, every country has ideas and beliefs connected to workers of magic, alongside fear and intrigue of such nebulous powers. I want to address Britain's own unique relationship with our witches through the land as I wander it.

Perhaps the witch will show me enchantment and trickery; perhaps I will see something of the wildness people saw in witches or that witches now may seek to embrace. When witches are hard to grasp, I'll be seeking in nature the deep roots many of these stories feed from. Perhaps in exploring the witch in the natural world, I may understand better how the two have become so intertwined and understand them both a little better. I can only hope so, as I set off with my hiking boots, notebook and pen. I'm going to walk to standing stones, through forests, over routes that accused witches walked and seek out graves, caves and marshes. I'm going to walk around the country (not around the whole country, you understand, but around very small bits, on separate occasions!) seeking the witch and the many ways she (and they) exists here. And the tales held within, and inspired by, these places. I'll seek facts, fairy stories and folklore, alongside snippets of superstitions and 'some once said', to carry me into the stories secreted in the landscape, that may capture something of the magic of a place.

*

Each county, era, village and even each family has its own ideas about witches. Some elements, like making a deal with the devil, once seemed to carry through the majority, especially during the medieval and early modern eras, when the British Isles saw its peak of witch hunts and witch trials. But then strange and fascinating variants seem to rise like steam from a cauldron. For example, in the county of Essex, care was taken to note the familiars of each accused witch, for these 'impes' were believed to be sent abroad by their mistresses to cause death and misfortune in the villages. It's amazing anyone managed to walk along Manningtree High Street during 1645, when it seems as though every woman was sending swarms of diabolical bunnies to do their bidding. In Cornwall, the witches raised storms and danced with fairies. In Scotland, they dined with fairy queens. These were accusations thrown at very real women; all these details are taken from trial notes and dubiously obtained 'confessions'.

Move into folk tales and you'll find in the Lake District, witches were turned to stone for misdemeanours, whereas in Oxfordshire, they turned others to stone and themselves into trees. You'd be forgiven for finding it hard to see the difference and the blurred lines between fact and fiction, history and myth and all the fraying edges in between. But what is true is that superstitions bled into action and accusations and the history of witchcraft has seeped into witch lore and modern practices – it is captivating chaos. But still, stories are what we have, so stories are what I shall seek. As for the 'truth' in each tale, I guess we'll have to take that one muddy footprint at a time. We'll be looking at everything from written accounts of real people who were thought to practise witchcraft, to the far less provable witchy presences in a place, as well as places of hanging, places of cursing and places where modern witches may gather.

It would be entirely possible, of course, to simply list the many places that are connected to the witch (and a very long list it would be). But I want to walk through these stories, feel them under my feet. Letting my experiences add their own lustre to the history, whispered stories and wayward practices. And maybe I will even find a little of what the creators and protagonists of these stories once felt: fear, uncertainty, hunger, weariness of travel as well as joy, hope and enchantment. I won't be putting myself in harm's way, but feel a need to experience these stories where they were first told, rather than just read about them in books. Every tale of the land tells us a little something about the relationship between mythology and the landscape, between us and our stories. Some folk history of the British Isles is intangible – stories, songs, beliefs and superstitions. And there is plenty that is very much tangible: stones said to be witches, trees said to sit atop their buried bodies, caves where they dwelled, plants that they coveted and earth a precious few may rest in. The stories we attach to these things may be open to much interpretation and speculation, but that, you may say is all part of the magic. I am drawn to explore the spaces where literary constructions can pass into folk belief and realms blend between history and magic, possibility and inspiration, and look forward to bringing you with me on the adventure.

What remains of us

Very little remains of real people accused and killed as witches; scant obvious markers because their 'crimes' were hearsay and superstition. It was often no more or less than their very *being* that aggrieved others – their age, manner, power, disability or poverty being just some variables that made them suspect.

Artefacts such as witch bottles, ritual protection marks, charms and poppets are particularly fascinating because they are all that is left to connect us with a past world where magical work was simply part of day-to-day life. The majority of accused witches were women (estimates vary from 80% to 95%) and often poor ones – things they materially left behind were modest but very human. There were no structures, churches, or temples specific to witches beyond the possibly sacred spaces accessible to them, be that grove or hearth. So, physical remnants are special. Perhaps we attach the myths and stories to larger monuments, stones and trees, as a way of bringing the witches and varied pagan ancestors back into the landscape. We are compelled, perhaps, to gather their stories, to create connections and to create places for stories of the witch to land.

*

For millennia, generations of people from many corners of the world have made their home here in Britain, bringing their own ideas of magic and creating their own stories, which have become part of the richly stocked treasury of British folklore and collective story heritage. This is one of many reasons our lore is so rich and fascinating. We have an amazing collection of monuments, artefacts, deities, stories and folklore from varied ancient tribes and religions, from Celts and Romans to Anglo-Saxons and Vikings. Over centuries, stories were and are shared, adapted, blended together and woven into new tales and specific origins lost to time. We'll never know every tale, because every time one is told new magic is woven into it. Tales change with the time, place and teller, I'm regularly reminded that I'll never know them all, as I discover endless iterations of the same tale, and there is a wonderful sense of possibility within that. I am excited to share both some tales that may be familiar to you and some that are more unusual and may be completely new to you.

Not only have witches and magical beings always lived in our stories and our lands; it's also ever-changing. The history of witchcraft is, like folklore (and indeed the landscape), not over, not past; it's here with us each day. Always growing, living, breathing. On this journey, I will meet living witches, pagans and wild storytellers alongside weathered stones and lost myths. Some walks start with a small piece of witch lore and then the journey takes me to other realms, far from the place I started. But I learn through this journey, the witch really is everywhere, even when I stray from the path or find myself lost, I'm still very much in Witch Country.

*

I'm wrapped up in this story as well. Since the end of the last lockdown in 2021 I have struggled to get back out in the world, as though the Covid-19 lockdowns butted up against an inertia I had been slowly building and as I ground to a halt, sometimes I think I am having trouble starting up again. I have found myself more nervous about simple daily tasks of catching buses and trains and going for hikes, as I had fallen out of practice. So, what better way to venture back out into the world than using inspiration from the books I write. I ponder if perhaps I am a bit lost. I have recently passed the milestone of forty – that middle point of things.

I have spent many years cultivating a peaceful, gentle way of life. But perhaps now is a good time to sneak out of my comfort zone. Am I having a midlife crisis? I'm not sure I have the energy for a crisis. This may all sound like a wildly 'first-world problem', with me, a white woman who gets to fill her days writing, walking and doing yoga, boohooing about losing enchantment and motivation. Which to be honest, it kind of is. It's all a frippery, a fritillary lantern in a storm of war and oppression, but as J.R.R. Tolkien's wisest magic worker Gandalf once said: "All we have to decide is what to do with the time that is given us."* So, with my time, part of my time, for a year, I decide to do this…

I moved out of my beloved city of Bath with my partner Dan, to the green outskirts of Wiltshire just a couple of months before the first lockdown began. Like most people, I went from rarely having a day that didn't involve being outside, to days without going outside at all and finding it harder and harder to do so. But alongside this, I was writing books, like *Kitchen Witch* (2022) and *The Witch and the Wildwood* (2024). My days were filled with

* J.R.R. Tolkien, *The Fellowship of the Ring* (1954)

researching and writing about witch women lurking in verdant pools, herb women, wild women and witches – and now, I want to find them, to meet them…to whatever extent that would be possible. I want to get outside and find this enchantment I was writing about. To find the witch in the wild (and in some cases, not so wild) landscape seems like the natural next step: moving from writing of the Cailleach and the Pendle witches, to seeking them in their natural habitats. From marsh witches who brew up morning mists, to witch hares that become women, as well as the rare words and stories that accused witches were allowed to speak: I want to find them and the many places that they may lead. I hope for a lot, maybe too much, but I won't know until I get out there.

Hidden stories & Hope

The journeys ahead may sit somewhere between pilgrimage, folkloric adventure, ramble and 'occult tourism' – terms that together can mean many things. Occult, once meaning hidden and secret, is now associated with all things magical, mystical and supernatural. I'm seeking it all: the magic that shimmers beneath the surface.

I have little doubt I am not alone in feeling that sometimes the modern world can push people to breaking point. That perhaps the constant notifications, emails, meetings, credit scores and commuting are not the way to happy bodies and minds. I find myself regularly frustrated at my own habits of wasting an hour or more scrolling through social media. Many of us may have, at some point, questioned whether a very different life may be better – one that connects us with wild open spaces and feeling the elements on our skin. It was not so very long ago that we as humans saw magic in nature and sought to be at one with it. In a relatively short period, technology has revolutionised the world and a new fast-paced lifestyle has been forced upon us, leaving many people stressed, frantic and out of control. I certainly feel this myself at times. But what if we were to return to lives lived more closely with green spaces and natural places? Even just for an afternoon? Or on a gentle sunny walk? What if we could tap into the deep magic that resides in the plants, trees and ancient places of this world? Could that be healing? Could we create a sort of occult osmosis allowing rich folklore to seep into lives lacking wonder? Magical practice and rural rituals may well be considered charming and quaint and now more closely thought of as the realm of druids, magical workers and ritual observers. But can enchantment, ritual, folklore and wellbeing come together in the natural magic that casts a subtle but powerful spell over us all? Can the witch help me rewild and reenchant myself? Or will she show me what I fear in striking out into the wilds? Maybe both. (Spoiler: it's both).

*

Landscape is always changing, but luckily, some markers of sacredness still stand – stone circles, dolmens, corpse roads and long barrows, for example. But how are we marking the landscape now? Motorways, houses, roundabouts, shopping centres… There is power, perhaps, in re-using sacred sites, reconnecting in the story and sacred ritual of these ancient places – like those who gather at Stonehenge, Avebury, Maeshowe and Newgrange, to treasure the sacred sites of the past so as not to allow them to be bulldozed and replaced with the temples of an uncaring present – another superstore or drive-thru.

I want to find and explore the places we may still see, hear and feel the stories of magic and mischief. To enjoy tales from small acts of rebellion to great grand magical happenings and everything in between. At the very least, this history reminds us that there are other ways of living, being and finding joy – it hasn't always been this way. And whilst we can't go back, we can remember as we move forward.

Is it possible that our love of folklore, often from more rural times, sings so sweetly to us because we are so busy living, rushing in the moment, that we've forgotten our connections with the landscape and how we fit into the natural world? Leaving us feeling lonely, disconnected, disheartened, disenchanted? Does it feel, at the same time, that as a nation we are so confident that we are at the pinnacle of civilisation, enlightenment, facts and science that we are actually missing the possibility and hope held in a past of magic and belief? Are we finding ourselves drawn to seeking something else? Maybe that leads us to pockets of pagan beliefs that still exist in these lands. Or a magic of a landscape that can mean a myriad of different things to different people. Exploring how a place feels – experiencing the spirit or energy of a place – it's all deeply personal and in finding the stories that connect to us and that resonate with us, we are finding our own personal connection and hopefully caring about the landscape.

There seems to me to have been a surge of interest in folklore in the last decade, a result, perhaps, of a desire or need to connect and reconnect to a land and its stories. And rural customs, where a large number of folk traditions and celebrations are born (as a nation, we've lived largely rural lives for far longer than we have urban ones). Maybe we appreciated the wild anew after tumbling back into it when released from our lockdown homes. Seeking with new fervour pathways we'd not (yet) walked, forgotten history, flowers and birds we wanted to learn more about. I know the witch might not be the obvious starting place for some. But for me personally, I can think of no finer guide; they have walked a long way. Their names are not always mentioned, remembered, or respected, but they offer an invitation to uncover all manner of secrets that we may or may not know we are seeking. And a large part of this invitation is to look at the natural world itself, that's where I'm seeking my witches.

I am searching for many things, especially something that is lost – maybe amongst it is the faded image of a rural, more pagan way of life, times of more widespread belief in magic. And something that never existed in the material world: the 'witches' of the witch hunts, as in the handmaidens of the devil, baby-boiling kind who to the best of our knowledge, never existed anywhere other than in fear and superstitions. But some things I seek still exist in the modern day: stories and those who name themselves witches, pagans and/or those who are interested in what we may call 'the old ways'. Witches and workers of magic are held in oscillating correlations of fascinating and fear-inducing – from the ancient past all the way up to today. Witch is still a relevant word, still used in good and bad ways and still a symbol of empowerment for some. The witch is also, I believe, a powerful way of talking about the nature of the earth and of society; the witch sits at the centre of the long histories of humans trying to figure out how the world works. When you look at the landscape, traces can be seen of what went before and who went before us. What we as humans celebrated and held sacred, how we honoured those we lost, how we lived and what we feared and what brought us hope. Magic in some form has been part of this history since the beginning, from temples, burial sites and carvings to charms, places of sacrifice and ritual. The story of the witch is just one of many in these lands, but I am excited to let her stories guide my adventures out onto it.

*

This journey will no doubt also be a journey of conflicts. I, like many, am interested, intrigued, enchanted and even inspired by the witch and their stories. But souls caught up in the witch hunts would have been desperate to not be called a witch. While some 'confessed', we've no idea if they truly believed that's what they were, surviving, as many were, as poor peasants – gathering herbs and making balms, or offering blessings and charms as ways of survival. Many accused considered themselves good Christians and good wives. They were often, as we may infer from the scant records, confused as to why they were being called witches at all. Conflicting ideas of law will come up too. In England now, legally speaking, witchcraft, malefic witches and magic do not exist, despite all those accused and killed for it, but how could the situation be brought to a close otherwise? How do you stop the fear and the false beliefs? How can you bring the stories into harmony? In accepting history in all its elements of good and bad, inspiring and horrific, then, the next part of the journey is what to do next when it comes to these once witches: how are we dealing with these controversies now?

Memorials, exploring options to pardon those executed for witchcraft, considering how to offer burial in a way that connects to past beliefs, displaying remains in respectful ways, trying to share their words and understanding the situations that led to such events are all playing a part. Harmonising with the witch in the modern day, authors, scholars and practitioners are exploring what witches were and what they did, from founders and forerunners of Wicca to modern *witchfluencers, witcherature, witchtokkers*. We can find something of a celebration of people who could not have imagined their histories being brought to light centuries on. I'd like to do my part by, as best I can in my rifling through resources, to give back to the accused – names other than witch: mother, sister, friend, healer, wife, wildlife enthusiast, nature lover, carer…and many more. And to share their words where possible.

Setting out

I have had great fun trawling through Ordnance Survey maps for such delights as various Witch Lanes (Dorset, Somerset, Essex), Witch Hills (county Durham, Yorkshire, Scotland), Witch Wood (Scotland, Essex, Cumbria), Witchery Hole (Worcestershire), Witchling Wood (Kent), Witchbrae (Scotland), Witchcraft Way (Norfolk), Witch Lake (Scotland) and Witches' Glen (Scotland) – this isn't all of them by a long way. Some are just innocuous squares of land and trees, some are residential streets, some are great monuments of natural beauty. The witch has certainly left her mark in the landscape and landforms.

Each month, I'll head out to explore a place and seek to experience and capture a sense of the landscape, memory and magic that dwells there. Some of the witches' presence in the land is very obvious: real history of very real people in specific places – like the group known as the Pendle witches from Pendle Hill in Lancashire, who journeyed from Lancaster Castle to Gallows Hill to be hung for the crime of witchcraft. To witches that exist only in the story of a place like Arthurian sorceresses and water witches.

And for some trips, I really have no idea what I may find. Some locations are not recognised on maps or official records but exist in the lore and stories of a wild place, whilst some are tourist attractions lit with neon lights. There are many varying interpretations of exactly how a certain place may be considered magical or 'witchy' and how one may see the witch in the landscape, so I'm exploring as many different ways as I can as I explore the legacy of the witch. And because they are so closely linked, I'll stumble across plentiful fairies and devils too.

Magic words

The words and ideas around myth and magic are not ones that can be easily tamed into single definitions; it's best to accept that now as we begin this journey. Witches both exist and don't exist – it's entirely dependent on one's definition of a witch (the same applies to their magical work, often called witchcraft). Some answers to the question "What is a witch?" can include, but are not limited to: the largely inaccurate, *a witch works with malevolent magic and worships the devil.* This was the historical religious approach to European witchcraft trials, which resulted in the torture and wrongful killing of accused witches. Much of witch persecution throughout the centuries is drawn from this root. And in certain countries, one may still be burned as a witch. *A witch honours gods and goddesses and practises magic for good:* this is the approach favoured by many modern Wiccans. *A witch is a folk healer, A witch is a supernatural entity, A witch is an archetype of power. A witch, or someone who practises witchcraft, may be interested in tarot, astrology, mediumship, divination, crystals, herbalism, charms, folk magic, healing, superstition, ritual and ceremonies.* You can see how this realm of magic and witchcraft can cover a lot within the realm of hidden, secret and somewhere apart from religion and or science (though they can both play a part in people's spiritual practices and personal beliefs as well).

In some of the oldest surviving English herbal healing manuscripts: the Anglo-Saxon Bald's Leechbook and the Lacnunga, both written about 900-950 CE, you'll find recipes for burning fragrant woods and dried herbs and spoken charms in which both Christ and Woden/Odin (Christian and pagan/heathen deities respectively) are mentioned. In the later herbals of Culpepper and Gerard (1597 and 1653), we find more herbs and charms that seem to skirt very closely to our ideas of magical work. (And did tip into it. Nicholas Culpepper had a mixed reputation and did experience informal accusations of witchcraft.) And we find a blend of Christian religious elements was mixed up with more pagan or rural ideas in common practice and noted in some witch trial accounts. And the difference between prayer, charms, magic and witchcraft?

This is much like the difference between being calling someone a herbalist, healer or seer and calling them a witch; it is all in the opinion of the person naming. Once in Europe many healers, herbwives and diviners existed and what they practised might be considered magical, but if you wanted to condemn them as a witch, you would call it witchcraft.

Life for our ancestors, from ancient to early modern Europe (and many places and times beyond), was magical. Unseen forces swirled around the edges and dark corners of commonplace life. Things happened beyond human understanding that were attributed to magic, demons, curses and bewitchment. Life was a constant interaction with the mysterious and unpredictable. Seeking to understand and appease these forces for protection, survival and finding meaning in a world that often seemed beyond human control may lead one to seek aid from all manner of sources: witches, healers, churches, temples and sacred groves. It still does. And today, some still slander and accuse with the word witch, but here in the West, it has also taken on far more positive associations of power. Some have adopted witchcraft as a practice and to some, it is a religion. Witchcraft could be considered a mix of folk magic, ritual and superstition. Witchcraft was once largely considered to be a purely malefic practice, but the line was always blurred, as wise women, cunning folk and even some church leaders offered charms and counter charms or rituals of their own to create material change by uncanny means.

This book is not intended to be an exhaustive list of all the places of the witch, it would take me the rest of my days to write that. Rather it is an idiosyncratic journey, shaped by my research, desires and the terribly dull variables of time, ease of public transportation and finances. There were so many more sites I would have liked to see and would still like to visit. But, I am, as always, comforted that any lacking in my travel dreams also act as inspirations for my next books. It is a special thing to always have another story to explore and another place to be inspired by anew.

I don't consider myself particularly brave, outdoorsy or adventurous (because I'm not) like the authors of some of my favourite books of travel, tracking and trespass. But I can walk, and I have the means to get to a few nice places within this land via public transport and a few borrowed lifts, and that's a privilege I want to acknowledge and enjoy and share some ideas about with you, the reader. I have no extensive skills in orienteering, bird and plant identification, geology or history and maybe that's rather the point: anyone can enjoy this land and nature and the wild stories it holds. I would love to show you that there is not a corner of this country that is not close to some element of nature that can evoke the witch, a story, spell or a certain magic (if that is what you seek). We are all allowed to walk the land and reflect on what it says to us. We need not be scholars or naturalists to do this (though I draw on wonderful works from both throughout the year). I can seek magic simply because I want to, because I can. Because I want to see and breathe fresh air and enchantment, and that is reason enough.

A wyrd year

This journey was never going to be an A to B trip, but I'm going to use the year and its seasons to help chart my route roughly from autumn to autumn. Folk magic intertwines with rural customs and lore as we journey around the Wheel of the Year. Folk customs seem to whisper of witches and remnants of a slightly more pagan way of life and are connected to times when fear of the witch, use of charms and a world that held demons were very real and present. Not that many generations ago, we got everything we needed from the landscape – food, fuel, medicine and clothing. But something else came from the environment too: stories, a resource, sustaining in a different kind of way, drawn distinctly from the natural world around the storytellers. The marshlands and coastlines of the south, the mountains of the north are mirrored in their stories and in their witches.

Can these journeys help us, help me, find wonder in the landscape? I hope so. I wanted to explore places that feel, as some may have been intended, like portals, places and waymarkers where a magical connection to the land is possible. I dreamed of discovering places where there's a palpable magic in the air, where the earth's connection feels enchanting and where beauty flourishes and wondrous things can grow. To remember traditions and festivals where the earth was an honoured partner, connect to a deeper sense of place and find glimpses of traditions, even when the origins of those traditions are lost.

Going out out

So, now I actually have to get out there. I have to put my walking shoes on, because the time has come to make a start and go outside. The sky is a brilliant blue, the light is taking on the golden hues of early autumn and Halloween decorations and pumpkins are in the shops. My home office is a wild mess, with books piling up on the windowsill so high that they are starting to obscure my view. There is plenty I could do here inside. But that's not my adventure; my adventure is out there. So, I go find some socks and faff around looking for sunglasses. I'm wearing the same yoga trousers and vest I slept in, but with a hoodie over the top, I imagine no one will notice. And I open my front door.

The maples that line the street are in the process of turning a vibrant orange-red and the sun is shining. I stand for a moment outside my front door and text Dan, that I'm going for a walk around the park and I'll be back in fifteen minutes.

I'm journeying south. A bird skims across the path in front of me, I think it's a robin at first. He sits in the undergrowth of a hedge, and I get a closer look. It's a dunnock, a hedge sparrow. I can hear the noise of the cars that run behind the hedgerow of hawthorn, their berries shining red. A magpie flies over me to the taller trees. I know a few birds from sight – the goldfinches, dunnocks, blue tits, great tits, round wood pigeons and magpies all frequent our garden to eat the seed Dan generously doles out to them. A prematurely purchased pumpkin has been smashed on the pavement and its orange seeds and flesh are scattered along the path. The magpie and at least one crow sit in two tall ash trees. There must be a hundred different rhymes for magpies throughout the country. The one that comes to mind right now of course is:

One for anger, two for mirth,
Three for a wedding, four for a birth,
Five for rich, six for poor,
Seven for a witch, I can tell you no more.

And maybe to counter the fact that I see just one…

Magpie, magpie, chatter and flee,
Turn up thy tail and good luck fall me. *

To see the white blossoms of the hawthorn *(Crataegus monogyna)* is a joyful herald of the end of winter and the beginning of summer, which is why you may well know hawthorn as May-tree and maythorn (other folk names include hagthorn and hedgethorn). But May is far off right now. The bushes are now covered with red hawthorn berries known as haws, haggle-berries, pixy-pears or cuckoo beads. I know this because I have recently finished writing a book all about folklore of the wildwood and how it connects to witches, revealing just some of the many places people saw witches: hidden amongst thorns and shining berries, woven through branches. From our earliest tribes, we have been drawing threads of mythology from the land like earthworms, carefully from the soil.

As part of their symbol of seasons changing and as common hedging plants,

* Both can be found in Frank H. Stauffer, *The Queer, the Quaint and the Quizzical: A Cabinet for the Curious* (1882).

hawthorn trees are also seen as gateways, places of boundary and boundary crossing and potential connectors to the spirit world. Like the blackthorn, cutting one down may disgruntle the fae folk. Our ancestors here in the British Isles told of thorn trees (both blackthorn and hawthorn) as connected to the witch. With a name like blackthorn *(Prunus spinosa)*, this woody, thorny tree was always going to have a slightly ominous reputation. Blackthorns can form dense scrub, an impenetrable tangle of thorns, a haven for birds and small wild animals. English witches reputedly used the sharp thorns to pierce poppets in their curses. Those who carried a blackthorn walking stick may well have been suspected of being a witch and it was feared they could cause illness or cause crops to whither with a point of this staff. The dark fruit of the blackthorn, sloes, are popular for creating drinks and jams; they also act as an astringent, making them popular naturopathic medicine to reduce inflammation. The fruits are sweetest harvested after a frost; some more magical Irish lore suggests the best time to harvest sloes is on the full moon nights of midwinter for this is when the *Lunantisidhe* fairies have left the tree to visit the moon goddess. Folk names for blackthorn include wishing thorn and faery tree.

I watch a blackbird and its brown mate eating the haws. The sandy gravel path turns to tarmac, still pooled with water from last night's rain. Another chunk of battered pumpkin. I walk round the dog park (I don't know if that is its official name, but it is a very popular spot for dog walking), more hedges, lots of brambles and bindweed and a collection of rosehips. I follow the leaf-lined path around the edge of the park; silver birch, trailing brambles and vines, two ash trees laden with drying clusters of ash keys that shine a copper orange in autumn and then swiftly turn brown. Then onwards past dry-stone walls and piled edges of wet leaves. When I take this walk at dusk, I might spot a toad or a bat flitting under the streetlights.

I am not adept at identifying flowers or trees, so I take pictures of many plants and trees I am unsure of to look up when I get home. The walk takes twice as long as usual. I call up an app on my phone that can identify birdsong – 'it' has heard a long-tailed tit, dunnock, robin, blue tit, great tit, magpie and goldcrest. Did I hear them too? I suppose I did, but only as a collective sound of birdsong, but it's nice to know they are there.

I make for home. I think the leaf litter and damp path smell like peeled satsumas, but that might just be because I'm thinking of my lunch. A red setter runs through brown leaves in an avenue of plane trees. I cross the road, and this is where I meet that mute witch decoration I mentioned earlier (replete with every common stereotype – striped tights, broom, buckled boots, pointy hat) splatted on a house window as if blocked in mid-flight.

So, by the time I make it back to my desk I can confirm I have seen at least one witch, plastic as she may have been. By the end of this journey through *Witch Country,* I will, somewhat to my amazement, have travelled over 2,000 miles via car, train, plane, bus and a more modest (but still satisfying) 200 miles by foot. I will have met professional witches, wassailers, priestesses, cave explorers, poets and storytellers and witnessed the witch image embodied in trees, stones, tors, pools and graves.

But I do not know this yet.

Now, in this modest walk of no more than a mile from my home, I have yet to make those journeys. But the stories I may draw of the witches are already plentiful, autumns of years past, hawthorn and blackthorn, magpies, hags, fairies and sloes. So, if such a small walk can evoke such wonders…well, where can we go next?

AUTUMN

September • October • November

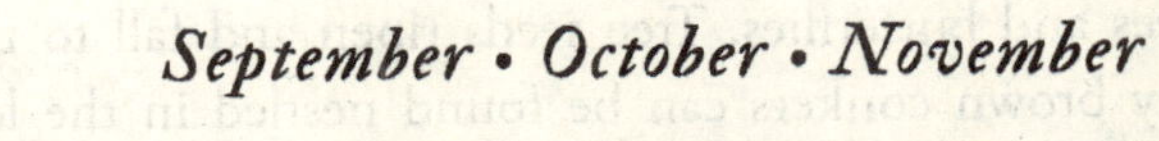

Clooties • Kings • Marshes • Witchfinders • Covens

FIELD NOTES: *THE SPELL OF AUTUMN*

Autumn is my favourite season. It murmurs at the edges of the last summer days, in gilded smoke curls and the scent of damp leaves, candle wax and fallen apples brown and half-chewed by animal foragers. The shift between the shining seasons of summer and autumn is the most beautiful and bittersweet of the year. Senses catch on wood smoke and stolen sunny days are savoured before the colder weather arrives. The countryside releases warming sparks in sprays of spiced colour: cinnamon, clove, nutmeg, ginger and golden saffron are woven through tree canopies. Cooler temperatures and dropping sunlight cause deciduous trees to stop producing the chlorophyll they use to convert light into energy in spring and summer. It's chlorophyll that gives leaves their green colour, so as the chlorophyll fades, yellow and red pigments are revealed.

Dark green ivy that trails over trees and old buildings flowers in the autumn, to the joy of bees and butterflies. Tree seeds ripen and fall to the ground: acorns and shiny brown conkers can be found nestled in the leaf litter at your feet; beechnuts, hazelnuts and chestnuts fatten and tumble from their cases and husks. Tasty morsels often connected to good fortune and wisdom. Blushing against late-autumn skies, clusters of bright berries announce winter is on the way. Glossy black elderberries, damsons, rosehips, blackberries and sloes all ooze sweet juices in hues of scarlets, purples and inky black. Flowers fade, but foragers will still find colour and nourishment. Berries of the rowan tree grow scarlet. Green carpets of lichens and mosses; silken strands of spider's webs; fairy rings of fungi fly agaric, the iconic red fairy tale toadstool and enchanting jade-green elf cups offer even more colours and magic to the autumnal palette. I have tried for many years to capture the magic I feel in the autumnal seasons. In my book *Kitchen Witch: Food, Folklore & Fairy Tale* I was already looking to the hedgerows: *"The morning mists lift slowly now; autumnal sunshine gleams on hedgerows and orchards bursting with crops. The last golden rays of summer have departed to make way for the russets, bronzes and ochres of autumn. Crows caw as they jump through harvested fields. The time of the second harvest is the last gathering of the grain and the fruits that have ripened under the summer sun. In the cauldron, these fruits become syrups, chutneys and jams to stock our winter cupboards."*

*

This autumn, my travel radius starts modestly with my home county, Wiltshire, then further out to the furthest east I will travel this year: Essex. And the furthest south: Hampshire and the New Forest. I will save my great northern journeys for summer.

It has been a long time since this land was scattered through with dense forest. By the eleventh century, pastureland was already fast replacing the oak, hazel, ash and birch forests, and timber was being felled for building and fuel. Common woodland was gathered up for the property of the Crown and nobility, shrinking forested areas down further.

I wonder if trees grieve for their lost ancestors. Trees communicate with each other – we know this now as a generally accepted truth – through the interconnected roots of mycorrhizal hyphae networks. So, do they feel the loss as one falls? One may feel the ghosts of lost woodland lingering at the edges of urban spaces and roadsides, on the edges of farmland and in old maps and stories. The landscape moves with time and leaves some things behind: old paths and the oldest of trees are standing alone. The quiet echoes of trees that have fallen: they are gone, but here, for now, we remain to hear their stories. And what better time to tell those tales than hallowed evenings?

> *There is a dream-beauty also in that lovely suspense between the last wild winds of the equinox and the snow-bringer, that period of hushed farewell… The glory of the heather is gone, but the gold and bronze of the bracken take on an equal beauty. The birch hangs her still tresses of pale gold, 'that beautiful wild woman of the hills', as a Gaelic poet says. The red and russet of rowan and bramble, the rich hues of the haw, the sloe, the briony, all the golds and browns and delicate ambers of entranced autumn are woven in a magic web. In the mornings, the gossamer hangs on every bush of gorse and juniper. Through the serene air, exquisitely fresh with the light frosts which from dayset to dawn have fallen idly, rings the sweet and thrilling song of the robin, that music of autumn so poignant, so infinitely winsome.*
>
> **Fiona Macleod, *Where The Forest Murmurs: Nature Essays* (1855-1905)**

SEPTEMBER

Root & Stone: Witch Trees

Grovely Wood, Wiltshire

We journey through Wiltshire, our home county, to Grovely Wood; Dan is driving and I am daydreaming as I look out the window. I'm thinking about witches and trees. We see witches in trees often it seems. We've already explored ideas of witches utilising blackthorn and hawthorn, but this is only the beginning of connecting witches with trees.

Here in September, I think of witches buried under trees (as they allegedly are in Grovely Wood, where we are headed) but also witches transforming into trees. I think back on a trip Dan and I took that I think of as recent, but upon reflection, I realise it was before the pandemic lockdowns, so a fair few years ago now. We went to the Rollright Stones, advised by the owner of the B&B we were staying at in the Cotswolds. It's an impressive stone circle that is also home to vivid stories of a witch and her presence in a place. The site itself hedge-rides the border of Oxfordshire and Warwickshire – a collection of standing stones known as the King's Men or Rollright Stone Circle, the King Stone, the Whispering Knights and collectively as the Rollright Stones. A witch was responsible for it all, apparently. Cotswold stone is famed for its soft set-honey hues and I wonder if this is why, in part, within the rolling green fields of the Cotswolds, witches have powers of calcification drawn from the earth of our quarrying heritage.

A few miles away from the Rollrights, you'll find the village of Adlestrop, where scattered stones are known as the Grey Geese, created when a woman who was driving a flock of geese to pasture refused an old witch who asked for one of the birds. In response, the witch cursed the flock, turning them all into stones, and there the Grey Geese of Adlestrop remain.

THE WITCH AND THE KING

There are many versions of the story of the Rollright Stones. This is a shortened version of one of my favourites, drawn from Round About and Long Ago: tales from the English counties *by Eileen Colwell (1972).*

Long ago there lived a king who, thinking his own kingdom small, wanted more land to call his own. So, he passed through England with his knights and killed any that stood in his way, burning crops and houses. Until they arrived at the edge of the village called Long Compton. They camped there and the king's men built a huge fire and killed cattle owned by a nearby farmer to feast upon. The villagers watched the fire burn from their homes. Feeling fearful and powerless against this strong band of knights and their king's plan to rule all of England. In their despair – the villagers went to the witch. And using all her skills, she mixed powerful spells in her cauldron. The spells bubbled and steamed as she uttered her incantations and traced symbols in the earth. She worked all through the night and as dawn was breaking, she climbed the hill above Long Compton to where the invading king and his men slept heavily after their feasting. As they awoke, they found themselves looking straight into the fierce eyes of the witch who stood before them. The wind blew her long hair and her cape billowed behind her.

"England shall not have you as king," she said.

"Who will stop me?" bellowed the king.

"I shall!" said the witch.

"My powerful spell is now set free
Thou and thy men cold stone shall be…"

The men watched as the king turned cold and hard, now he stood as stone. The men scattered in fear, but it was too late. One by one, the king's men too, became stone. Knights who had hung back whispering their concern in a cluster were last to be turned, but turn they did. Rain began to fall, but they no longer felt it, wind began howling, but they no longer heard it. The witch's work was done and triumphantly her final act of transformation was for herself, she cried, "And I shall be an elder tree!" Her outstretched arms became branches, her fingers twigs and her body reached tall into bark and bough. And the stones remain there to this day, watched over by the witch, just to keep an eye on things. As a tree she grows stronger with every rainfall and sunbeam. Which tree is the witch tree you ask? She has long been lost amongst her sister trees and if we do not know which is the witch, then perhaps any tree surrounding these stones may be watching us…

In other versions of the Rollright Witch story, that could well whisper of masculine ambition and sense of entitlement and about female resistance, the witch challenges the king to make it to Long Compton.

"Seven long strides shalt thou take and if Long Compton thou can see, King of England thou shalt be!" proclaims the witch.

The king thinks this so easy a task, but he misjudges the land and the size of the hill and, he fails, so the witch turns them all to stone.

There is no one around when we come to wander around the stones. The large stone circle is our first stop – these are the King's Men: weathered, local oolite limestone positioned in a ring a little over 100 feet across, according to signage, like a yawning mouth of ragged teeth. The stones provide a home to lichen, which adds to their mottled, pointillist surface. As at several sites like this, it is said to be impossible to count the King's Men. These are certainly active stones: there are tales of the King's Men returning to life, dancing at midnight. (They should take care, maidens and witches are turned to stone for doing the same.) Within the circle of jagged stones is a path worn smooth in the grass where people have walked the inner circuit. We admire just to the south of the circle, between the stones and farmland, a modern willow weaving of three dancing women looking over green fields that froth at the edges with the last of the season's meadowsweet. I look back on photos of the Rollright trip before we head to Grovely and notice the sky is much the same as it is today – warm, low-hanging, soft and grey. September is holding onto the heat of summer.

The eight-foot-tall King Stone is now across a busy road from the circle, standing on his own inside a roundel of railings. The King is a curving pillar like a solid wave of smoke, it is thought perhaps that his odd shape is due to pieces of stone being chipped off in centuries past as good-luck charms and amulets before the site was protected. Finally, we walk round the edge of the fields to see the Whispering Knights east of the stone circle. It is thought that they, like the King Stone, pre-date the circle. The Whispering Knights were once a portal dolmen: a burial chamber that consists of four upright stones and a large (now fallen and broken) capstone. They too are encircled by rusting railings. These tall stones are well named, they do indeed look like whispering figures, all the stones have a certain curve to them that lends both a sense of movement and the ideas of myths that they move, dance or turn their heads to speak at certain times of year.

The Whispering Knights too, became more interesting as oracles. An old woman, one Betsy Hughes, whose mother had been murdered as a witch, confessed to Sir Arthur that when she was a girl, she and her friends would slip off to the stones at the time of the barley harvest, when they were working until dusk. There, with a good deal of giggling, they would take it in turns to lay their ears to a crevice and listen for the whispering; another old crone completed the picture by recalling that the Whispering Knights were used to tell the future. 'Time after time I have heard them whisper – but perhaps after all it was only the wind.'

Jacquetta Hawkes, *History in Earth and Stone: Prehistoric and Roman Monuments in England and Wales* (1952)

The king and witches have not ended their relationship, it seems, or maybe inevitably, as a local saying once claimed, there were enough witches in Long Compton to draw a "wagon-load of hay up Long Compton Hill."* Local legends also say that the King Stone is a meeting place of Long Compton's witches. Women may question the Whispering Knights, pressing an ear against a stone to receive their whispered wisdom and even seek entrance to the fairy halls under the stone circle, where fae may be seen coming out to dance around the King Stone on full moon nights. And at midsummer, people may gather and cut one of the nearby elder trees so that sap bleeds from it, letting the witch's blood flow, weakening her spell for a moment and allowing the king to move his head from its stone form. (This sounds like risky business all round to be honest, potentially invoking the wrath of both witches and a tyrant king.)

* *Ghosts and Witches of the Cotswolds*, John Attwood Brooks (1986).

Ancient Magic

To further the occult associations of this place, in 2015, a skeleton of a young Saxon woman was found, dated to around 1,400 years old. The items in her grave – a circular deer antler disc, a large amber bead, a bronze ladle and an amethyst mounted in silver – suggest wealth and status, as well as being a magical practitioner of some kind, indicating she was may have been a priestess or wise woman figure.

We know very little about Paleolithic or Mesolithic gods in Britain. But when we find remains like ritual offerings around sacred sites, we get a tiny sense of the magic that may have taken place at these sites, remnants of rituals long vanished, revealing a little of their religious and spiritual interests, rituals and venerations.

The Neolithic and Bronze Age are the eras of stone circles, which can still be seen across the entirety of Britain in great number – there are over three hundred in both England and Ireland and around eighty in Wales. Many of them appear to be connected in some way to solar, lunar and stellar alignments, that may have connected beliefs and cultures that varied through communities. The 2015 find gives some insight into the continuation of ceremonial activity at the site. Like the witch of Wookey Hole (who we'll meet in February), the remains strongly suggest magic and ceremony took place here, but not necessarily, the kind of magic described in the area's most popular folktales.

In folk practice, apologies should be made if one intends to cut into or cut down an elder tree (*Sambucus nigra*) – lest one incur bad luck or worse; the wrath of all manner of beings who held the elder in high regard or dwelled within it. Witches, elves, fairies, and the Germanic 'elder mother' were all thought to make their homes among its branches and roots.

As with many trees and within the wealth of tree folklore, we find contradictions of uses, so although connected to witches, the elder was also used as a protective charm against them. Crosses made from elder wood were hung inside stables, doors and windows of the house, to scupper any diabolical designs, deter witches and protect the inhabitants. Elderberries collected on Midsummer's Eve saved their possessor from witchcraft and awarded magic powers. All parts of the elder can be useful and powerful in healing. So perhaps the beliefs evolved to protect a valuable resource. And perhaps it became so closely connected to witches and wise women as they were very likely to use the elder in works of medicine or charms. An elder tree is among the many things witches were thought able to transform themselves into. In Ireland particularly, witches rode elder branches in the wind, rather than besom broomsticks, and were known to lurk beneath the shadow of their branches, or within them.

*

Now it's time to take a new walk to see different trees – this time, it's Grovely Wood in Wiltshire and another witching tree – Beech.

This time the lore says that they are buried under the trees. The story of the beeches of Grovely Wood sees women as victims rather than the victor, as in the case of the Long Compton witch.

Of the legends associated with the beech trees of Grovely woods, the most well-known may well be that of four sister witches. The tale is this: around the 1700s an outbreak of smallpox hit the town of Wilton, Wiltshire, killing over a hundred locals. The Handsel sisters from Denmark, who were newcomers to the village, were blamed for the sickness. Convinced that the four sisters were responsible for the deaths, the remaining fearful villagers accused them of witchcraft and collaboration with the devil. Without any form of trial, the sisters were hauled from their homes and out into the woods before being beaten to death. Following their brutal murder, the sisters were buried apart, separated, for safety in the minds of superstitious villagers so that they may not conspire after their death to bring about more misfortunes. The beech trees were planted to mark each grave, or, in some versions of the tale, the trees mysteriously grew up on top of the sisters' muddy gravesites to remind the villagers of their dreadful deeds. This gruesome tale no doubt fed ghost stories, and sightings of the sisters haunting their funerary woods have been recounted over the years. With a history dating back far into the Iron Age, it's clear that many stories were made and told here, and much haunts this place.

Whilst, if one were to dive deeper into this story one may find no records of Handsels in the area. Scatterings of Danish people did indeed reside in Wiltshire as a result of various battles and invasions through the Middle Ages, and smallpox outbreaks were recorded in later eras. So, some aspects of truth may lie at the story's roots.

In England the beech tree *(Fagus sylvatica)* is considered a protection from lightning and thunder and in fact so powerful a protector is the beech tree that some lore suggests that no harm of any kind could befall a traveller who sought shelter under the branches of a beech tree. So, if they truly were planted over the bodies of the sisters, protection was most likely being sought *from* them, not *for* them.

We park up to begin our walk to the witch trees of Grovely Wood. I anxiously check my map and directions, keen not to lead poor Dan on a wild goose chase. But the path is simple to follow as houses give way to a track and a hedge-lined path, furrowed by vehicles, flanked by hedges of brambles, field maple, blackberries, hawthorn and opening out into golden fields beyond. The dark green of the woods loom ahead, noticeably darker. Soon we plunge into a shadowed walk along the Roman road that runs through the spine of Grovely Wood, lined by a huge number of beeches and some conifers, crumbling prickly beech shells crunch underfoot.

The first witch tree is easy to spot, it is the largest and richly adorned with clooties and charms. A circle of twigs around the tree creates a boundary I cross over, moving through moss-covered lower branches heavy with story.

The tradition of tying cloth and ribbons as a petition, prayer, spell or wish to trees in certain sacred and magical places has a long history on these isles. These trees are known as 'clootie trees' and can be found throughout the country. Traditionally made from cotton or linen, as the 'clooties' degraded and fell from the trees, sympathetic magic suggested the charm or spell was then complete.

The clooties and charms hung upon the first (and most laden) witch tree are a thousand hopes, prayers and ideas. A witch figurine (that many would call a kitchen witch) swings from a branch. Another charm seems almost ironic – a little note in a synthetic, coloured bag reads, "I believe that nature brings peace to all of our troubles". Many of these charms would not biodegrade and seem to skirt on the edge of littering (if not careering straight into it) – they may not be immediately considered harmful but fly in the face of the best 'leave no trace' advice.

There is a petite older lady in hiking gear at this tree when we arrive. She has short grey hair, glasses and a practical raincoat. I say hello and it transpires that she is a guide to a local rambler's club and was planning out the route for a special Halloween walk. She was pondering whether she might craft some wreaths out of wild clematis (also called old man's beard) as offerings, which I say sounds like a very good idea.

Before heading off, the guide happily shares with us the story of the headless huntsman who haunts the woods. She explains how she would share with her groups, *you know he's near when you can hear the crack of twigs.* And how she'd get someone at the back of the group to crack a twig to give everyone a little start – testament to how much we love a little scary tale. She points us on course from the first tree to the second. "Once you have found the first, you will see her sisters soon enough," she says. A straight walk through ferns and bracken takes us to number two and then three, (number four has fallen and we do not find it).

Hallowed trees and gallows trees

We have woven so much lore around the trunk, roots and branches of trees. To touch or knock on wood is an apotropaic* tradition of literally touching, tapping, or knocking on a tree for good luck. As with many folk customs, there are many conflicting stories about its origin. One is that it is a remnant of ritual from Europe's pagan past, once an appeal to tree-dwelling spirits and connected deities for protection, celebration or warding. People might tap or touch the trees to let them know they were there, seeking guidance or making offerings. Other suggestions of the origin of touching wood for luck include (but are not limited to) as a symbol of the Christian cross, by superstitious sailors for smooth sailing and miners who knocked on the supportive rafters to ensure they weren't rotten. The tree remains a place of safety, blessings and a lasting symbol of love in the custom of carving initials of lovers into trees.†

Wishing trees have a long history in Britain. A wish tree might be distinguished by species, location or appearance as an object of offerings to seek wishes granted or prayers answered from such beings as fairies, nature spirits, saints, goddesses or the tree itself. To leave offerings on sacred trees or beseech them in prayer is something we have long done in the Western world. Ovid speaks of it in his *Metamorphoses*, written somewhere around 8 CE.

> *Among these trees, there stood a huge oak, which had grown sturdy and strong in the course of years, a forest in itself, hung round with wreaths and garlands and votive tablets, tributes for prayers that had been granted. Under this tree the dryads often held their festive dances, often they joined hands in a circle and embraced its trunk.*

The tradition of hammering coins into the bark of trees is another form of giving offerings to the trees. In England it was custom to place coins, needles and pins in the bark of certain trees as offerings to the local spirit or fairy folk and particularly popular in trees near holy wells. Coin trees can still be found throughout the British Isles, but this practice is now actively discouraged, as coins can damage live trees and disrupt living creatures living in both live and dead trees. To wassail trees (as we will discover later) is a ritual of song and

* The word 'apotropaic' comes from the Greek word *apotropaios* which means to turn away, as in turning away unwanted things.

† Current wisdom suggests that not all the old practices are in the best interest of the tree – so these practices should not be taken as a suggestion for future customs.

pouring of the wassail brew of warm apple and ale onto roots, to bless the apple trees and wish them good health for an abundant harvest.

In his book *The Forest in Folklore and Mythology,* Alexander Porteous says,

> *In Croatia, witches were formally buried under old trees in the forest and it was believed that their souls passed into these trees.*

Croatians, like many cultures, held trees to be sacred and, in some cases, guardians. Perhaps it was thought the trees would hold the witches' spirits safely. Or perhaps these old stories are drawn from superstition or folk and fairy tales; many involve the dead being buried under trees, or trees growing from burial sites. Some examples of these tales are "The Juniper Tree" and "Ashenputtel"‡ *(Grimms' Fairy Tales)* and versions of the Russian story of "Aliona and the Crystal Apple"§. There are tales through Europe of 'witches trees' that may have been used by witches and healers as a precious resource as well as specific trees colloquially called 'witch trees' with attached folklore of witches being hung from, hidden in, or buried underneath.

A gallows tree could serve as the place of execution for accused witches. Picking apart which trees were actually used and which are surrounded by superstition may well be impossible, but is certainly, something to consider. Hanging places throughout the British Isles hold names such as Hangman's Hill, Gallows Hill, Gallows-Fey and Hill of the Gallows, still whispering of their history (gallows saw the end to many people's lives, accused witches being just one group). Although a hanging tree or hangman's tree is any tree used to perform executions by hanging, the term is also used colloquially to refer to constructed gallows, like London's famous Tyburn Tree, which was never a tree but a wooden gallows frame that hanged many an accused witch and heretic. And some are a little more ambiguous, like the area of Heavitree in Exeter. The name Heavitree may come from the old English of *heafod-treow*, 'head tree', or literally 'heavy tree', referring to the consequences of hanging bodies from branches. A plaque can be seen in Exeter, round the corner from where I once lived as a student (Exeter was hanging witches from the 1500s through to the end of the 1600s):

> *The Devon Witches. In memory of Temperance Lloyd, Susannah Edwards,*

‡ A version of Cinderella.

§ You can read a version of this story in my book *Kitchen Witch: Food, Folklore and Fairy Tale.*

*Mary Trembles, of Bideford, died 1682, Alice Molland, died 1685, the last people in England to be executed for witchcraft, tried here and hanged at Heavitree. In the hope of an end to persecution and intolerance.**

In Scotland, trees were regularly used as gallows, known as *dule* or *dool* trees (meaning sorrow or grief). The trees selected were usually growing in prominent positions or at busy crossroads. Beeches, elms and sycamores still grow in Scotland that are considered historical dule trees. In one more unhappy connection, as well as wood forming a structure to hang witches from, they may also be burned on pyres of wood (in England, accused witches were more likely to be hanged, in Scotland and Europe, it was burning). So, the use of trees in magical or healing work may lead one to be accused of witchcraft and may also be the means of their execution.

*

As we make our way out of the dense woods, the light slowly begins to filter through the trees and we return once more to the open space of wide fields and distant horizons.

This month we've met witches of elder and accused witches under beeches. Our first journey has taken in a heady mix of lore, history and superstitions, speaking to the enduring power of memory and emotion, and of memory and place. It has been a good reminder that stories and folklore, like embers, can be revisited and revived regardless of how much time has passed. The witch is still with us, and sometimes it does not take much to reignite the embers of her memory. Her spells can still be found if we are willing to go out and seek them.

* The text of the memorial sign that can be found at the gatehouse ruins of Rougemont Castle, Castle Street, Exeter.

OCTOBER

Dying Light

Manningtree, Essex

October is the season of the witch, if ever there was one. It's close to the end of the month and the rabble of *mischief nights,* the dark evenings of All Hallows, All Soul's Day, Halloween and Samhain. These festivals mark summer's end and are a time both to remember and honour the dead and raise merry hell at a seasonal threshold. This is when many a folkloric gathering of witches danced, feasted and chanted around fires, along with all the many creatures they were connected with via superstition and lore: ghosts and ghouls, mischievous spirits, cats, bats and familiars.

Today, it is the Eve of Samhain, October 30th, and I am off to Manningtree, in Essex – the county with the dubious honour of killing the most witches of the English counties during the period of the European witch trials.

There are so many tales of witches from Essex, from amazing to horrifying, it's hard to know where to start. In the Assizes* from around 1560-1680, some 545 people were accused of witchcraft. A significant chunk of these deaths occurred in 1645-46 and would have been the handiwork of the self-titled Witchfinder General, Matthew Hopkins, who feared that covens of witches in Manningtree were trying to kill him. So he got in there first, along with his colleague John Stearne, seeking to rid Essex of witches, before trying to do the same in surrounding counties.

But 'witches' were persecuted before Hopkins got stuck into his own campaign and Essex (like all of England at the time) was a dangerous place to do anything noteworthy enough to draw attention. Reports of witch hunts may well have inspired Hopkins' concern of witches abounding everywhere and distrusting feelings about women in general. In September 1643, a pamphlet reported a witch had been discovered (and dispatched) by Roundhead soldiers, claiming to be "A Most Certain, Strange and True Discovery of a Witch: Being taken by some of the Parliament forces, as she was standing on a small planck-board and sayling on it over the river of Newbury: together with the strange and true manner of her death, with the propheticall words and speeches she used at the same time" (these pamphleteers sure did love a wordy title!)

The article's opening lines are a classic conflicting image of society's view of women, who were deemed both incompetent and threatening at the same time: "Many are in a belief that this silly sex of women can by no means attaine to that so vile and damned a practice as sorcery and witchcraft, in regard to their illiterateness and want of learning."

* A court which formerly sat at intervals in each county of England and Wales to administer the civil and criminal law.

The pamphlet describes how a group of foraging Parliamentary soldiers spied a woman and, with "no little amazement" saw her floating upon the surface of a river. Now, it turned out, on closer inspection, that she was standing upon a plank of wood; she might have been trying to cross the water, look for fish, or maybe she was just entertaining herself. But the onlookers surmised that she was clearly a "divellish woman" – and when she reached the shore, the soldiers ambushed and interrogated her, demanding to know "what she was", though clearly they had already decided, so her refusal to answer made little difference. They decided to shoot her, and her final words formed the title's 'propheticall words': "and is it come to passe, that I must dye? why then his Excellency the Early of Essex shall be fortunate and win the field." And she sank to the ground "her legacy of a detested carcase to the wormes, her soul were ought not to judge of, though the evils of her wicked life can scape no censure."

It's impossible to know if the woman existed. Still, it shows it is considered worthy of print that a woman was shot for what she is, rather than anything close to a criminal act and that floating on a plank should be considered proof enough that she led a *wicked life*. Certainly, it echoes other witch beliefs of swimming witches that we'll revisit later. At this time, as the witchfinder and trials were about to build pace at terrifying speed, being a witch was a criminal act and came with the assumption that you were evil. A wave of witch hunts followed the publication of the story of the Newbury witch and once accused as a witch, it was battling against a strong current to convince people otherwise.

*

The destruction caused by the infamous Witchfinder General was substantial. He was in his twenties and seemingly had a real issue with women and completely unearned superiority. (Can you already see echoes of present-day issues?) But of the many hundreds[†] of people killed in the English witch trials, Hopkins and his associates were responsible for up to three hundred in a period of barely over a year. So, it felt important that I tell this story, even just the outline. Hopkins wrought terror through Norfolk, Cambridgeshire,

† Witch hunting numbers will always be only guesses, a horrible tribute to how little respect was held for those accused. Often no one bothered to even record their names. Many records were lost, mob justice played a part, many died in prison, some waiting months or even years in squalid conditions to even be heard in a court (not that, in many cases, they would have a chance to speak).

Northamptonshire, Suffolk, Essex, Bedfordshire and Huntingdonshire and it took a clergyman, usually no friend to the witch, to question what the hell he was up to. When an email arrived in my inbox advertising a writing workshop in Essex – "Walking in the Footsteps of Witches" at Manningtree – I was inspired to explore Manningtree, where it all began for the Witchfinder.

*

All in, it's about three hours from my west country home to Manningtree by train. It's an hour to London Paddington, a hop over to Liverpool Street on the Tube. A pause to treat myself to an iced oat latte with hazelnut syrup at Starbucks, as it becomes clear that I am indeed capable of catching the train and navigating the Underground, things I have done just a handful of times since the lockdown. Then it's onward for one more hour from Liverpool Street to Manningtree, Essex.

The train goes through Colchester before Manningtree, but I cannot see the infamous castle from the train windows. It rained heavily recently and there are flooded grasslands between Colchester and Manningtree; trees and hedgerows whizz by; a large bonfire burns in a dry corner of a field.

While travelling, I listen to the audiobook of *The Ash Tree* by M. R James. A story set in the East of England, featuring a 'Mrs Mothersole' killed as a witch, and her intoned curse connected to an ash tree. This haunting and gently creeping ghost story seemed appropriate for the time of year and was surely inspired, at least in part, by the witch hunts of East Anglia.

I arrive at Manningtree at 11.30, ready for meeting at noon at the Red Lion and our tour of the area. I walk from the station, a little disoriented, past warehouses and housing estates. I know the sea is somewhere to my left, but there are too many buildings to see it. This is a land of estuaries and marshes, though I have yet to see them. I walk down a High Street of red brick shops, a chippy and a red phone box, barrels and baskets planted with flowers, a grand-looking library with white columns framing its door. At a crossroads, I catch a glimpse of the Stour estuary but turn the other way to head uphill to the Red Lion pub.

Soon enough, I am settled amongst a group of writers in a warm little room at the back of the pub, the oldest pub in town apparently. It was established in 1605, and I marvel at the fact that one could, from these very windows, have seen people hung as witches on the tiny triangle of grass nearby, known as the green, in 1645.

How it begins…

In July 1645, four local women were hanged – Anne West, Hellen Clark, Marian Hockett and Ann Cooper – for the crime of witchcraft and this was very much just the beginning.

According to historical records, around a hundred witnesses testified against these first four women – a considerable investment of their time, money and reputations, to make sure these women hung. The women were arrested, interrogated and imprisoned in the cramped cells of Colchester Castle before being tried at the Assize courts. They weren't alone. At the same time, fifteen others were killed in Chelmsford, but Anne, Hellen, Marian and Ann were brought to Manningtree to be hung by short drop* here on the village green before a gathered crowd.

Our guide gives us a short introduction to the Manningtree witches in the pub, with some readings offered by the group, before we head into town, down roads that the accused would have once walked. We stand at the green where many lost their lives. Three relatively young trees grow on the green now: three observers from a green island of grass, too young to know of the horrors of the earth they grow on. The tallest of the three has red roses propped at its base, left over from another witch-themed walking tour. We journey down the road to a plaque dedicated to some of the witches, where Stour and South streets cross. It's an odd choice of location, it's not by the green but underneath the Manningtree Ox; a metal armature of an ox connected to a Shakespeare quote that sits underneath the witches plaque – which presents quite the contrast. The quote chosen by the Rotary Club is, in the play, an insult offered in reference to gluttony and excess.†

The two plaques read:

---

* A short drop hanging, where one dangles until they asphyxiate (as opposed to the long drop, where your neck snaps), led family members to be forced into acts of torturous mercy to pull on the dying's legs to speed up the process.

† The full quote, from a comedic argument between friends Prince Hal and Sir John Falstaff is quite the insult! "Swearest thou, ungracious boy? Henceforth ne'er look on me. Thou art violently carried away from grace. There is a devil haunts thee in the likeness of an old fat man. A tun of man is thy companion. Why dost thou converse with that trunk of humours, that bolting-hutch of beastliness, that swollen parcel of dropsies, that huge bombard of sack, that stuffed cloak-bag of guts, that roasted Manningtree ox with the pudding in his belly." But amazingly, even this I can bring back to witches because Sir John Falstaff, who features in several of Shakespeare's plays, has a nickname, (after his favourite drink of sherry wine, called sack, mixed with sugar and cinnamon) its "Sack and Sugar" – a name we'll see given to a witch's familiar very shortly…

"That roasted Manningtree Ox with a pudding in his belly."
Wm. Shakespeare: Henry IV. pt. I.
Erected by The Rotary Club Manningtree Stour Valley

And

Manningtree Witch Hunt 1645
Below are the names of local women who were accused of practising witchcraft.
As victims of the ignorance and hysteria of this time, they were cruelly treated and imprisoned in the dungeons of Colchester Castle.
Subsequent trial by judge and jury at Chelmsford Assizes on the July 17th led to their conviction and execution.
This plaque is erected to remember those women and all people who have suffered intolerance and persecution on account of their gender, religion, ethnicity or social standing.
SARAH BRIGHT from Manningtree, executed Chelmsford,
ELIZABETH CLARK from Manningtree, executed Chelmsford,
HELLEN CLARK from Manningtree, executed Manningtree,
ANN COOPER from Great Clacton, executed Manningtree,
ELIZABETH GOODING from Manningtree, executed Chelmsford,
MARION HOCKETT from Ramsey, executed Manningtree,
ANNE LEECH from Mistley, executed Chelmsford,
*ANNE WEST from Lawford, executed Manningtree.**

We are given time to walk on our own, finding our own places to walk, sit and observe in and around the Red Lion and its infamous green. On my meandering walk, I stroll past the aforementioned Rotary Club: a crowd of members is standing on the small balcony, drinking and laughing. One can't help but think of the full-bellied men of wealth and means who decided the fates of so many souls, often poor and hungry.

* Manningtree Museum and Local History Group.

Trialling times

I find an area called Mistley Walls that looks out over the silty, salty waters of the River Stour. Where, according to a sign, one may see grey plover, redshank and black-tailed godwits around the mudflats. I don't. Instead, I see three seagulls and a spherical wood pigeon pottering under a holm oak. And a spray of long-tailed tits fly above me, like a sprinkle of white teaspoons thrown from a feast.

The same sign helps me pick out sea lavender and sea milkwort along the salt marshes. Apparently, from July, there is a haze from the blooms of the sea lavender and aster, but they match the grey of the silt here today at the tipping point of October and November. Marsh samphire grows along the salt marshes, which can be eaten; if samphire grew here in the days of Anne West and Hellen Clark, I have no doubt they would have treasured it as a foodstuff, especially now, long past its fresh phase of green new shoots of spring, (it should, it is said, be harvested before the summer solstice,) but if any last tough stems remained in October, they would be valuable to the poor and hungry, facing down the winter and the ever-present threat of starvation. This is all my own speculation of course, but I try to imagine what it would have been like for people living here who looked out over these same waters. There is something to be said for what we may call psychogeography. To be in the place where such fear and horror took place. To offer what respect we may in our own imperfect way, to try and understand what they may have felt, these desperate daughters and outcast mothers.

In any place of witch trials, it's hard to look at bodies of water like this one and not think of the 'no-win' test of near drowning to prove guilt or innocence, ironically called 'swimming the witches'. The theory was that the purity of the water would reject those who had renounced God and were in league with the Devil and so would float. The victim would be tied up, their thumbs tied to opposite big toes. Support for this practice came from no less than King James I of England (known as King James VI in Scotland). In King James' book, *Daemonologie*, he suggested two reliable proofs of witchcraft: the devil's or witches' mark and the result of 'swimming' the accused.

One of the Witchfinder General's favourite techniques of witch identification was *watching* the accused for several days straight, depriving them of sleep and walking them back and forth to a point of delirium and exhaustion to catch addled confessions, as well as through familiars arriving to meet their masters.

Familiars

Animals play a vivid part in the Manningtree and Essex witch trials and wider stories and suspicions of the witch trials. The witch, it was feared, would often have an animal that was, in fact, a demon of some kind, called a familiar. The witch's familiar was usually a small animal, no oxen, more likely a cat, dog, toad, or rabbit, but sometimes as tiny as a housefly or butterfly. The witch fed the familiar from teats on her body and in return, it might act out her commands.

Of the thousands of witchcraft trials that took place across the length and breadth of Britain, a significant number of 'confessions' detailed descriptions of encounters with some spirit – their spirit-familiar might be variously described as a familiar, imp, demon, fairy, all connected to the devil. There was a strong folkloric component to familiar beliefs connected to the prevalence of images of devils and demons in both folklore, fairy belief and religion of the time. And some people wanted to believe it so much that perhaps their minds created such ideas, whether as a witchfinder wanting to find proof or a delirious accused person under the power of suggestion.

Searching was another popular method of witch detection, which included probing the bodies of the accused for physical evidence, specifically teats, which were used to suckle their familiars. This could also amount to 'proof' that could be used against them. Sometimes, but not always, midwives and women of good standing searched the accused witches for the marks. As women could also be accused for practising midwifery – there seemed a hare's breadth (pun intended) of difference between the accused and the accusers at times.

The discovery of witches

It is so easy to get lost amongst all the strange stories and superstitions that surround each person accused of witchcraft. All the half-told things – the half-truths and half-cut documentations, often you read of an accused witch and her fate is never recorded, or her words are cut off by record keepers. This is all just fragments of what I can find out, what I can journey with, what snippets can be found.

The woodcut frontispiece to *The Discovery of Witches* written by Matthew Hopkins and published in 1647 (both Hopkins and Stearne wrote books of their escapades, which offer us, whilst biased, first-hand accounts from those involved) shows him standing in the middle of a room with two women sitting either side of him and five animals, identified as their familiars.

One of these women, we can assume, is his first victim, Elizabeth Clarke, a poor one-legged woman from Manningtree, as she sits alongside the animals she named in her confessions. Elizabeth had been accused, among other things, of placing a spell of illness on a woman. Clarke was placed under the 'care' of Hopkins and his inhumane methods until she could take no more and told him what he wanted to hear, along with naming another five people. This witch hunt soon grew to implicate many more. Hopkins was invited to use Colchester Castle as a base to interrogate the witches who were accused in Manningtree, and they would be incarcerated there for months while awaiting trial.

Elizabeth Clarke named other women in implication of witchcraft, but the most amazing part of 'the watching' was that she would call her imps and records suggest that the 'watchers' (who too may have been very sleep deprived) saw these animals as Elizabeth named them. They feature in Hopkins' woodcut: *Holt*, who looked like a little white kitling (a word for kitten); *Jarmara*, the fat hairy dog without any visible legs; *Vinegar Tom*, the long-legged greyhound with a head like an ox; *Sacke and Sugar*, the black rabbit; *Newes*, the polecat. Further names mentioned include: *Ilemauzar, Pyewackett, Pecke in the Crowne* and *Griezzell Greedigutt*. Apparently so outlandish were their names, Hopkins said, *"which no mortall could invent"* (that just shows a lack of imagination, I'd say). Further notes say Clarke had three brown imps from her mother (who was killed as a witch – tragically, this world of witch accusation was not unfamiliar to Elizabeth Clarke).

Of the women that grace the Manningtree memorial, each had her own streams of familiars – Hellen Clark confessed that the devil appeared to her in her house in the likeness of a white dog called *Elemanzer/Ilemauzar;* whom she often fed milk-pottage (this name suggests she could be the other woman on the book's frontispiece). Sarah Barton, the sister of Marian Hocket, said Marian had given her three imps by the names of Littleman, Prettyman and Dainty. Anne West spoke of seeing black rabbits leaping at her door on a moonlit night.

See how complicated it can all get? Lives tied together, accused mothers and daughters, sisters and friends. Communities that can be both tied together and torn apart by fear and accusations. And ripples of rumours and superstitions that jump down the High Street as black hares and white dogs in a bizarre interaction of reality and myth all combined in the process of *discovering* a witch.

Subsequent accused Essex witches commanded more imps who lurked in doorways. A woman called Mary Johnson was accused of carrying a rat-like imp in her pocket causing the death of a child. It was said to have entered the victim's house before Michaelmas and at Mary's bidding rocked the cradle of a child who shortly after sickened and died. Margaret Moone confessed that she had twelve imps, their names including *Jesus, Jockey, Sandy, Mrs Elizabeth* and *Collyn*. And Johan Cooper, widow, who died in jail, confessed she'd been a witch about twenty years and "hath three Familiars, two like Mouses and the third like a Frog." Anne Cate of Maidenhead said she had four familiars for over twenty years, three mouse-like imps called *James, Prickeare, Robyn* and a fourth like a sparrow and named *Sparrow*.*

All these imps were apparently sent round to do such mischief as kill children, make people sick and kill livestock. The streets of Essex must have been teaming with magical imps, so many there seem to be! There's something almost whimsical, looking back now at these accounts of cute names and funny animals – but it does little to temper the history, which, even softened by time, is still horrifying.

Hope and despair

As well as revealing the fears and fantasies of interrogators, confessions offer an insight into those of the accused as well – whether these were visions they had truly had, or they were making them up during interrogation – what were they hoping for during their supposed demonic trysts? Did they fantasise about the possibility of companionship, power, wealth, revenge, hope…? In the 1645 trials of Bury St Edmunds (some thirty miles from Manningtree and also overseen by Hopkins), Mary Skipper confessed to becoming a witch

* *A true and exact relation of the severall informations, examinations and confessions of the late witches, arraigned and executed in the county of Essex,* Charles Clarke (1837).

when the devil appeared to her in the shape of a man after her husband's death, telling her if she entered a covenant with him, he would pay her debts, carry her to heaven and that she would never want for anything.[†] Here was the promise of relief from poverty, debt and the endless toil of life, as well as an escape from her grief, perhaps.

Margaret Moore of Cambridgeshire (the county above Essex) was a poor woman who had watched three of her four children die in infancy. As the last lay sick, she awoke from sleeping by their side at hearing the call of her own dead children to her, "Mother, good sweet Mother, lett me in,"[‡] on opening the door she meets a spirit she calls *Annys*, who offered to save the life of her remaining child in exchange for her soul. She agreed, offering up the only thing she possessed in return for her child's life. She was hanged as a witch in Ely in the summer of 1647.

Othering

History has a tendency to make witches weird, wizened and cantankerous. Perhaps we make assumptions to soothe ourselves by making the accused just a little more 'other' by adding age or disability, devaluing them even further than they have already been. Making them 'other' helps us reassure ourselves that it couldn't happen to us. Except, of course, subtle, sinister ideas still permeate our news narratives (and less subtle conspiracy theories prove we still believe wild and outlandish things without a shred of proof).

A case in point is that of Elizabeth Clarke, Hopkins first victim. If you have read about her before, it's very possible, you've come across a lot of writing, like I have, that suggests she was elderly, eighty years old or more. Elizabeth Clarke is described as having only one leg and being very poor. But no description of her age is actually mentioned in either Hopkins' or Stearne's accounts of their witch hunts. Historians may have inferred her age, based on her status as a widow and the physical description provided in later sources. I believe that writers retelling the Manningtree story went on to estimate Bess's

† As found in *Godly Zeal and Furious Rage: The Witch in Early Modern Europe*, Geoffrey Quaife.

‡ Margaret Moore's confession, May 1647. As found in *Witchfinders: a seventeenth-century English Tragedy*, Malcolm Gaskill.

age – eighty – as a general age to signify she was an old hag. I say this because, through this journey, as I trawl through all manner of writing – I find that some of my long-held beliefs about witches and their stories, are challenged. Regarding the story of Elizabeth Clarke, among the many revelations of this trip was reading the excellent book *Witchcraft: A History in Thirteen Trials* by Professor Marion Gibson.

Professor Gibson found in Manningtree-with-Mistley's parish register a baptismal record from 1643: "Jane Clarke (alias Applegate) daughter & bastard of Elizabeth Clarke (by Joseph Applegate) was baptized on the 12th day of Februarie." Going through parish records Gibson found just this one Elizabeth Clarke – born in 1606. Is this our Elizabeth? This would mean when Hopkins put her through her ordeal of sleep deprivation, she was also a new mother. And that when she was hanged in 1645, she was aged just thirty-nine, meaning she died younger than I am now. This certainly presents a very different image of her.

Discoveries like this pepper my journey, challenging things I thought I knew. So, which is it? Was Elizabeth Clarke a twittering old crone or a wily mother? Or both? One thing is true, she was seen as different, a bundle of contradictions, ever the *delicate firebrand-darling.*[*] During our writing workshop at the Red Lion, one woman says, "We don't have room for different," she saw links with modern-day treatment of neurodivergence and the trials of women and witches. When people are scared, they condemn others, fearing what they don't understand and feeling their own reality challenged by all those they may call 'other'. How can people be so cruel? Because they are afraid. It was true then and it's true now.

So much has been lost and forgotten. So many individuals turned into myths. But the places where these things happened still remain. There is a footpath connecting Manningtree and Mistley. Villagers would have been familiar with it, visiting each other, perhaps walking along it, seeking foraged food or charity or snippets of news of the day. The path passes where St Mary's Church at Mistley Heath once stood and where Matthew Hopkins is said to be buried. But there is nothing to see now, the church, graveyard and the Witchfinder are all lost. (Though local superstitions abound of Hopkins

* Hopkins, in his book *The Discovery of Witches* (1647) wrote this term as what the devil called his witches. Thirty years earlier Thomas Potts, author of *The Wonderfull Discoverie of Witches in the Countie of Lancaster* (1613) of the Pendle witch case also used it to refer to "that wicked fire-brand of mischiefe, old Demdike."

haunting the area in his snappy seventeenth-century garb.) Those killed as witches, of course, are not in the lost churchyard: their resting places are lost too. Accused witches may have been buried at crossroads, in unconsecrated ground, beneath gallows, at the margins of communities or in marshes or intertidal spaces, any markers intended more as warnings than memorials. But despite their whereabouts being lost, they still remain, hidden beneath the ground we walk on today.

How it ends, for now

> *Every old woman with a wrinkled face, a furrowed brow, a hairy lip, a gobber tooth, a squint eye, a squeaking voice or scolding tongue, having a rugged coat on her back, a skull-cap on her head, a spindle in her hand and a dog or cat by her side, is not only suspect but pronounced for a witch.*
>
> **John Gaule, *Select Cases of Conscience towards Witches and Witchcraft* (1646)**

Many more people in and around Manningtree were accused of witchcraft, found guilty and hanged. I feel sometimes, like the elusive art of counting stones in ancient stone circles, I'm never quite sure I've got the numbers right when it comes to those who lost their lives in any one area during the witch trials. But emboldened by his 'successes', Hopkins began hunting for witches all over East Anglia that would lead the casualties into the hundreds. If they were found guilty they faced public execution. But their appalling treatment meant that some died solely from their imprisonment or from the swimming test.

Opposition rose against these Witchfinders. In the spring of 1646, the Reverend John Gaule of Great Staughton published a work in objection of Hopkins' methods – "Select Cases of Conscience towards Witches and Witchcraft." Gaule's complaints helped lead to Hopkins being formally questioned about his punitive methods (and Hopkins wrote his book in part to counter criticism). He was already in poor health and so Hopkins disbanded his team in May 1646 and retired to the village of Mistley. He died of tuberculosis and was buried just over a year later, in August 1647.

*

After sharing our thoughts and writing, I leave the warm words and welcome of the Essex Writing Group. Manningtree is a place of water and I want to seek the famed marshes before I take the train home. It is 3.30 pm, and it already feels like dusk is falling, the clocks went back yesterday, so I am keen to make it to the marshes quickly before I retrace my steps back towards the train station.

The RSPB reserve of Cattawade Marshes lies between two arms of the River Stour on the Essex/Suffolk border. It is something adrift, as a place – there's no public access to the reserve itself, but a footpath on the south side of the river allows views of the reserve, which is where I am headed. There are no formal viewing points here, I think there is a car park that would afford better views if one was driving. And the OS maps suggest better circular routes than the route I take, which is a poor one, along a very busy A-road.

So here at dusk on the eve of Halloween, I scuttle under a low bridge with no pavement and cross over the road. Fields filled with silent sheep run along my right. I weave to cross back and forth over the road a few times as the pavement evaporates and reappears in streaks of fragile sanctuary, flickering in and out like a mirage. I have been quite alone for the past twenty minutes when suddenly a man appears with a black dog at his side. I pick up my pace, crossing over the road once more, my heart racing.

Ahead, I spot the narrow footpath snaking behind a house, a skinny, muddy trail leading me to the marshes. The light is fading fast, shadows creeping like spectres. Long-tailed tits skitter through shabby, browning maple trees, while a white egret, ghostly against the dusk, dips along the water's edge. A sudden flap of heavy wings startles me – a goose takes flight, silhouetted in the gathering gloom, its form soon melting into the darkness. It feels like the marsh itself is rising up, dark wings unfurling, sending a shiver down my spine. So, I take flight too, back toward the train station, I do not wish to linger long at these dark and dusky marshlands.

The bright lights of the station stutter into view, as I hurry past a cacophony of sparrows dancing from scraggly buddleia and hawthorn bushes. I consider how easily fear can twist the familiar into the sinister. Nightfall breeds phantoms, turning innocuous sights into grotesque figures. Shadows stretch and writhe, transforming every rustle into a lurking threat – a busy road becomes a perilous chasm, a stranger morphs into an unseen menace, the black dog a harbinger of dread. Fear can push people to become monstrous and see monsters everywhere in swarms of black rabbits and prowling hounds, witches and devils – in the grip of fear, the world teeters on the edge of terror.

The train judders onwards as night falls to black. I am swept at high speed toward the bright lights of bigger cities and hubbub of the capital. The moon shines brightly, almost full. I think of fairy tales of moons and marshlands as I shuttle back home to the West Country and Halloween beckons.

The Buried Moon

A folktale popular throughout England, but particularly relevant to areas of marshlands. You can find versions of this story in More English Fairy Tales *by Joseph Jacobs (1894). Note the echoes of swimming witches and intertidal burials.*

Long ago, in the liminal lands of marshes and tidepools, bogs, black-water and creeping green algae; the moon shone and she lit up the marshlands so folks could walk safely at night in the embrace of her light. But whenever she didn't shine, then, out came the things that dwelt in the darkness seeking to do harm: bogles, boggarts and bad spirits.

Well, the moon, being kind and virtuous, wanted to see these tricksy beings for herself and see perhaps if she could send them away for good. And so, she stepped down to earth in the glimmer of starlight, wrapped up in a black cloak that covered her shining hair. To the marsh's edge she went to look about her. But as she stepped, she slipped and tumbled in. Tangled and twined in the cold marsh, a snaggle of snarling branches and roots and in a flash the moon's light was lost. Dark things leapt out with screeches and howls. The marsh witches shrieked and the crawling things snaked themselves around the moon's knees, holding her fast. The bogles fetched a big stone and rolled it on top of the moon to keep her from rising. The will-o'-the-wisps were instructed to keep watch, to see that she remained trapped in her watery prison.

The days passed and the village folk looked forward to the paths soon being safe again under the light of the moon. But days turned to weeks and the moonlight never came. The poor folk were afeared, so they went to the Wise Woman who dwelt in the old mill. "Well," said she, after looking from her brew pot to her mirror to her book.

"Go, all of ye, as the night gathers, with a stone in your mouth and hazel-twig in hand and speak not a word till you're safe home again. Walk far into the midst of the marsh, till ye find a cross, a candle and a coffin. Look there and find the moon."

So, the following night in the darkling gloom, the folk set out – with a stone in their mouths and a hazel twig in hand and they came nigh to the pool and they stopped as one, for there it was: a will-o'-the-wisp flickering like a candle flame, above a great stone that looked like a strange coffin below black branches stretching out two arms to form a dark, gruesome cross. This surely must be where the moon lay buried. Without speaking a word, the villagers rolled the stone away. And they saw a luminous face looking up at them out of the black water, the moon was smiling with relief; the folk stepped back, dazzled and there, then, the full moon was returned to the sky.

And from that night on, the moon shone brighter over the marshes than anywhere else and evil spirits again cowered from her light.

NOVEMBER

Just an Ordinary Witch

New Forest, Hampshire

It has that mysteriousness, that spell, with which in imagination we endow the noon silences, the eves and dawns of faery twilights. Still, the silence and the witchery of the forest solitudes in November are of the spell of autumn. The last enchantment of midwinter is not yet come. It is in 'the death months' that the forest permits the last disguises to fall away.

Fiona Macleod, *Where the Forest Murmurs: Nature Essays* (1855-1905)

In November I head to the New Forest, an area of protected forest land in the county of Hampshire, on the south coast of England. The forest is, contrary to its name, far from new. In fact it was designated as a royal hunting ground as far back as 1079, in the era of William the Conqueror and the Domesday Book, its name deriving from the Latin *nova foresta* – literally new hunting ground. It is an area of ancient woodlands, heathlands and wetlands, and a place where animals are afforded safe protection (once for the purposes of hunting, now for the protection of endangered and treasured species). It is a place that is rich in natural beauty, wildlife, history and for me, childhood memories – from the green grasses and babbling brooks of Beaulieu by which I have eaten many an ice cream to sites of various ill-fated rope swings.

This is a place I think I know well. And I'm looking forward to beginning my weekend adventure with a seven-mile walk from the train station at Brockenhurst to the village of Burley. It's golden autumn. Dan has gone to Mauritius for the week for work, but I am content and excited for my own adventure. However, my enthusiasm is quickly dampened by the British weather. When I get off the train at Brockenhurst the rain is coursing down in sheets and the roads are flooded. I get thoroughly flustered and head off in the wrong direction several times before getting my phone out and allowing the map app to lead me down a road (my app looks for driving roads rather than footpaths, I must get a footpath app I think, though it is too late in this moment).

The New Forest has retained its medieval traditions of *commoning*, where locals can still graze livestock freely, preserving a very tangible sense of an older, rural way of life. The forest boundaries, of around 200 square miles, hold within them wild ponies, deer and rare bird species. The boundaries lead all the way to the ocean on the south coast. I think of the New Forest as something of a haven, and a little set apart from modern life: peaceful and protected, time moves a little slower perhaps here as some 'old ways' still feature in the living practice of its people. The ponies roam freely here, as they have done for centuries, managed by local commoners, helping to maintain the forest ecosystem (alongside some donkeys and pigs). These hardy semi-wild ponies are an iconic symbol of the New Forest (they feature on the logo for the New Forest National Park) and they are both a connection to the rural heritage of the forest and a lovely feature of local life in the present.

So, why the New Forest, you may ask, other than my rather romanticised fondness for it? Where are we headed? Well, this ancient place has some very notable claims connected to modern movements of witchcraft and its followers and, in the words of a 1963 BBC documentary, "is absolutely steeped in witchcraft."* So, I am looking forward to going and finding sites of interest to historians of witchcraft and its modern incarnation in the form of Wicca.

The New Forest, and more particularly the village of Burley, where I am headed, was the home of Sybil Leek, who once described herself in an interview as "just an ordinary witch from the New Forest in England." This was underplaying her hand to some degree. In the 1963 BBC report she is described as "a housewife, a mother, forty-one, an antiques dealer and self-confessed white witch." She was also an accomplished astrologer and occult author of over sixty books on witchcraft, who was known for her public persona as a modern-day witch and openly discussed her practices and her coven at a time when witchcraft was still considered very fringe. She owned an antique shop in Burley and worked for the local television station. She was an advocate of nature-based spirituality and living in harmony with the earth.

There are excellent photos of Sybil with her bird familiar, Mr Hotfoot Jackson, in the New Forest, with arms wide to spread her black cape behind her and her jackdaw atop her head. Apparently, when she attended events with Mr Hotfoot Jackson, he would croak loudly from her shoulder whenever something was said of which she disapproved. In various interviews and writings, she mentioned her fondness for crows and ravens and how they played a significant role in her spiritual practices, as messengers and guides between the physical and spiritual realms and as symbols of magic and intuition. To my mind, all the photos I have seen of Sybil and indeed her many interviews, some of which can be found on YouTube, portray her as someone who would be very fine company.

I still have the postcard Leslie sent me, telling me he had just met Sybil. It depicts Burley's famous antique shop, called 'A Coven of Witches'. Stags'

* "1963: A witches' coven on Halloween", BBC, bbc.com/videos/cqqpr4d50qgo – you can see Sybil with her jackdaw familiar in this short clip.

antlers ornament one wall, while over the door hangs a sign representing a witch riding a broomstick. Housed in one of the New Forest's most picturesque villages, it must have been the perfect setting for their meeting. They became firm friends and I soon had the pleasure of meeting Sybil myself, together with her 'familiar', Mr Hotfoot Jackson.

Doreen Valiente, *The Rebirth of Witchcraft* (1989)

Sybil was born, as she tells us in her book, *Diary of a Witch* (1968): "in the classic place for witches, at a crossroads where three rivers also meet, a wild, desolate, witch-ridden part of Staffordshire. Three counties also meet there at the base of the Pennine Range…it is a tough, wild part of the country, with the blue-grey mountains dominating the landscape, where acres of heather make a purple carpet, where fairy rings are found." Like the mythical witch, Leek's beliefs and practices were rooted in a reverence for nature and the land, viewing it as a source of spiritual guidance and power. She was the modern embodiment of the Wise Woman living in the woods (or, as was actually the case, in a very charming village within an ancient forest).

Just at the edge of the New Forest, in Highcliffe, lived another luminary of modern British witchcraft, Gerald Gardner. A revered English occultist and author, he is widely considered the founder of the modern pagan religion of Wicca. In the 1950s, Gardner self-identified as a witch and began the process of founding Wicca as a religion with help from notable witches such as Wiccan High Priestess, Doreen Valiente, creating a pagan faith religion with ideas drawn from many realms, including folk practices and ceremonial magic. In his book *Witchcraft Today* (1954), Gardner's work laid the foundation for Wicca as a structured belief system, emphasising nature worship, seasonal rituals and the practice of magic. This played a large part in bringing modern witchcraft into mainstream awareness. Followers of the religion of Wicca call themselves witches. The word "wicca" was thought to come from Old English roots meaning "to weave/bend" and was later used to refer to a witch or worker of magic. We also have Wicca, Gardner and his peers to thank for the very popular 'Wheel of the Year', a circular calendar of eight festivals, common with pagans, druids and witches. Agricultural points of the year are planted in between observable solar events of equinoxes and solstices, featuring echoes of pre-Christian and pagan practices, once common folk-festivals and a few more idiosyncratic ideas drawn from folklore: Yule/Winter Solstice, Imbolc, Ostara/Spring Equinox, Beltane, Litha/Summer Solstice, Lammas/Lughnasadh, Mabon/Autumn Equinox, and Samhain.

Part of the story Gardner told of his own introduction to witchcraft was that he encountered a coven in the New Forest, where he was captivated by the rituals, the connection to nature, the spiritual beliefs he encountered, and what he saw as the craft's ancient roots and connection to pre-Christian traditions. His experiences greatly influenced his writings, and he was initiated into the New Forest coven in 1939, the same year World War II began.

And that leads us neatly into an event that took place in the New Forest on August 1st 1940 known as the 'Lammas Ritual', or 'Operation Cone of Power'. The story goes something like this…

> *A great circle of witches gathered at night, including the members of the New Forest Coven. They met at a Wilverley Plain in the New Forest, at a former gallows tree called The Naked Man. Also naked, or 'skyclad' those gathered began to dance in a spiralling pattern around the circle, building up to the communal ecstatic state that they believed could control magical forces, raising magical energy known as a "great cone of power". Together they chanted commands directed at the Nazis in Germany, along the lines of "you cannot cross the sea, you cannot cross the sea, you cannot come, you cannot come."*

The number of witches involved ranged from seventeen up to a cast of hundreds, dependent on the teller. Other additions and embellishments to the story include, but are not limited to: the work was so exhausting that several witches died in the time following the ritual. And deceased German soldiers washed up on the southern shores of England immediately after the ritual. The children's film *Bedknobs and Broomsticks* (1971) featuring Angela Lansbury ends with a long scene that brings this event to mind – where a witch on the south coast of England conjures a spell that saves England's shores from the invading Nazis.

The story of this ritual has become legend, between newspaper reports and books by notable names in the Wiccan and occult movements of the 1940s, 50s and 60s – Gerald Gardner, Cecil Williamson, Doreen Valiente, Janet and Stewart Farrer. All gave slightly shifting accounts of the story creating a tale that has passed into folklore, but, I imagine, born from seeds of truth. I have no doubt that those present in the New Forest during wartime offered up prayers and rituals of some kind to banish Hitler, just as Christians pray and modern-day witches may hex corrupt leaders* and warmongers – you do what you can with what you believe. But the story of Operation Cone of Power most likely involves some exaggeration and mythic elements.

One can see why it would be such a favourite story for Wiccans, as an example of how modern witchcraft may be used for what could be considered noble purposes, to show Gardner's patriotism when neopagan witchcraft was routinely associated in the British media with more sordid stories of Satanism and ritual murder.

I should add here that this was all a little before Sybil's time, who moved to the New Forest in the 1950s, and Gardner moved to London in the mid-1950s. So, while two very notable figures in witchcraft inhabited the New Forest at the same time in history, they did not move in the same covens. Sybil respected Gardner's *panache*, as she called it, but considered his propensity for naked rituals a bit tiresome to her ladylike sensibilities. One can relate.

*

I arrive at the edge of the Wilverley Inclosure, which is a fenced area of around 500 acres that is open to the public. It's a mixed area of groves, grassland, marshland, heathers and hedgerows. The terms "enclosure" and "inclosure" are often used interchangeably, older signs seem to say enclosure, where the more modern ones are inclosure. It was, as one sign says "enclosed in 1775 and in 1809" and "thrown open in 1846", and has gone through various periods of enclosure and thrown-open-ness, all tied in to land management, conservation and the regulation of livestock grazing. Within the inclosure is the open grassland known as Wilverley Plain where Operation Cone of Power may well have taken place in 1940.

To get into the inclosure, I have to climb over a fence because the stile is flooded so deeply I don't want to wade into it. The wind blasts the rain so hard into my face that it stings, my steps falter and I swear, but I've no choice but to keep going. My navigation is further challenged as the flood water has turned every path into a stream, so I can't distinguish the path at all anymore and end up crunching through heather on sloping banks. I see a family of deer up a hill in front of me – stag, doe and a fawn – and for a moment, my spirits are lifted:

* In 2017, a mass binding spell towards Donald Trump was organised on social media and performed by witches in the U.S. and around the world, so group magical workings are still going strong in the twenty-first century.

they surely wouldn't be here if the day was bright and busy with walkers. But then I step knee-deep into a bog and swear again. The deer make their escape from this human disturbing their peace and I am mildly panicked. I can't go back. I don't want to sink or step into more bogland, but I am sure there is a path around here somewhere. I use my walking stick to prod in front of me until, with great relief, I feel the more solid ground of a path beneath me and heave myself from the marshy depths. I make my way over the hill.

I come up to a fenced, thickly wooded, coniferous area and there's another gate to pass through. Here, I meet three New Forest ponies sheltering, seeking some protection from the elements in the lee of the dense conifer trees.

A white pony breaks from his group to come and smell my walking stick with his dark velvety nose, I assume, to assess its edibility. My walking stick was made by Dan's dad, who is a skilled woodworker and often makes us amazing gifts: a hedgehog house, a bird house and a wood store all grace our garden. And we each have a very special walking stick. Mine is made of a solid piece of Elder, the white horse nuzzled its carved handle. "Hello, you're nice," I say, and I stand still and calm in the driving rain until he loses interest and wanders off. † I bid him farewell and continue on my way. I thought the pony was just checking if I had snacks to offer. Looking back, maybe I did well to be polite and carry a stick of elder, or maybe he already assumed I was half drowned so his work was done.

It would not be until months after this trip that I read and learnt about the Colt Pixie.‡ In Dorset, Hampshire, Somerset and Wiltshire folklore they are a fairy or spirit fond of shape-changing into equine form. The Colt Pixie as horse is pale and shaggy furred; in the New Forest, you may even still find a few locals who use the term "as ragged as a Colt Pixie" for those who look, as I did during my hike, a bit ruffled. The Colt Pixie has a keenness for luring travellers and even other animals astray into bogs and marshlands; in some accounts, they do this by exuding a light similar to will-o-the-wisp, or they may invite a traveller to ride on their backs only to leap into deep water and drown the poor soul. There's a shimmer of Kelpie stories and the Scandinavian *Bäckahästen* (brook horse) who has the ability to grow to allow as many children on their back as possible before jumping into drowning pools. Did I get away lightly? Maybe not. After meeting the white horse and getting

---

† The advice from the New Forest Park Authority is not to approach, feed or pet the wild ponies (or pigs).

‡ Spelling variations include 'colt pixey' and 'colepixie'.

through the gate, I am walking through the thick-needled conifers. A heavy silence descends as the dark trees buffer the sounds of the roads and the rain. I think I catch a glimpse of a figure behind a tree trunk through the clustered treeline. Spooked, I walk on and don't look back.

*

Past the conifers the grove opens up again into a wide expanse of grassy common dappled with gorse, where a few brave souls are walking their dogs. At this point, I have zero clue where The Naked Man tree – the main reason I came here – may be. And I am definitely past caring. Luckily, along the Wilverley road, I begin to see signs of 'civilisation': a golf course, then a cricket pitch. The rain has stopped. Pools of water reflect trees and hedges. Dusted black-blue sloes sit in tall blackthorn hedgerows, not quite ready for harvest by possible foragers, as we've not yet had the first frost.

At last, I make it into Burley and like a soggy homing pigeon, I find a steamy-windowed café to enjoy an oat milk hot chocolate and peel off my waterproof jacket. My leggings and socks are soaked through but steaming and all is well with the world. I realise I am sitting directly opposite a shop called 'A Coven of Witches', a white-painted brick building, with shining black woodwork and an *olde worlde* sign. During the late 1950s, when Sybil Leek lived in the village, she caused much outraged gossip by walking its streets in her long black cloak with Mr Hotfoot Jackson sitting on her shoulder. Befriending the local gypsies of the forest, she learned stories and lore from them. And she most definitely made her mark on this sleepy town, in the stories still told of her and the shop she named 'A Coven of Witches'.

After I finish my drink. I walk around the corner to my country house hotel. There is a fire crackling before me as I open the door to reception. This was not, by many definitions, a particularly harrowing adventure, but I am delighted to have made it to my destination and pleased with my progress. The hotel is one of cosy, faded grandeur and delightfully warm. Once in my room, I run a bath and place my hiking boots on top of the radiator and all my other clothing over chairs, window hooks and wardrobe doors, the rain and my bog-stumbling have soaked my rucksack through its waterproof cover.

Later that evening, as everything dries out, I have celebratory bread and olives in the bar for tea (and book into the local pub for lunch the next day because what I really wanted was a burger and chips). Out of the window, I watch the resident deer herd on the edge of the hotel's land, as dusk falls. The deer are inexplicably being herded, possibly towards their own supper or shelter, by a man on a penny-farthing bike. I think Sybil would have liked him.

*

The next day I am the picture of smugness. I've had coffee and breakfast in my hotel and the sun is out; it feels positively tropical for November. I walk through an area called Berry Wood and onwards, seeking the Mouse's Cupboard, which is marked on my map by name only; I have no idea what it means and can find limited clues in internet searches, but I am inspired to seek it out. On the journey through the Berry Wood, brown leaves lie settled in circular pools of undulating vibrant mosses, many more wild ponies and gossamer threads dancing from bronze bracken. I see just a single person on the way, walking her dog.

I am on the lookout for pigs, I don't meet any during my visit, but they are around because it is the time of the year special to the New Forest known as *pannage*. Pannage is an old rural practice, started in the era of William the Conqueror where pigs are released to roam in the forest to forage for acorns, beech mast and other nuts, helping to clear the forest floor and reduce the risk of poisoning for ponies and cattle. Through autumn, the New Forest is one the very few places in England to still observe pannage and hundreds of pigs join the free-roaming ponies, donkeys and cattle foraging the forest. Pannage was once one of six ancient rights bestowed to commoners; the others being that one could collect wood, stone, peat for fuel, graze livestock and fish in rivers on common land.

I wander off labelled paths through thick layers of brown leaves for some time before finding what I believe is the Mouse's Cupboard: it's a tree and the sun is shining on it as I approach. Its trunk is hollowed out and weather worn, and two spars of bark rise up before the opening like two little figures. Peering inside, I discover a dark passage that travels deep down into the earth – surely a palace where a mouse might stash their treasures… I know this has nothing to do with witches, but I enjoyed this mouse-sized adventure led by names on a map that can inspire us all.

Then, I finally get my burger and chips. At the pub I booked yesterday, another beautiful building, another roaring fire and I feel I have won the seating lottery as I get a comfy chair right next to it. The village's retired fire chief is in the pub and proudly tells me he'd started the fire and we discuss his skills in both starting fires and putting them out.

*

It was rare not to hear the phone ring in the middle of the night or hear a knock at the door when the rest of the family had gone to bed; another frightened person was seeking the aid of a witch in the Forest. No one was ever turned away from my door. The local police were always nice to me and indeed several members of the constabulary would come to talk about witchcraft. There was no persecution at this time or evidence that we were not honored members of our communities. Sometimes as I walked through the Forest, I would see the large stacks of logs which the Foresters prepared for the winter and I could never repress a little shiver when I thought how many logs had been used from forests like ours to burn witches in the old days. Shortly after I became High Priestess of the Horsa Coven, the Witchcraft Laws were repealed. Although no one had been prosecuted for many years in the New Forest, it is not pleasant to live under the threat of a possible death sentence. I began to feel that I could pass the logs in the Forest without averting my head. In the days just after the repeal of the laws, I think we lived in a fool's paradise. I, for one, was deluded into thinking that now we witches could emerge into the light to show the world what we knew about witchcraft and to offer the tenets of the faith openly for all to examine and decide upon their validity. I have to admit that I was wrong. The world even now is not yet ready for witchcraft, as I know all too well. But then I was wildly enthusiastic, young enough to believe that the injustice of centuries could be wiped out in a few years.

Sybil Leek, *Diary of a Witch* (1968)

I think Sybil had a hopeful vision of acceptance but was realistic and aware of the tensions her work raised, and the harsh reality of enduring prejudice. In her lifetime she saw the repeal of the Witchcraft Laws that allowed her to name herself a witch. But her hope that witches could openly practice without judgment was tempered by a society that wasn't ready to fully embrace or understand witchcraft. Whilst she saw legal protections change, deep-seated prejudices were slower to evolve. Her optimism in her writing, though, reveals something of the resilience of those who practice witchcraft, as well as Sybil's own dedication to her craft and her hopes for the movement.

After lunch I head back to Burley through the village. I can take a proper look at the Coven of Witches shop, now I am not sodden, nor weighed down as I was yesterday. Outside, it is painted white with black framed windows and shutters. I can see from old photos it has changed little since its founding by Sybil. A symbol of a witch on a broomstick hangs on one wall between two sets of antlers, and another witch hangs above the door. A dragon sits on the roof. As far as I understand it, up a bramble and holly-edged forest track behind the shop is the red brick house that once was Sybil's home. I'm here outside of the popular tourist summer season, so the shop, like the village, is quite empty. It smells of dusty books, as many fine curio shops do. Figurines of fairies and dragons, crystal and tarot cards, sit in glass cabinets and shine in the low autumnal sunlight filtering through the windows. It is very quiet in the shop, and I am very aware of the floorboards squeaking under my boots. I want to buy something in small support of the business, so I get some greeting cards with swooping owls on them. There is a lovely framed collection of photos of Sybil at the entrance of the shop. But I didn't feel compelled to quiz the nice lady behind the counter about Sybil, maybe because I'd watched several YouTube videos where presenters had already done so, so I didn't want to bother her with what I'm sure were the same questions she always gets.

Overall, Burley doesn't tout its connection to this famous modern witch that strongly; I wonder if it's connected to the fact that Sybil herself said she left as she was never made to feel particularly welcome in the village. Her landlord wouldn't allow her to renew her lease on her shop, some locals were upset by her presence and not all the villagers were friendly to her. Eventually Sybil moved to America, where she continued studying and writing about the occult and astrology. She arguably became more famous in America as the quirky English white witch and she lived there for the rest of her life. Maybe this lack of Sybil's presence in Burley is just how it feels outwardly to me, the tourist. There may well be hidden practices held by covens connected to Sybil's own Horsa Tradition, of which strands are still thought to exist where she taught in both England and America.

There's a second witch shop called 'Cobwebs and Cauldrons' and a fairy shop called 'Away with the Fairies' too, that I don't go in, but I know Burley is also the location for the annual New Forest Fairy Festival, so maybe the magical focus has shifted more faewards. But I like to think Sybil's influence still settles faintly on one's shoulder here.

Recently we were forced to move from the cottage at the back of our antique shop in Burley and the circumstances of the removal were far from happy.

We had no sooner recovered from the shock of having notice to quit when we had another notice from the landlord of the shop telling us he would not be renewing the lease.

The witchcraft laws of Great Britain were repealed a little over ten years ago but there is still an element of suspicion attached to a subject about which the layman knows very little.

We were fortunate enough to find a tiny, seventeenth-century cottage with a thatched roof, two-foot thick walls slitted with tiny windows and an aviary in the garden, several miles away from the shop and just on the fringe of the Forest.

Sybil Leek, *The Jackdaw and the Witch: a true fable* (1966)

In the 1970s, when Sybil was writing books in an America that was gripped by the "Satanic Panic", she was horrified at some of the terrible crimes committed by people claiming to be witches and Satanists. That centuries-old tradition of connecting witches with devils continues. Witchcraft will continue, no doubt, to be a very personal and varied practice and ideas people have of witches and witchcraft continue to be at every point on the spectrum, from devilish to delightful. But Sybil said she had no desire to appear cackling or cruel.

Sybil played a potent part in a new era of how we view witches, the magical and spiritual paths that can lead us all the way up to the present day, where we see the major modern pagan religions of Wicca and druidry drawn from remnants of pagan precedents. Like many faiths and religions, there are countless strands to such practices, but within many is the folk magic, rites and customs that offer a reverence for the natural world as divine.

Just as the word *witch* means different things to different people, from foraging for herbs by moonlight to hexing political figures, with witchcraft, magic and the many ways such work is being used today, people are hungry I think, for practical solutions to deal with issues that can seem out of our control, such as lifting spirits (or raising spirits) as a way to uplift themselves. Much as magic workers of centuries past did, practical spells, charms and divination can be employed to feel a little stronger in a society that has a habit of pushing people down (especially those considered outsiders). Modern-day interpretations of the witch figure as an icon of power offer resistance to a paradigm of culture that, whilst it has much to recommend in terms of healthcare and standard of living, also still clings to sexism, racism, capitalism and the destruction of the earth.

To be a witch today seems often to be based around being present, mindful and involved in the processes in the natural world – a simple but powerful idea. We perhaps seek the rural and the beautiful and the powers of common folk to help us explore our capacity to embrace magic and to accommodate hope. Hope that it all won't fall apart, that the old ways have not been fully lost to the haste of modern life, and that we won't lose our most precious of natural wonders to accommodate yet another motorway.

*

Sybil died quite young, at the age of sixty-five, by which time she had authored an incredible sixty books. She wrote way more books than I realised. When mentioned on tours of Burley, she is sometimes painted as a bit of a kook. But she was also a prolific author and businesswoman.

Many of the witches and forest beings one might come across are superstition and myth, but Sybil Leek was very real. A witch of a forest, perhaps not quite how many imagine them, but witches rarely are. And I have had a lovely time doing perhaps what Sybil loved most: walking through the New Forest and enjoying the simple and powerful magic of its beauty. And so, when I walk out from Burley onto forest tracks, I like to think these may well be the paths she also walked.

> *Witches being simple people close to nature do indeed believe wholeheartedly in magic, which is all around us. There is alchemy in love – the mysterious feeling which no one is ever quite sure about but which contains all kinds of magical ingredients. There is the magic which drives illness from bodies in pain, there is the magic of a great name, of music, of spring. Magic is a joyous exceptional experience which leads to a sense of well-being and there is nothing we witches love more. So we strive to bring this about by the use of our particular religion, by keeping close to nature, by seeking harmony in ourselves and our environment.*
>
> **Sybil Leek, *Diary of a Witch* (1968)**

WINTER

December • January • February

Witch Marks • Toad Witches • Mists • Underworlds • Witches Kitchen

FIELD NOTES:
WEST COUNTRY MAGIC

Winter lies over the northern world, the greens of meadows and field sleep under a blanket of snow and veils of frost and mist. In winter, we carry the wildwood inside – for fires, light, warmth and cheer – with rich colours and scents of holly, pine and ivy. The tall firs in the dark forest wear sparkling dresses of white hoarfrost, silently guarding the woods and their inhabitants. With the pause button pressed, the year falls quiet and the forest sleeps. I walk gently through crackling frozen leaf piles and frosted paths. I know hares and foxes might be seen, while hedgehogs, dormice and bats are still hibernating, but I have not had the good luck to spot them this season. But deer I see often – they graze in the field opposite my house, very close to where I wait for my bus that goes into town. I watch them from the corner of my eye –if I look directly at them, their heads shoot up and they freeze, ready to bolt, staring back.

Staying close to home in this season, I'll visit Wiltshire, Devon and Somerset.

The West Country is an area of the south-western part of England – it's a term that usually encompasses the counties of Cornwall, Devon, Somerset and Dorset, and , for some (me included), Wiltshire too. These are places of rural landscapes, dramatic coastlines and stone circles. A large part of my relatively small family was born and still lives in the West Country, centred around the city of Bath, Somerset. And I have always considered it my home, despite the fact that I was born two hours south in the city of Portsmouth. I remember for well over a decade of my childhood, every dark Christmas morning barely past the witching hour, in something that feels a little bit like a folk tale itself, we would bundle into the car, and Dad drove us to see our family in and around Bath, arriving before sunrise on Christmas Day. There is a point on this drive from Portsmouth, on the edges of Salisbury, we would pass a village called Nomansland that, to my mind as a child, was like a portal. When Nomanslands was crossed, we were in the 'West', after which everything became a sweeping slideshow of Cotswold stone, cottages and farms decked in fairy lights. Small, still-sleeping villages of churches and chip shops rolled by in cold pre-dawn light. I moved to Bath for university, and after a few stints living in America, I returned to the West Country about fifteen years ago and have lived here ever since. It's a wonderful and magical place to live in and roam around, and a very easy place to love. Folk traditions here still sing raucously, swaying with a cider or two in hand. Of course, the whole point of this book is that there are magical places to be found anywhere and everywhere, but the West Country is certainly blessed with a wealth of magic, and absolutely holds my heart.

In an edition of *The Horn Book* magazine in 1947, Elizabeth Goudge wrote an essay called "West Country Magic" that I will share from here as I cross through a West Country winter, as her love of these counties echo my own, and all the magic she saw here certainly builds my excitement for my paths ahead.

> *The West Country is a kingdom to itself with an indescribable spirit that is all its own… There is magic in all four counties… It shines in the exquisite silvery light, it breathes in the soft air, it is in the woods and orchards and the old deep lanes, in the running of the streams and the singing of the birds. It is – except on wild, frightening Dartmoor – a very gentle magic, suited to this pastoral country of round green hills dotted with grazing sheep, ploughed fields of wallflower-coloured earth where flocks of white sea gulls follow the plough, sheltered villages of white-washed cottages, beautiful manor houses and very old churches with tall towers rising in springtime from a mass of apple blossom. And this gentle magic is essentially a fairy magic. I have always half believed in fairies, but since I have lived in Devon I have believed in them entirely. I have not actually seen one yet, but I expect to any day. Everything I see makes me want to write a story…*

DECEMBER

By a Witches Marke

Bradford on Avon, Wiltshire

It's Friday, and the shortest day of the year. The sun rose at 8.12am this morning, and I was already cradling my first coffee of the day in Bath, to meet my friends and bid them a happy solstice and merry Christmas. Every Friday we meet here, they, after a virtuous early morning yoga class and I, after embarking on the limit of my abilities at 7.30 in the morning, getting on a bus into town. From here, I take the very short train journey to the very beautiful Bradford on Avon.

I am on my way to see a medieval building, hugged close between the Kennet and Avon canal and the River Avon; the two water courses swoop and swerve, staying close, winding and flowing closely together all the way from Bradford on Avon to Bath, where they finally get to embrace and the canal joins the river in Bath. The tithe barn has been here for around seven hundred years, the canal for only two hundred. And the River Avon, which flows through the south-western part of England, passing through cities like Bristol and Bath, has been a significant watercourse for thousands of years.

The great barn

Arriving in town, I take the short walk along the canal to the tithe barn, one of the largest medieval barns in England, built around 1330 to store the 'tithe' – agricultural produce given by local people to support the church. The barn passed through the ownership of several families before arriving into the National Trust's care.

It's dark inside the cavernous barn, except for where light filters in through narrow windows along the barn and at each end, far apart: it is a big space – over fifty metres long, with a great ceiling supported by curving dark wood beams. There are windows shaped like capsized crosses, narrow like those used by archers in castles. And with the veiled cloudy light of the solstice shining through, they remind me of the sword Excalibur, glowing as it's drawn from the lake or from a stone. But where the light really streams in, from the large barn doors, is where I find what I am looking for: witch marks. Lots of them, daisy wheels mainly; I trace my finger over the spirograph-style flowers.

I was excited to discover, in my search for witches that there were tales of markings that many call "witch marks" or "witches marks" in this tithe barn near my Wiltshire home. Not only are they close to home for ease of midwinter travel, but also will afford me a very jolly day of perusing festive wares around the barns (the tithe barn is surrounded by lovely artisan stores and is a delight decked out for winter).

Obviously, Bradford on Avon is conveniently close to me, so travelling here was a factor in picking this location specifically to seek witch marks. But another factor is that the marks at tithe barn are very clear and easy to spot, and can be touched, which felt special; magical workings in plain and touchable sight. The tithe barn is such a well-preserved medieval structure, and its original purpose – collecting tithes from local farmers – ties it to the daily lives and superstitions of medieval communities. To see and touch these historical markings in their original context offered me a tangible connection, a real sense of the value of the tithe within the barn and the protection sought for it (with charms that one may well call witchcraft, always with the contradictions). There is a very real connection between medieval/early modern witch beliefs and the stones of this building, and the physical records within that stone.

Witch marks

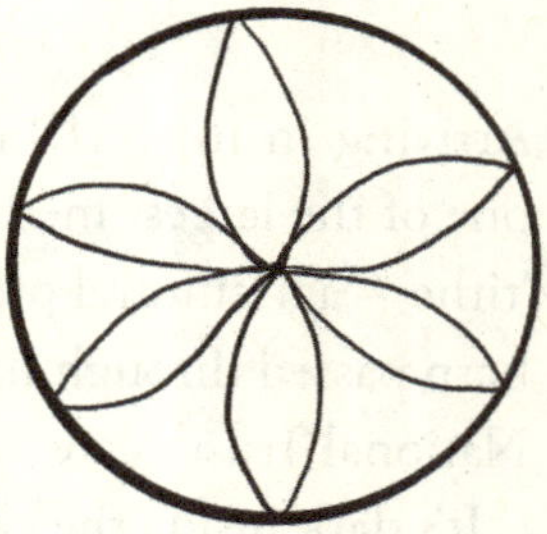

Witch marks are not made *by* witches, but *against* them – they are considered apotropaic – ritual protection markings that were believed to ward off evil spirits, or to trap them. They can be found etched into stone, plaster, woodwork of walls, windows, doorways and chimneys of houses, churches and barns, locations that were considered the most vulnerable and potential entrance points for demons, witches and evil spirits. The marks were created to provide protection to the buildings and those who lived or worked within them.

The evil that was being 'turned away' may have been demons, witches, maleficia or any bad fortune like fire, flood or fever, and to encapsulate all these things using the singular word of 'witch' was, a helpful shorthand, one people have long used especially during the period of the witch trials to encapsulate or represent any misfortune that may befall them. It is unfair, but true that anything from a hangover to adultery, storms, sickness to seduction (both failed and successful attempts at) have been blamed on witches at some point or other.

The types of witch marks in the barn are the daisy wheel, also known as the hexfoil or hexafoil. As the name suggests, the symbol takes the form of a six petalled flower carved using a hand compass and as such looks very geometrical in design. Those familiar with sacred geometry will recognise similarity with design such as the 'flower of life'. Whereas some witch marks are warding in nature, daisy wheels are thought to be a little like dream catchers, somewhere a spirit may get trapped. Demonic spirits would be drawn to follow the lines, becoming trapped – going round and round and be unable to get out again.

Daisy wheels can vary in size and complexity from a single floret to an interlinked group – and it is a group of daisy wheels I am here at tithe barn to see. I have been to this barn before, but I have never seen the daisy wheels, carved into stone walls beside the wooden doors. Now I am looking for them, I can't believe I ever missed them. They are small but beautiful, scattered in seemingly random clusters, overlapping and conjoining. The stone is cold and chalky under my fingertips as I trace the wheeled pattern. But I remain untrapped, which must be a good sign.

Other common witch marks of protection and warding include overlapping Vs, to create icons that look like W's or M's – known as Marian marks or *Virgo Virginum* (Virgin of virgins). It is thought that these marks were invocations to the Virgin Mary to protect the site where they were found. Other types of marks appear as pentagons and pentagrams, mazes, dots, diagonal lines and crosses. All are part of a tradition and ritual of creating symbols and patterns for protective purposes.

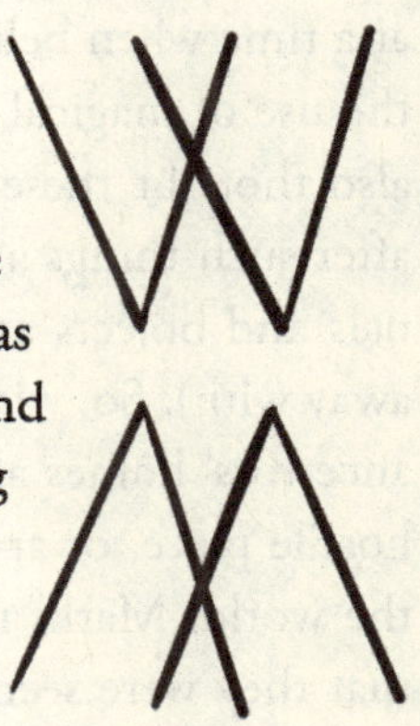

Did everyone believe these marks would trap or ward off a devil or witch? Probably not, but they may well have thought it was better to be on the safe side when it comes to the amorphous world of spirits or luck, much like how, even today, many will try to avoid opening umbrellas indoors or breaking mirrors (two common British suspicions considered unlucky). Few would wish to invite bad luck into their life.

This modern term "witch marks" is not considered particularly helpful by some scholars, but in repelling evil spirits, 'witch' was, as we have seen, a bit of a catch-all term. And these symbols are most well-known to us today as witch marks.

Our contemporary understanding of these markings is surprisingly new. Historian Violet Pritchard, included them in her interpretations of inscriptions and incisions that could be found in all kinds of buildings in her book, *English Medieval Graffiti* (1967). Works such as these prompted many people who, for the first time, took notice of these ritual protection marks that for centuries had been hiding in plain sight; people had dismissed them as pointless graffiti or marks made by builders, rather than warding magic.

Our curiosity about them has only grown since then. In 2016 (on theme, the project launched on October 31st), English Heritage launched a public appeal for information and pictures of witch marks. The idea was/is to learn more about the regional location of marks and to build a record of England's apotropaic marks, to locate marks in buildings around the country, in order to try and better understand why they were used. We are potentially seeing physical proof of a fear of witches, or at least a desire not to go inviting them in.

Witch marks can also be found in caves: Creswell Crags is a well-known example, and I am delighted to discover they are also in Wookey Hole Caves because I have already planned to visit in February. Witch marks were made at a time when belief in witchcraft and the supernatural was widespread and the use of magical symbols and ritual objects was part of everyday life. It is also thought these symbols may have seen a boom after the Reformation, after such things as holy water and consecrated candles were abolished (rituals and objects associated with fripperies of Catholic tradition were done away with). So, witch marks may have been cut, scratched or carved into our ancestors' homes and churches in the hope of making the world a safer, less hostile place, or at least feeling so: a physical clue to how our ancestors saw the world. Marks may well have been such a common part of everyday life that they were seen as unremarkable and, then in time, so easy to overlook, like horseshoes* above front doors. These are very everyday magics.

Running my fingertips over the cold, creamy Bath stone, the local limestone, I cannot help but think of an idea of haunting called Stone Tape Theory. It is a paranormal hypothesis suggesting that certain physical material, like stone or buildings, can absorb and store energy from past events, particularly from traumatic or emotional events, presumably ones that raise the most intense energy. Stone Tape Theory has been something of a buzzword over the

* Horseshoes were once made of iron, a metal believed to have protective qualities and to ward off evil spirits.

past years, revived by popular ghost and folkloric podcasts and TV shows in part. According to the theory, stored energies can later be "replayed" under the right conditions, leading to ghostly apparitions or hauntings. The fact that the name and idea was inspired by a 1972 British TV play called *The Stone Tape,* probably doesn't help its credibility. But the ideas are, nonetheless, tantalising. I don't know if witches can haunt buildings but the remains of what was done to protect oneself from them can still be seen in this stone. Can that replaying of energy stored be *felt* by sensitive individuals perhaps? Like my aunt for example, who I have mentioned in previous books, who cannot visit Avebury Stone Circle because her one visit had her feeling like her skin was burning. I am sure there are countless accounts of places where people can feel an energy of a place, both good and bad. After all, in this very real mark I run my fingers over, there is a physical remnant of fear, uncertainty and protection; I know this: can I feel it? Am I the record player needle reading the grooves of recorded magic? The messages are still here for any who wish to read them, a form of intentional interaction with the supernatural realm. We can interpret witch marks as attempting to control or repel unseen energies – the marks that were carved could be seen as absorbing or holding protective intent. So maybe there is something in the idea of memories held in stone.

Other forms of protection from evil included charms and hidden objects. Such things as single shoes, dolls, dead cats and witch bottles are sometimes discovered hidden away within buildings during renovations.

Other kinds of witch marks...

Before this relatively modern practice of identifying apotropaic marks as "witch marks", when one spoke of witches' marks, one was more likely referring to marks upon the body of an accused witch. Thought to be a mark created by the devil whereby the witch's imp, or familiars suckled, they were called "witches' marks" or "devil's marks". And an accused witch could be proved so "By a Witches marke, which is upon these baser sort of witches…"† Sometimes the search of a body was done by local women, sometimes

† *A Guide to Grand-Jury Men, Divided Into Two Bookes,* Richard Bernard (1627).

midwives, or by witch prickers who would also pierce marks with needles, pins or blades to see if the mark bled or caused the accused witch pain. According to superstition, the witch could not feel the prick, or bleed from the mark – which could be anything from a mole or skin tag, to a scar or boil. To be "Try'd by Pricking"* was particularly popular practice in Scotland where witch prickers such as John Kinkade had something of a reputation in the same way as Matthew Hopkins for his witchfinding in the South of England.

Yule tide

A lit Christmas tree stands outside of the tithe barn and over the grass yard there is the granary, now a shop of Christmas garlands, trinkets, sparkly baubles and candles.

Christmas, as a holiday is, for many of us common folk, a mishmash of customs: pagan, Roman, Germanic, Christian, with a sprinkling of folk magic. Similarly, an assortment of ideas from Roman, Germanic, Celtic, Norse, and rural customs have also created stories of witches and witchcraft, demons and familiars. All mingle together in our stories and imagery of the witch. This is just one reason why both Christmas and the image of the witch are so rich and multi-layered and endlessly fascinating. To keep the many fears of the cold dark nights at bay we may sing songs, tell stories, make the witch marks, warding charms and hang holly boughs. I walk into the granary to admire beams strewn with holly, lights and baubles. These green branches are, intended or not, some far distant cousins of the boughs of greenery, herbs and charms hung during pagan festivities.

A range of plants enjoy connections with Christmas due to their status as evergreens: coniferous trees, holly, mistletoe and ivy all spring to mind. All hold value as both decorative and magical plants. Some tree and plant folklore is connected directly to witches, other snippets of tales and superstition are parts of rural superstition, folk magic and practice that may well have led someone to be suspected of being a witch themselves.

* "A relation of the diabolical practices of above twenty wizards and witches of the sheriffdom of Renfrew in the kingdom of Scotland, contain'd in their tryalls, examinations and confessions and for which several of them have been executed this present year" (1697).

My grandmother used to say that a sure way to keep a witch outside your home was to hang a garland of holly and bay outside the front door at Christmas: the witch would remain there, counting the holly berries – indefinitely, presumably, since witches only count up to four before starting again at one.

Kathleen Wiltshire, *Wiltshire Folklore* (1975)

My aunt brings holly *(Ilex aquifolium)* into her house every year at Yule. This must be done, according to her, before the new year, to ensure good luck for the coming year ahead. People also hung boughs of holly leaves and berries around the house to bring colour to the dark days of Yule, as well as keeping evil spirits away. Holly brought into the house may also allow faeries who wished to join in the festivities, a place to shelter in the home and thus avoid conflict between them and the human occupants. Holly trees may be used as boundary trees planted in the hedgerows to prevent the passage of witches, who were known to fly or run along the top of hedges – the spikes would stop them in their path, a belief particularly popular in Germanic lore. Similar theories were held to other spiky plants like gooseberry bushes, which may be planted to ward witches away from livestock.

Holly is the tree of the gentle folk. Scottish people decorated their houses with branches to protect themselves from fairy mischief during Hogmanay, leaving an offering (usually a silver coin) at the base of the tree to appease the spirits. Every part of the plant is toxic, but folklore still finds it indispensable. Leaves were burned like incense to strengthen magic and it was said a holly wand added protection to a practitioner while performing magic.

Sandra Lawrence, *Witch's Garden: Plants in Folklore, Magic and Traditional Medicine* (2020)

In our pagan past in Europe, the mistletoe *(Viscum album)* was perhaps considered a magical plant because it grows in an 'in-between' place, between earth and sky. It can be found growing on hawthorn and ash and more rarely, on oak trees. In the UK it seems particularly fond of cultivated apple trees. Mistletoe was considered magical to the ancient druids because the evergreen mistletoe bears its fruit in winter, it is an emblem of fertility and a symbol of rebirth. Traditionally it was hung over the doorway at Yule, tied with red ribbon for harmony and to represent a welcome to all who visit. In England the tradition of kissing under mistletoe began to feature in written works around the 1700s – the mistletoe formed part of the 'kissing bough' and with each kiss, a berry had to be plucked off, for luck.

We have two native species of ivy in the UK: *Hedera helix* and *Hedera Hibernica,* common ivy and Atlantic ivy respectively. In some traditions, carrying a piece of ivy was believed to bring good luck and prevent misfortune. Its evergreen nature means ivy may be a symbol of undying love and fidelity. Ivy should be brought into the house only at Christmas and it may stay in the home, along with holly garlands until Candlemas (also called Imbolc, Feb 1st/2nd) when it should be burnt, to not do so would invite in mischief in forms of fairies, pixies and poor luck. And if you make an ivy wreath and wear it on May Day, you'll be able see witches.*

> *Evergreens and holly, box, mistletoe, ivy and yew, all are popular decorations. Holly is said to discourage witches and tax collectors… Superstition dictates that on no account may holly (or mistletoe, in some places) be brought indoors prior to Christmas, lest bad luck result. By Candlemas, according to old tradition, all greens must be removed and burned.*
>
> **Dorothy Gladys Spicer, *Yearbook of English Festivals* (1954)**

*

After some festive mooching and lunch, I set off past the tithe barn, along the Kennet and Avon canal to walk all the way back to Bath. There are families, friends walking in groups, lots of runners and dog walkers. The path from Bradford on Avon along to Avoncliff is busy and pretty in winter muted tones. Bare trees reach out over the water, a few dressed in green moss and ivy – whose leaves are dancing in the cold wind. A distant cousin of mine lives on a houseboat in London called the Baba Yaga, so I'm on the lookout for witchy boat names; they run by almost like poetry of personal passions: *Narrow Escape, Barn Owl, Elm, Sloe Gin Palace, Midsummer Spirit, Wayward Angel* and *Aelfwenn*, two *Merlins* (so that's two wizards at least) *Blackthorn, Eleftheria* (which means freedom in Greek).

I had visions of frosty misty air hovering over the water and the narrowboats. It's not frosty, but there's a bitterly cold wind – the tail end of a storm that has caused the windows in our house to scream and whistle is finally losing its edge. The canal boat chimneys still cast plumes of woodsmoke through the air and scent the breeze. The River Avon is to my right as I walk to Avon-

* *Treadwell's Book of Plant Magic*, Christina Oakley Harrington (2020).

cliff, I can see its surface rippling in the wind. At a brief few moments during the walk, the sun shines for just a flash, at one point lighting up an apple tree bare of all its leaves but holding on to so many round golden apples. (These apples are a gleaming yellow, but actual golden apples feature in classical folklore, and I've delighted in writing of them in previous books.)

Wild clematis *(Clematis vitalba)* makes white plumes in the tree-lined walk, the occasional puff flying free on the wind. Also known as 'old man's beard', the old man in question is the devil, inspired by the plants intrusive and weed-like growing habits, often killing other plants. The devil pops up often in plant folk names along with witches and fairies. Other regional names for wild clematis include devil's guts, devil's twine and hag rope. Early Christians, however, said the plant had sheltered the Holy Family on their flight into Egypt, variously referring to it as lady's bower, maiden's hair and shepherd's delight. It was also known as traveller's joy, a name quoted by John Gerard in his "Herball", first published in 1597, where he enthused that "each seed having a fine white plume like a feather fastened to it, which maketh in the winter a goodly show, covering the hedges white all over with his feather-like tops."

I am enjoying today's opportunity to re-tread steps on a much-loved path that I have not walked for many years. Swans glide past, some still with the soft brown colouring of recent growth from cygnetry. I think of the Christmas carol, "The Twelve Days of Christmas" – *seven swans a swimming.* A lime green canal boat has a giant Christmas wreath upon its prow. Once I've crossed over the Avoncliff canal bridge, the river is now on my left and the railway line is sandwiched between the two waterways. The path becomes very empty and quiet. Even though I set off just before one, here on the shortest day there is a feeling that dusk is just round the corner. I have a torch in my bag just in case.

I walk past the charming canal-side gardens of the narrowboat residents – wind chimes, seats made of logs and fashioned into toadstools and swings made of rope. I see a heron ahead of me and try to walk past very slowly so as not to disturb his vigil. He turns his head to cast me a side-eye as I pass behind him, and he returns to his focus. A second heron on the far side bank is completely unfazed by my presence.

There are bewitching beings that are said to inhabit the waters of Britain, these water witches are more often portrayed as feral creatures in wilder bodies of water like rivers and stagnant pools or the kind of mossy bogs that might hold corpse lights and will-o'-the-wisps. And all could be seen as cautionary figures that may well have been invoked by parents to warn their children from playing near water. Waterways, just as with trees and other natural features, are each guarded by their own *genius loci* – a spirit of a place. The physical characteristics reflecting their particular habitat and sometimes fearsome characteristics.

*

Time passes at a different pace along canals, as I imagine anyone who has piloted a canal boat will tell you; things take time and boats can be overtaken by walkers. I overtook a few myself as I marched onwards past the stone bridge of Dundas Aqueduct, not that anyone much minds because we are not in a rush in this place. My walking takes on a meditative quality and I am put to mind the magical-tinged practices of celebrating Yuletide, the winter solstice…

Mother Night

Mother Night, is, we believe an Anglo-Saxon festival, but we know so very, very little about it. Like some of our most treasured stories, for me at least, the idea of Mother Night is caught somewhere, like silken threads in tree branches on a dark and windy night. It is an enchanting notion and a glimpse of something perhaps a little more matriarchal and mystical in the dark nights of December.

Some of the most tantalising snippets of past celebrations in these lands are from the medieval English historian and monk we know as the Venerable Bede, who wrote *De Temporum Ratione (The Reckoning of Time)*, a history of the calendar written in the early eighth century. He stated that the pagan Anglo-Saxons celebrated *Modranicht*, or Mother Night, in the depths of winter around the time of the winter solstice, after which the days would begin to lengthen again.

In *De Temporum Ratione,* Bede writes:

> *…began the year on the 8th calends of January [25 December], when we celebrate the birth of the Lord. That very night, which we hold so sacred, they used to call by the heathen word Modranicht, that is, "mother's night", because (we suspect) of the ceremonies they enacted all that night…*

And...that's it. That's all we have on Mother Night from any historical written source. Bede, to our knowledge, is the only person to mention Mother Night, and even his knowledge of it seems scant. In most sources up until 1038, Anglo-Saxons referred to 'midwinter' (*midne winter* or *middum wintra*) and then in 1038 the first recorded appearance of *Cristes Maessan* (Christmas). Nonetheless, Modranicht remains an intriguing and enchanting idea that has been picked up by some. Some modern pagans/heathens celebrate on December 24 or the eve of the winter solstice; no details of the original festival survive, so it's pretty open to personal interpretation. It may have been a new year celebration. The "mothers" referred to may well be ancestral mother goddesses, matrilineal ancestors or Mother Earth. And I think many find it quite easy to accept as an idea because there are echoes of 'mother' themes coming in from other religious festivals – the Christian feast of the Nativity and the Virgin Mary, and older myths featuring winter crone goddesses such as the *Cailleach* (Celtic/Gaelic) and *Holle/Holda* (Germanic).

So it may be that Modranicht was a time of both religious and cultural significance for the Anglo-Saxons, the beginning of the Yule season. It may have been considered a shimmering time when rituals and ceremonies were performed to ensure protection, fertility and blessings for the coming year. Winter solstice, Mother Night or even New Year's Eve were a time for divination rituals, the threshold times being when spirits and supernatural beings abounded and the veils between worlds were thin; allowing a walker access into the foreshadowing power of the season.

Årsgång, the 'Year Walk' is a Swedish tradition of a solitary, midnight walk in the dark and silent paths of winter woodlands or forest. One would take themselves far from the village lights and the chatter of winter festivities and a vision may be sought of the year ahead. The Year Walk is a form of divination and recorded in documents dating back to the 1600s, but these texts also suggest the tradition goes back far further into history. A walker may hear songs coming from the woods or see spirits, but would try to avoid pesky elves, fairies or more frightening entities, all of whom may distract a year walker from their quest. In some descriptions of the ritual, the walker would leave their home in the middle of the night and in silence, walk through a forest or woodland toward a sacred space (such as a church) and if the spirits allowed it, you would see your future, seeing what was ahead personally or for your community. Similar practices can no doubt be seen across the world. In another tradition that has made its way into English customs, the 26th of

December to January 6th are when signs from the natural world can be read as omens for the year ahead; I have heard these called the Omen Days. In the last decade this time has been called *twixtmas* – we still use this as a sort of time out of time, betwixt and between, apart from our daily lives, a perfect time to pause and reflect – how much divination we bring into this time is variable, but it is common to craft a resolution or two, a hope we may seek to manifest for the year ahead. The conventions suggested for Omen Days vary, but each day may be considered to correspond to one of the twelve months in the coming year. Any omens, dreams or portents observed on the given date foretell what will transpire in the corresponding month; similar practices can be seen the world over as we have long sought to gather information on what the future may hold. Today, newspapers and magazines often use this slow news time at the end of the year, when journalists are on their Christmas holidays, to forecast what lies ahead in the new year, from horoscopes to forthcoming books, films, fashions or trends, predicting what will make it 'big'.

> *It appears certain, from some passages in the Vedas, that twelve nights about the winter solstice were regarded as prefiguring the character of the weather for the whole year. A Sanscrit text is noticed by Weber, which says expressly, 'The twelve nights are an image of the year.' The very same belief exists at this day in Northern Germany. The peasants say that the calendar for the whole year is made in the twelve days between Christmas and Epiphany, and that as the weather is on each of these days so will it be on the corresponding month of the ensuing year. They believe also that whatever one dreams on any of the twelve nights will come to pass within the next year.*
>
> **Charles Hardwick, *Traditions, superstitions, and folk-lore, (chiefly Lancashire and the north of England:) Their affinity to others in widely-distributed localities; their eastern origin and mythical significance*** (1872)

*

After I cross over Dundas Aqueduct, I head to Bathhampton to get my bus home. By the time my Fitbit buzzes to tell me I've made it to the ten-mile point, I'm feeling ready to settle onto a soft bus seat and be carried back to my house. By 3.40pm, the moon has risen and the clouds are turning a rich creamy gold reflected in the water, the colour of crème caramel. The festive lights of Bathampton village are shining. I cross over the bridge to the village and catch my bus. I get home just as the sun is setting at 4.02pm, ready for a hot bath and to climb into my Christmas pyjamas. Merry Midwinter to all, and to all a good night!

JANUARY

By Mist and Moor

Dartmoor, Devon

So far we've encountered witch marks, witch trees, magical stones, vivid history, enchanting folk tales and fascinating remains that can contribute to the rich archive of a place's...what's the word? Energy? Composition? Layers? It sometimes feels like we struggle, I know I do, to find the right words to describe something just beyond our grasp, leading us to gather a group of fun words to dance around the description. I've noticed terms like *psychogeography, sense of place* and *hauntology* cropping up on my journeys. While they weren't created to describe the same thing exactly, they certainly touch on similar ideas from different viewpoints. For example, can a place hold past events within its cracks and crevices, enchanting and connecting us to a deeper sense of place? Hauntology suggests that certain spectres from the past can loiter in the present, with echoes of history reverberating through landscapes. Like the Stone Tape Theory, I mentioned in December. Can places and structures hold onto their own history in ways we can't quite yet fathom?

Psychogeography, on the other hand, involves the psychological exploration of spaces, delving into the hidden layers of both urban or natural landscapes and tracing connections between people and their environments. Our experience of any place is part of its psychogeography, influencing how we feel and how the place affects us. The act of seeing what is around us is a way of seeking the extraordinary within the ordinary. As humans, we inject symbolism and meaning into our surroundings and any space can offer symbolism and meaning set down and reflected back to us. Can the stories of witches bewitch the land itself? Is there an element of dissonance involved when sites that enchant in the present have been a place of violence in the past. Can we see them in new light? Is it human nature to seek light in the dark? To walk through past pains with respect to honour present beauty, as nature returns, growing and building new life over horrors?

Being part of a place's story invites us to consider how we act and how we might reinscribe a place's unspoken histories and experiences. All places have a story, not necessarily of a witch, but certainly of mystery and maybe a sprinkle of magic. If seeking magic in the landscape, it's like experiencing nature in general – there's no wrong way to do it (within the brackets of the leave-no-trace mentality, of course). Whether it's finding magic in the first light of dawn, opening a window, growing a snowdrop on a windowsill, walking a path, or sitting under an elder tree, it's about appreciating what is around us.

*

It is nice to start a new journey in January, when all is white. Frosts, ice, and snow swathe the landscape to create a blank canvas: the new year stands before us. Awaiting explorations not quite formed, I seek to step out of the fog of the year just past, carrying gifts and gratitudes and trying to shuffle the piles of half-forgotten life lessons like one too many library books. With trees stripped bare of leaves and the foliage died back, this is a season of crackling, frosted footsteps, storms, dark, starry skies and rolling mists. The perfect time to visit Dartmoor.

Dartmoor is a vast, wild and beautiful expanse of moorland in Devon, in south-west England, a landscape threaded with rivers, and peppered with stone circles and standing stones, boasting over twenty stone circles and the largest concentration of stone rows in Britain. "Our miles of broad and almost deserted moorland, the deep valleys, the dark combes, and our stormy iron-bound coasts, may to a certain extent have inclined the Devonians of the past to a firmer belief in the miraculous, than would be found in a more populous and less rugged county..."* The iconic granite-topped hills, known as tors, rise sharply from the surrounding moorland. The very names of these tors – Hound Tor, Crow Tor, Kings Tor, Dartmeet Tor, and Merrivale Tor – hint at the rich folklore and wild stories of this place. Each tor and standing stone carries its own stories and superstitions, many of which are intertwined with tales of witches and magic.

There are a lot of excellent books on the folklore of Dartmoor, a place tumbling with legends, strewn in every stone. For Christmas, my dad gave me a book called *Walking the Stories & Legends of Dartmoor: A Guide to 20 Walks Retracing the Stories and Legends of Dartmoor* by Michael Bennie; it's brilliant and exactly what I'm looking for. So, along with *Witchcraft and Folklore of Dartmoor* by Ruth St. Leger-Gordon, I have two guiding texts of Dartmoor that give me far more witches in the landscape than I can hope to cover in one trip.

*

On Thursday, Dan drives us down to Dartmoor National Park. Our first stop is the Nine Maidens; a stone circle that can be found on the sloping banks of Belstone Common, that is peaked with tors, on the edge of the village of Belstone. It is freezing so we walk quickly to warm our bones. After parking

* *Devonshire Witches*, Paul Karkeek (1874).

up at the Belstone car park, we walk past beautiful stone and thatch cottages. Several groups of walkers are about, including a few leaving the warmth of an appealing-looking pub. We walk past the church and up a frosted lane, flowing water in a gulley at the lanes edge is topped with a crust of ice like a crème brûlée (this is not the first or last time I use desserts to describe the delicious visual delights of nature!) We enter Belstone Common, past a sign warning us that the land is part of a military training area. From the sign we learn that in 1939, with the beginning of the Second World War, nearly all of Dartmoor's unenclosed land was used for training. Still today, Dartmoor provides a training landscape for soldiers, sailors and airmen. The red flag of warning is flying, but there are also quite a few dog walkers up on the Common, so we take this to mean we can go on the Common but stick to the paths. We walk uphill on a very small, about one-mile, section of the Tarka Trail,† a route that includes the Nine Maidens (called Nine Stones on the OS map). The stone circle is on our left, the stones smaller than I was expecting.

The first thing that hits me about the Nine Maidens is that there are far more than nine stones, which I wasn't expecting (confusingly, Seventeen Brothers is another name for this circle). The legend of the Nine Maidens says that they are the petrified remains of young women who had the temerity to dance on the Sabbath. Other versions of the story include that they were turned to stone either for disturbing a coven of witches or for practising witchcraft themselves. And of course, we all want to see proof of this magic, which is also worked into the stories. It is said that they can still be seen dancing. According to various tales, this is at noon, at night, or at the Hunter's Moon, or that all nine maiden stones shift their position very slightly at midday – as they are damned to dance every noon for eternity as a punishment for dancing on the Sabbath, or is it the ringing of the nearby church bells that brings them to life? And is it this constant dancing which is to blame for so many guesses towards their number?

Stone circles take serious time and effort to construct. So, whilst it is a hugely common cautionary folktale of folks dancing too vigorously on Sabbaths/Sundays/holy days, these stones were in fact once made to be sacred – to hold rituals, possibly not riotous dancing but certainly celebrations of sorts – so I think it's not beyond the realms of possibility that people once danced

† The Tarka Trail is a 180-mile, figure-of-eight walking and cycling route around North Devon, inspired by the route travelled by Tarka the Otter in Henry Williamson's popular 1927 novel of the same name.

within these stones before tales were retold as a punishment or warning for revelry. (And you may now dance to your heart's delight around these stones, so we've come full circle!)

Like many of the named stones of Dartmoor, the names are often shadowed versions of less enchanting titles. Michael Bennie considers the maidens, like many others, almost certainly a corruption of the Celtic *maen*, meaning 'stone'. The stones were part of the retaining wall of an ancient burial chamber, which would originally have been covered with earth. Today, we count just sixteen stones, though it's possible to up the tally to twenty if we include smaller and toppled stones. And the closer we get to Belstone Tor, the more granite stones we see, they are scattered everywhere and we have to pick our way through them.

In *Witchcraft and Folklore of Dartmoor*, Ruth St. Leger-Gordon quotes this poem from the *Book of Avis* trilogy by Eden Phillpotts as supposedly inspired by the Nine Maiden stone circle (she acknowledges that the number has changed again and Phillpots reduces the Belstone maidens to seven, suggesting that if this number resulted from a personal count, Phillpots must have been badly pixie-led).

And now at every Hunter's Moon
That haggard cirque of stones so still
Awakens to immortal thrill
And seven small maidens in silver shoon
Twixt dark of night and white of day
Twinkle upon the sere old heath
Like living blossoms in a wreath
Then shrink again to granite grey.
So blue-eyed Dian shall ever dance
With Linnette, Bethkin, Jennifer,
Arisa, Petronell and Nance.

The Hunter's Moon is usually the name of the full moon in October, which comes after the Harvest Full Moon. Here on our visit in January, the moon is visible in the clear blue sky for most of the day; it is waxing towards the full Wolf Moon. Symbolic of howling hungers, wild animals and wailing winds, perfect for this trip to see wild dancing women, hounds and devils…

The stone circles on Dartmoor, are said to have been made "when there were wolves on the hills and winged serpents in the low lands." On the side of Belstone Tor, near Oakhampton, is a small grave circle called "Nine Stones." It is said to dance every day at noon.

***Notes and Queries: A Medium of Inter-Communication For Literary Men, Artists, Antiquaries, Genealogists, Etc.* Issue 61 (1850)**

But why do we say the number of stones total nine, regardless of the actual number? The number nine is considered powerful and is found in many myths. The use of the number nine when there are actually seventeen stones may have connotations of witchcraft: "These nine maidens are, of course, another embodiment of the three times three mystic number, seen again in the nine Muses and the nine Valkyries, for example," says Ruth St. Leger-Gordon. After all this, it's still not entirely clear to me how many stones there are supposed to be here. And how many there once were, maybe like the Rollright King's Men and Long Meg and her daughters (who we'll meet in August), we aren't supposed to know...with so many stories, it seems there is no single answer.

From the Nine Maidens, we head up to the scattered stones on Belstone Tor. Picking our way through many more granite rocks. As we approach the tor there is standing ice where water would have flowed a few days previously and icicles spill off the edges of the rounded rocks. The cold wind bites but beautiful views surround us. We head back down to the village of Belstone and back into the car to retreat to an enchanting hotel and a glass of fizz. We are certainly well-cosseted from the wild and icy winds as evening falls.

*

On Friday, we park up at the wonderfully named Pork Hill car park (there must be a story somewhere as to why it is titled as such, but as yet it has eluded me), which is busy but not full. We walk over short green grass to Pew Tor first. The sky is a vivid blue and the famed mists of Dartmoor can be seen in sweeping bands over the grasslands and farms, lush green pastures, in the distance.

The hoar frost arrived and settled in the clear, still night. When we woke this morning, everything was covered with sparkling gems of crystalline ice. By mid-morning in the sun, it was slowly departing. But the Gorse bushes with golden flowers that dot the landscape still hold sprinkled sparklings of frosted shadows, and frost can still be seen in the lee of each bush and stone and frosted feathers of icy twigs hide out at the bottom of each plant. Anywhere where the sun has not yet hit is still white and glimmering with nature's glitter.

Frosts and ice have helped to sculpt Dartmoor's unique landscape. After the last Ice Age, there was a long cold period when rainwater seeped into the cracks in the granite. Through the freeze-thaw process, massive pressure meant stones cracked open and sections crumbled away. Over tens of millions of years of being eroded by wind, rain and ice, the stunning stones and dramatic rock stacks of Dartmoor were created.

*

From the rocks of Pew Tor, we can see all the way to the sea at Plymouth; it shines golden in the sunshine. The huge stones of Pew Tor make a rough circle, creating a sheltered grassy area at their centre. The rock formations of Pew Tor lend themselves to stories of early Druid temples with stone seats surrounding the natural rock basin for rituals, or a palace of the pixie king perhaps, with many a potential doorway into another realm within the crevices and crags of the distinctive Dartmoor granite.

Onwards from Pew Tor, we walk to the next tor in our sightlines – Heckwood Tor and from here we have a fantastic view of the ground that sweeps all the way down to Vixen Tor, home to the witch I came to meet. Sadly, it must be from a distance as we cannot get to Vixen Tor herself. The tor is on private land and since 2003 access by the public has been banned, causing protests and mass trespassing by hikers and climbers, which I'm sure the witch would approve of – both the acts of righteous rebellion and the chance for more prey to walk her way.

Vixen Tor's shape has been likened to a Sphinx and of course, a vixen or a witch's face. All considered tricksy creatures, as reflected in the story of Vixana the Witch…

> *On Vixen Tor, there once lived a witch called Vixana; she lived in a cave at the foot of Vixen Tor, built for her by the earth-dwelling gnomes. Vixana's coven would gather to dance at the tor's peak, revelling in their dastardly plans. She delighted in calling up a mist to surround travellers. As they passed the foot of the tor, they would lose their way, wandering into the bog and marshes, sucked down to their death.*

One fateful day, a young man walked past Vixen Tor, and Vixana brought down the mist as usual. But this young man was not the usual traveller – for he had recently rescued a pixie from a bog and as a reward the pixie had gifted him a ring, a ring that when worn, made him invisible and gave him the power to see through mists and fogs and enchantments. So, as the mists fell he slipped on his magic ring, and this is how he was able to find his way undetected behind Vixana. He toppled her from her rocks and she died amidst the boggy mire and voracious rocks below.

On our loop back to the car park, we find the old lichen-coated Windy Post cross, with its unmistakable lilt. It stands above a glassy stream which is being enjoyed by a string of Dartmoor ponies. Dartmoor ponies are a hardy, semi-wild breed native specifically to Dartmoor National Park. These strong, stocky little ponies have adapted, with thick manes and coats, to the wild winds and weather of Dartmoor. Historically, they have carried loads and pulled carts, but today, they are valued for their contribution to the landscape and biodiversity of Dartmoor, as well as their role, like the New Forest ponies, in local tourism and culture.

A little old cross on the windy heather,
Roughly hewn out of granite gray,
Fretted and worn by the wind and the weather,
Carved by the monks of a bygone day.

V. Phillips, "The Windy Post"

We see other crosses on our drive and looked up later the fact that the crosses were medieval waymarkers on the old monastic track which connected the abbeys of Buckfast and Tavistock.

Our next stop is the Two Bridges Hotel, where we've booked a traditional Devonshire cream tea – I'm already looking forward to freshly made, warm scones with jam and thick cream and a steaming pot of tea. Our bellies are rumbling in anticipation, but first we must walk a long straight track past fluffy cows to the very small patch of trees which is all that remains of Wistman's Wood: a grey-green cluster of English, or pedunculate, oak *(Quercus robur)* trees cowering over moss-covered rocks with just a few holly, hazel and rowan scattered in between. These oaks are notable because they are so short: twisted and stunted by the great winds that whistle over Dartmoor. The mist brings moisture that covers everything in rich mosses that look like green felt, blanketing rocks and trees alike. The moss and stunted trees create a somewhat otherworldly look to Wistman's Wood, supported by local tales, of course. It is said that the devil (also known locally as Old Dewer) sallies forth from Wistman's Wood at night, riding his headless black horse and accompanied by his pack of black wisht hounds. But this is no ordinary hunt: he is after human – not animal – prey. When darkness falls, the devil's wisht hounds hunt unwary travellers and drive them deeper into the woods, never to be seen again. And on the howling night winds, one may hear the baying hounds, thunderclaps and laughter of the devilish troop.

The image of the devil dog and spectral hell hound(s) runs rampant through British folklore, with different areas and counties having different takes on the beasts, including, but not limited to (there are so many!): the Wisht (a word that can mean ghostly/haunted/sorrow); Hounds of Devon and Somerset; the Yell or Yeth (Heath) Hounds also found in Devon; the Wish or Witch Hounds of Sussex. And then there are the singular huge dogs often with sharp teeth and glowing red eyes: Black Shuck who stalks the dark lanes of East Anglia; Old Scarfe who howls and rattles his chains around Norfolk; and the Barghest who prowls the Yorkshire Dales.

There is something a little haunted and melancholy about Wistman's Wood, it has been withering in size for centuries. This could be a reassuring metaphor for the devil's home shrinking, except woods shrinking is never a heartening sight. Wistman's Wood has enjoyed a boom in popularity featuring on many Instagram and YouTube accounts. Its otherworldly beauty chiming with ideas of whimsy, eeriness, magic and natural beauty that are popular with many online. But this has put the very small space under pressure and slow-growing mosses are being disturbed. There are signs asking sightseers not to go into the woods, the moss and trees being so delicate, those who have seen the woods on social media will know that people do not always heed this request. I am unsure what to do, how to experience this place. There are no eerie mists this afternoon, just a crisp cold blue sky. I decide to sit beside the path to take in the woods and admire the oaks and their clawing curling branches cloaked in moss from a distance.

If there was a question in my mind about this being the right thing to, it is swiftly answered. I do not meet the devil but a very inquisitive robin, feathers puffed up to make him particularly round to protect from the cold winds. He sits first on a low branch of a tree then drops down onto the edge of the stone I am sitting on. I take the robin as a good omen, as many do – the robin has long been a symbol of luck and love and can be a meaningful bird in British cultural traditions. You may well be familiar with the saying: "When robins appear, loved ones are near", connected to ideas that the robin is a messenger offering symbolic comfort that lost loved ones are at peace and may watch over us. I take the little robin as a sign of good luck for our journey today and my ongoing journey, which comes into almost immediate effect as we make it back to the Two Bridges Hotel in time to sit by the fire, on a very squashy sofa and devour our long-awaited and well-earned cream tea.

The landscape is obviously a big influence on the amazing folklore of Dartmoor. But animals like our robin, are also drawn into many stories, from the wild roaming hounds to more modest, but magical, toads…

Toad Witches

In the journal *Devon Notes & Queries* (1901) can be found the intriguing tale of a witch living and working in the village of North Bovey, Dartmoor. Her name was Ann, and she was of that special class of West Country magical practitioner: a toad witch. To work her spells and enchantments, she employed the aid of her toads *Croppy, Rumbo* and one considered greatly wicked, *Krant*, and maybe a dozen more.

Her works with 'em in the churchyard at midnight when it is very dark. Her can tell you all you wants to know about the land.

When her wants to do an injury her first takes the Bible and puts the door-key in the leaves and then ties the book tightly together, then with the handle of the key her sets the Bible on edge and if it does not move her knows it is useless to go on, but if the book turns round her takes out her toads and begins.

The details of Ann's magical work, her mode of operation and how she employed her toads, like all good witch's tales, remain shrouded in mystery, due to some deliberate secrecy on Ann's part no doubt. Apparently, her preferred location for magical workings was North Bovey churchyard. When Ann had a spell or charm to work, she would make her way there with her toads, under the cover of midnight's dark. Of course, no one in the village would have been brave enough to follow

Ann into the churchyard at the dead of night to find out what the old witch and her toads were up to.

Toad magic was not just contained within Dartmoor. In the east of England, in the Fens, it was a complex skill, involving ritual ceremonies and training to become a toadman or toadwoman – where it was said that the owner of a *toad bone* would be granted the power to control horses, pigs and cattle. (In times when livestock were essential to survival, having some sort of control over their prosperity was a longed-for gift.)

In Yorkshire,

If you make friends with a toad and place him carefully in running water (such as a brook or a stream) at midnight, you will, according to folk lore, become a Toadman or Toadwoman. This means that you will know how to speak to animals and will have power over them and all living things.

And in Somerset,

There was an old witch over to Broomfield used to keep cats and toads and if she didn't like you she'd send the toads after you. She lived in the cottages at Rose Hill – they've fallen down now and if anyone did anything she didn't like she'd say, 'I'll toad 'ee,' and people was all afraid I s'pose. *

* From *Magical Animals: Folklore and Legends from a Yorkshire Wisewoman*, Claire Nahmad and *Somerset Folklore*, Ruth L. Tongue, respectively. Tongue's work, though sometimes criticised for blending fact and personal interpretation, still captures a spirit of regional belief. Like all the folklorists I explore, her words aren't presented as absolute truth, but as reflections worth appreciating.

*

On our final day of Dartmoor adventures, we park in the shadow of the dark stone church at the village of Manaton. I spot snowdrops on grassy banks as we walk up an ever-narrowing track onto the grassland and slope up Hayne Down and to the rock clusters that include Bowerman's Nose. Depending on the weather, you may see snowdrops as early as December; these are the first

I have seen. In British folklore, snowdrops symbolise hope as one of the first signs of new growth in winter.

The following story has long been told on Dartmoor to explain how the tall, rather human-looking stone column came to be:

Long ago, upon the wild moors, there lived a man called Bowerman the Hunter. Bowerman was a tall, powerful man who owned a pack of large, fierce hounds and whose chief delight was in hunting on the moors he loved so well. One dark, cold evening Bowerman was out with his pack, hot on the scent of a hare. Just as they looked like catching it, the hare turned into a dark and shadowed valley, closely followed by hounds and by Bowerman himself. Now this valley was one where the witches used to hold their Sabbaths and they were in the middle of their rites when the hare, pack and Bowerman burst in through their coven, disturbing their sacred rituals. The hare ran on through, the hounds barked, and the hunter roared with laughter as he continued the chase, leaving the witches shrieking with rage. But they would brew up a scheme to make sure he met with suitable retribution for his disrespect.

So, the next time he went out hunting, one of the witches, Levera by name, turned herself into a white hare, particularly prized by hunters. And she led Bowerman on a tremendous chase by bright cold moonlight, over the moors and through the valleys, until eventually, when he was well and truly exhausted, she enticed him into an ambush of the other witches. They promptly used their combined powers to turn him into the massive rock now called Bowerman's Nose. His hounds did not escape punishment, and they were turned into the rocks at the top of the neighbouring Hound Tor. You can still see the stone figure that was Bowerman with his pack of stone hounds scattered around just as they were that fateful night. But when the twilight falls misty or moonless, you might just hear Bowerman and his pack following some new quarry, hoping to escape the notice of the wild witches of the moors…

This is the story, told in my own words, of the tale of the Bowerman. And the dire consequences of his disregard for the witches' sacred space, which could be seen as a cautionary reminder of the importance of respect for nature and the mystical elements that inhabit it. The natural world holds both beauty and peril; those who fail to acknowledge this balance may find themselves forever altered. So we would do well to tread lightly in both the physical and spiritual realms.

At one time, there was suggestion that this rock was an ancient, man-made idol, due to its resemblance to carved stone figures, like those on Easter Island in the South Pacific. However, we know now that it is a natural formation and just as the geologists have proved its physical origins, etymologists have come up with a very mundane explanation for the origins of the stones name. It is apparently a corruption of the Celtic *var-maen*, meaning simply 'great stone' – much like the maidens really being a version of the 'maen' name for stone.

Standing on top of Hayne Down you can see in all directions. Bowerman stands facing north-ish. Hound Tor stands over to the south like a ragged castle as the wind carries howling gusts and rolling mizzle around us, blurring the higher peaks beyond. And amidst the thrashing rain and wind, one can easily imagine howling, gnashing hounds running through the mists. So we beat a hasty retreat, first to lower ground and then we follow the road home, to the gentler magic of our West Country home.

FEBRUARY

Hocus Pocus

Wookey Hole, Somerset

Imbolc has passed and bubbles of blossom hang on bare branches like pink puffed popcorn. Snowdrops are out in swathes and daffodils, primroses and crocuses are offering snippets of colour around the hedgerows. The green fields are dressed in dew, as I set out in the morning, journeying through the gently undulating countryside of Somerset. By the time I arrive at Wookey Hole; which is the name of both the little village in Somerset and the caves that lie beneath it, the sun has burned away the morning dew and haze and a blue sky shines above me. I am preparing to go underground into the caves of Wookey Hole, where more than one witch can be found…

The Witch of Wookey Hole

There are many versions of the story told of the witch within Wookey Hole, this is my own telling based on the many I have heard over the years…

They say that in her youth, she was a very beautiful woman, yet no man fell in love with her and so, growing bitter, she made a bargain for powers of evil, so that she might wreak her vengeance upon all mankind. Her devilish imps, dogs and goats no doubt assisted her in her wicked work and she, along with her loathly helpers, sat in Wookey Hole caves, plotting misery for all the countryside. She blighted the crops, soured milk, sent illness among the flocks and herds, she wove spells that created suspicion and unease in happy homes.

Some stories claim she was just an old woman who lived in the caves, blamed for everything that went wrong by the locals, but others say she was a witch who tormented the whole village and her cackling laughter could be heard emanating from deep with the caves of Wookey Hole. Hearing of the villagers' distress, the abbot of nearby Glastonbury sent a monk called Father Barnard to the caves. Off he went, up to Wookey to seek the hag in her den. He entered the cave, chanting his psalms, but the witch and her cave dwellers did not welcome this intrusion. She threw spell after spell at Father Barnard, but he seemed shielded by some air of goodness, so she tried to flee. Father Barnard dipped his chalice in the waters of the River Axe that flows through the caves and blessed it, making it holy water. He threw this liquid at the witch and all around her. The witch let out a blood curdling scream, followed by an eerie silence. Shining his candle in the direction of the scream, he saw that the witch had been turned to stone.

Father Barnard proudly returned to the abbey. Whilst the monk succeeded in ridding the villagers of their enemy, at Wookey Hole caves today, they like to think the witch got the last word. She is still spoken of in legend, whilst Father Barnard is largely forgotten.

And, if you go to Wookey Hole caves, you may see, as many have over the centuries, the petrified witch in her kitchen. It is said that from the moment she was frozen, no further evil has issued from the caves at Wookey, and that anyone may enter and emerge unharmed. But who knows, with so many hidden caverns under the earth, this place has never truly lain silent…

Let's hear the story from the Witch of Wookey herself, shall we? Okay, the first thing to say is that there is more than one. There always has been, it seems. Today, several witches are actually employed by the tourist attraction of Wookey Hole, and I'm honoured to speak to one, the wonderful and enchanting Sarah Mooney, before my planned visit during half term (the witch only appears at Wookey during school holidays: more children to devour, I imagine). So this is a very busy time for her and her sister witches in the caves. I'm a bit nervous about speaking to Sarah, not because she's a witch, or that she has been anything other than kind and generous to me via email setting up our call, but because I've never done this kind of interview for a book I am writing.

We speak virtually, both of us cradling mugs of tea and wrapped in layers as it's a cold day in the West Country. Sarah has spent the morning telling tales of witches and magic. It's National Storytelling Week, and Sarah is busier than ever sharing her skills. (You can enjoy her exceptional storytelling anytime via Mooney's Mystic Podcast – a favourite of mine to listen to.) She invites me to tell her a little about myself and this book. I stumble over my words and ramble a bit about seeking stories in the land. She says we are like mirrors of each other: she can speak and weave stories aloud, whereas I am much better taking months to craft a sentence, able to share my words far better on the page than speaking them. "So, do you see yourself as a witch?" I ask.

"I'm a keeper of myth," she tells me. "My work is storytelling. I honour the seasons, and ritual is very important to me. But excavating myth is what's most important. When asking the question, are you a witch, you really need to know who is asking it: what does witch mean to them? And what does it mean to you?"

"Do you ever feel judged harshly as a witch?" I ask her, curious as to how she is received by the public in her role.

"Often, I get a man saying, *'Oh, it's your mother-in-law!'* to their wives. And I might reply *'Yes, I know her; she is very powerful, so you better watch out!'*

"People can ask me any questions and I respond in rhyme. Sometimes people try to make it really hard, which is fine, because I'm very good at rhyming. But I often think, I'm a woman dressed in costume, there are a thousand people here today…why are you doing this? But I send them blessings for their ongoing journeys, I do lots of blessings there. And model how to be generous, open and warm and welcoming, in the face of any judgement people may have about being a witch…"

She tells me of two of her favourite memories of her Wookey witch role: "A mum had written in and said how much her little girl wanted to be the apprentice of the Wookey Hole witch for the day. So, she came in dressed impeccably; she looked incredible. But she was so nervous, she was shaking like a leaf, she was quivering from her toes to her nose. And she didn't speak; I was telling her jokes, and she was just looking at me. Her mum said she was so excited but has got a bit overwhelmed. So, I asked her what it was that she liked about being a witch, and suddenly she just shouts out: 'THE POWER!' and I was just like, *wow, amazing!*

"The other thing I really love doing is releasing the ducks for the annual Wookey Hole duck race. I get to tip two hundred rubber ducks into the River Axe, it's very entertaining and part of the witch persona is kind of adjudicator, compère."

In my head I am thinking of the Wicked Witch of the West from *The Wizard of Oz* saying, "Fly my pretties!" but over rubber ducks instead of flying monkeys. Though Sarah is definitely not wicked, instead, she's like a peacemaker, creating glue for the community, I reflect, thinking of some the central roles that wise women, elders, healers and midwives played in communities before some were accused of witchcraft for such roles. I tell Sarah this thought, and she replies,"Yes, I feel honoured to be this central part of the community for that moment, and it feels very healing."

Finally, I ask Sarah where she would go if she were seeking the witch in the landscape. "I went to the Long Barrow[*], next to Avebury and the stones said to me, 'We've been waiting a long time for you to come here'. The stones there felt like an ancient part of me that had never been seen before. And somehow, they could meet that part of me, recognising it.

"It feels to me that to be a witch with integrity I have to stay in connection with the land, so that's been a brilliant invitation: to keep listening to the land. Women embody this role in different ways, I walk the site as a powerful and open embodiment of the witch and that just feels like the biggest work I could do for the earth and for my life. And that just feels like it's changing the world."

I think she's right. So, on this wise witch's advice, listening to the land is what I shall do, and will most definitely take her advice and go to Avebury as part of this adventure.

But for now, I am excited to enter the caves at last…

Underland

The caves at Wookey Hole formed over millions of years, as rainwater percolated through the hillside and wore away the porous, sedimentary rock below; this process slowly created the chambers of caves. The Mendip Hills spread from Bristol to Bath, and under the hills are a network of hidden caves, chambers and labyrinths, used as shelter and burial since the time of Neanderthals 50,000 years ago.[†] This is a vast underworld place of caving and graving, quarrying and mining, alongside burial sites and long barrows. And the famed caves of Wookey Hole have been a popular attraction for many centuries, alongside their resident witch. The logo of Wookey Hole caves is a witch, smiling and friendly; she reminds me of the two-tailed mermaid logo of Starbucks. In *Myths, Scenes & Worthies of Somerset* by Mrs E. Boger, published in 1887, she speaks to how fiction can so easily, unwittingly, glide into fact, story can become history and how it can be near impossible to define the limits and edges of story. Like how the shadowy images of King Arthur blend with real history of King Alfred and mingle into a mist of truth and fable in the story of each. And if one tries to tear away the layers of myth and leave

* Long barrows are long prehistoric burial mounds that are used for multiple burials.

† wookey.co.uk/caves

only provable facts – you are left with only a distorted picture, losing the *rare beauty* of Somerset legends. And speaking of rare beauty, Boger considered the caves of Wookey Hole, lit with lanterns:

> *A stalactite cavern, pre-eminently beautiful, with its semi-transparent lime deposits formed into fantastic shapes, to which imagination has given various names. Lighted most judiciously with gas artistically placed, it looks like a fairy palace, with its tiny grottoes and unexpected beauties surprising one on every side… But of all these caves, one alone, Wookey or Ockey Hole, near Wells, has, as far as I know, any legend connected with it… The approach to it is extremely picturesque and the surrounding scenery wildly magnificent. A semi-oval arch cut transversely and about two hundred feet from point to point, the central point being nearly two hundred feet high and an assemblage of vast perpendicular rocks almost covered with trees and shrubs springing from between the fissures, is reached by a walk from Wells over Milton Hill, from which can be seen a fine view. On winding round the foot of the hill, this lovely dell, scooped out of the limestone rocks, comes in sight… William of Worcester, who wrote his travels in these parts in the year 1473, gives the following description:*
>
> *"The kitchen apartment before the entrance into the hall is vaulted to an unaccountable number of feet in breadth and covered with stone. There is an ost for drying malt and the figure of a woman, apparelled with a spinning distaff under her girdle. Thence folks pass another aisle a hundred steps in length and a man may go here dry shod over the stones. And then the apartment of the parlour follows, which is round, built of huge rocks above twenty steps in breadth. In the north part of this parlour is what is called in English – Holy Hole or Well, arched over and full of fine water, the depth of which has never been ascertained."*

Boger references William of Worcester's account, thought to be the earliest mention of the figure we now call the witch. He describes her not as a witch, but simply as a woman, noting a pillar-like deposit he names a distaff,* the kitchen realm, and drying malt. For at least half a millennium, this space and its figures have carried a distinctly feminine identity. 'She' is a stalagmite, formed by water droplets falling over centuries, each one charged with carbonate of lime and other minerals, slowly building mounds and towers on the cave floor. And with this drip, drip, drip of time and language, the shapes are formed – not just by water, but by words layered around them. The image

* A distaff is a stick on to which wool or flax is wound for spinning. The term "distaff" is also used metaphorically to refer to women or feminine activities, drawn from its historical association with women's work with textiles.

that emerges is one of a witch in her kitchen: the witch herself, her distaff, the pillar of salt, the bread oven, the cauldron, the dog. And by the time English traveller Celia Fiennes wrote of "Oakey Hole" around 1695, 'she' was the witch. The formation became a woman and then a witch and has been so for many centuries.

Bones

In 1912, archaeologist, naturalist, caver and geologist Herbert Balch discovered an apparent burial site. Scientists analysed the bones and concluded that the remains had lain in the Wookey Hole Caves for over 1,000 years. The finds included human bones, goat bones, a black bowl, a polished stone ball, a comb and a brooch. An iron sickle and a knife lay in a pit beneath the site. Speculation was rife that this was the tomb of the Witch of Wookey.

Upon closer, more recent analysis the finds are most likely a collection of burials. The skeleton of 'the witch' produced different dates, some bones are Roman, others date to the Iron Age and the bones appeared to be from a male. (This doesn't mean this wasn't a witch; ever since people have been named witches, there have been male witches and magic workers.) But the other finds have made even more speculations possible – a Romano-British goat herder perhaps? That was Balch's theory.

Over the years more items have been discovered in the caves. Many more human bones, pottery and Roman coins suggesting that humans occupied the cave from the Iron Age into the Roman occupation. Many of these finds are on display at the Wells & Mendip Museum in Wells, Somerset. And further witchy discoveries were to follow – in 2017, witch marks were found carved into the cave walls.

Cave dwellers

"There's never been a better time to be a witch," Chris Binding tells me and I think there's probably no better time to have met Chris. Diver and cave explorer, he has also spent many years under the spell of the witch and, serendipitously, he is just weeks away, from revealing more secrets of those that were called the witches of Wookey… Chris is a font of knowledge and enthusiasm: a technical advisor and caving instructor at Wookey for many years.

In 2017, Chris and his team found witch marks carved into the walls at Wookey Hole while they were mapping out new routes for visitors to travel through the caves. The marks dated between 1550 and 1750 and until the discovery of marks at Creswell Crags in 2019, they were the largest concentration of protective marks in any British cave. It was the invention of LED torches, he tells me, that really helped uncover all the many witch marks of the caves of Wookey; they showed up the markings far more clearly than older filament bulb torches had. But continuing the influences of light technology, he also tells me that it was candlelight that really brought the stalagmite known as the witch to life. The flickering of candlelight on her face, adding an illusion of movement.

When light was brought into these caves, even clergy were transported to a little fairy magic: "Whilst we peered into the gloom, the limelight was burning up, and now it flashed across the cavern to where the black scowling head of the Witch overshadowed terraces, basins, and wild images of spectral stalagmite.

"A glow! a gleam!
A broader beam
Startles those realms of endless night,
While bats whirl round on slanting wing,
Astonished at this awful thing.
The rocky roofs reflected rays
Are caught up in the waterways,
And every jewelled stalactite
Is bathed in that stupendous light,
One moment only; then the caves
Are plunged again in Stygian waves ;
The fairy dream has passed away
*And night resumes her ancient sway."**

* A vicar wrote this poem after seeing Wookey Hole lit up. Noted in Herbert Balch's own account of their discoveries in *The Netherworld of Mendip; explorations in the great caverns of Somerset, Yorkshire, Derbyshire, and elsewhere,* E. A. Baker and H. E. Balch (1907).

*

In a matter of weeks, Chris will be hosting an exhibition at the Wells & Mendip Museum, the museum founded by Balch to house many of his discoveries and artefacts, showing the stories of the many witches of Wookey, the stones, the humans, the bones and the myths. I honestly can't believe my luck. Chris has been researching the witch in depth for years and this exhibition is part of what he hopes will become a museum of witchcraft at the Wookey Hole site. We both agreed, as the fascination for folklore and witchcraft continues to grow, that this is a wonderful idea.

Yet again, I try to explain to someone kind enough to lend me their time and expertise what it is I am doing and seeking. But the Wookey Caves illustrate my disparate ideas nicely. Here, within one space, the witch is present in a myriad of ways: there are ritual protection marks (apotropaic magic), folktales of witches transformed into stone and many bones of real people, amongst fascinating artefacts of crystal balls and daggers, at least hinting at possibly magical or ritual connections and that's in addition to utterly amazing natural formations of the caves themselves, many of which are named for witches. All this hidden deep underground, in an intricate network of chambers formed over millions of years, joined by dark passages, and filled with stalactites and stalagmites. These all add a certain magic to this place that may be seen, felt and experienced by visitors.

And right now, sneaking behind a tour group of visitors, Chris and I enter the caves ourselves.

The show caves of Wookey, the largest show cave system in the UK, were created 1927, a show cave being parts of the cave system that are open and accessible to regular folks. The original wooden door from 1927 guards the entrance, and we are soon on crunching gravel with glowing lights luring us deeper. Dusty bottles and a prop cauldron sit on natural ledges in the rock. Past the props we come first to the area where Herbert Balch found, in 1912, some very real artefacts – the bones of goats, alongside a collection of human bones that he called 'the goatherder' but many others would call the 'Witch of Wookey'. Balch also found fascinating items nearby, which included a metal dagger and a man-made crystal ball, suggesting very strongly some kind of divination or ritual practice. Next, we descend to the Witch's Kitchen via a secret darkened passageway up to the left, not open to the public, called Hell's Ladder.

This is part of the old show caves that became too small to accommodate the huge numbers of visitors that now pass through Wookey. The steps are very steep and green moss and small ferns drip water from the roof. Chris demonstrates the acoustics by calling out, it is ominous, particularly with a crystal chorus of observers as we reach the top of the steps. Calcite towers look like figures, rounded and humanoid, watching us and sparkling water spills and spreads onto the floor, over frills and tiered pools of deposits that fan out like crystalline flowers. Since Roman times people seem to have heard otherworldly sounds from these caves caused by the water rising and falling echoing around the caves; Chris said the Romans thought it was the gods, speaking to them, in later eras, who knows – ghosts, demons, witches?

We descend the stairs carefully to the Witch's Kitchen, first we meet The Dog formation, shaped like a resting animal, rounded head and curling tail. Chris says there were bones laid at this formation, as if, perhaps not in the offering, but honouring, or maybe to appease the witch. And the witch is here too, or a witch. This is the stalagmite now called The Witch – she looks out over a lake with a boat floating atop milky water lit with beams of light from under the water's surface, which bathe the rocks in purples, blues and oranges giving it an eerie, otherworldly feel.

Chris points out a small cross marking on the rock directly behind her, a witch mark to bind her from moving perhaps.

Low rocks force you to stoop a little as you pass the clear water in The Witch's Cauldron, complete with white stone froth, seemingly bubbling up from the brew. To her left, there is a formation that resembles a stone oven. There is a whole narrative of magic once being cooked up here, each stone creating part of a scene of devilish domesticity.

Next is the Great Hall, one of the highest chambers in Wookey Hole. A vast craggy, grey rock sky towers above us. The air is cool and damp throughout the caves carrying with it the earthy scent of ancient limestone. The sound of dripping echoes softly in the darkness, a constant reminder of the ceaseless work of nature shaping these subterranean landscapes. We journey under a low rock roof to The Witch's Chimney, a narrow rising hole through the stone above us. The majority of the witches marks are here: over fifty in fact. Overlapping Vs, *Virgo Virginium* (virgin of virgins), and Ms (Marion marks) – both thought to be invocation of the protection of Mary, mother of Jesus, to banish evil spirits and witches. These are the apotropaic 'turning away' marks. No ornate daisy wheels of the tithe barn here, perhaps the straight lines are quicker and easier to create in the dark, they seem more urgent in intent. Most likely, in this case I imagine, seeking to keep the witch in the cave, preventing her escape through the chimney, hoping to trap her in here. Or perhaps seeking to ward off witches from the whole area.

Chris tells me to stand in the corner of the Chimney, in the narrow space where a tunnel rises upwards; I look up through vivid green moss and ferns and peer closely at the marks made on slick, smooth rock. Of the plentiful witchery of this place, this is a phenomenon that one can physically feel: a convection draught. Caused by a trick of body heat of those standing in the chimney displacing the cooler surrounding air, one can feel the temperature suddenly drop – and I can indeed feel a chill wrap around my neck. It is believed that this ominous effect would have been more pronounced years ago, before a low rock lip was removed to make it easier for visitors to pass through, but it can still be felt today. Was it the proximity to the witch, the cold chill felt or the similarity to a chimney (which, you may recall, is a place where witches were thought to gain entry) that prompted all the witch marks? Very possibly all three.

In using Marion marks to call on Mary for protection, we are presented with two opposing female images: the Virgin Mary and the witch, the very strongest embodiments at one time, of female sanctity and female sinfulness, respectively. Mary is an archetype, a patriarchally imposed idea of how a woman should behave 'properly' in society – she is youthful, meek, motherly, and nurturing. And the witch is the opposite: all ancient shrieking power ready to cause chaos and break out of such confining feminine roles. But Mary clearly holds a certain power, for her intervention is called on here by those who seek her protection and divine grace. The sacred feminine (Mary) is revered against the backdrop of the feared and marginalised feminine (the witch). It's a mirror still, of how society continues to navigate the complexities of female identity, balancing reverence for traditional roles with the recognition of women's inherent power. And clue as to how and why perhaps, more and more women are empathising with witches…

We move on to The Witch's Parlour where ancient whirlpools have created a beautiful dome-shaped cave. The waters are still now, though beneath them is an entrance to other caves, obscured by water levels, reflecting the sweeping curve of the rock roof. Lit today in blues and purple, it is like being within a rounded opal.

Caves of cheese

What has the witch been cooking up in her kitchen? We weave down a man-made corridor through the subterranean rock, at the end of which is…vast amounts of cheese! This may seem strange to those not from Europe, but in rural England, France and Italy, cheeses are often nestled in natural caves to age. This area is home to wildly popular Cheddar cheese, its place of origin being the village of Cheddar just a few miles away. Cheese-making in this region dates back to at least the 12th century, with local farmers developing techniques to create the distinctive, hard cheese we know and love today.

The cheese room shines with an electric hue, as one might expect from a smart lab in a prehistoric cave, with glass doors and bright lights. And it is not just here at Wookey that tales of witches and cheese seem to glance askance at each other. The fortunes of dairy products are actually pretty intertwined with witches, as with many foodstuffs. Butter, milk, cream and cheese often feature in fears and accusations of witchcraft because of their high value. Malevolent witches, it was feared, could meddle with milk and cheese with curses and spells, especially at those fleeting thresholds of festival days, equinoxes and solstices (when more otherworldly beings may abound). For our ancestors, it was a serious business if your butter wasn't churning or your cheese production was threatened.

All foods carry a certain magic, but the alchemical processes involved in the transformation of milk to cheese, cream to butter, rising bread and brewing beer, for example, made them particularly special and also valuable, with the time and care needed to create them and their high-calorie content, they would have been vital in surviving a long winter. There are tales through the British Isles and beyond into Europe of witches stealing milk through magical means – including turning themselves into hares to suckle milk directly from the cows, skimming the morning dew of farmers' fields and in this way magically 'skimming' milk from their stores. The fairy folk too, if not appeased, could also make milk mischief: causing cows' udders to dry up, spoiling cream or cursing the butter churn. As a defence for such attacks, housewives might wrap rowan or mountain ash around their butter churns and milk pails to prevent their contents from being stolen by both fairies and witches. And witch marks and horseshoes may still be spotted at the doors of old milking houses and dairies.

We leave the cheese and walk on clanking metal walkways over the pearlescent waters of the River Axe into the Cathedral Chamber. Water flows underneath us, and surrounds us with the pattering sounds of falling water. Here the cave walls are red. The flowstone – sheet-like deposits of calcite or other carbonate minerals formed where water flows down the walls or along the floors of a cave – is coloured with iron oxide.

In 2015, a thousand tons of rock were blasted to make way into Chamber 20 into which we are now emerging. It is breathtaking. Surrounding a static subterranean lake, the rocks are shaped in flutes and peaked channels. The word for this effect of water on rock is delightful and new to me; these are 'rillenkarren' stones, which as a word, feels just on the cusp of being onomatopoeic, spilling off the tongue like trickling waters. Rillenkarren are patterns of tightly packed rills found upon the bare, sloping surfaces of soluble rocks. The fluting is caused by water running over the limestone rock. Rows upon rows of these rocks stand together, as if they had been combed by unseen hands into little running peaks. It is an otherworldly place for sure.

There is so much magic and mystery here…and still so much yet to discover. Much of the cave system lies underwater, Chris tells me, so even he and his colleagues don't know the full extent of the labyrinth of caves or what secrets they may hide.

We emerge blinking out into the sun, and I remember what Sarah Mooney told me: *"as you come out of the cave, the River Axe comes out from underneath. It's a very special place, because it's where the underground and the overground and the water meet. For me it's a very liminal space. If I've got any activity in the other realms that I want to do…any songs, or stories, or listening, I find that a very special place to do it."*

I go over to the yew tree that she told me about (yews can live for a thousand years or more and are often associated with witches and graveyards). *"As you come out of the cave,"* she said, *"on your left there's a huge yew tree with chairs all around it. I spend a lot of time there as well. It's a very old tree and I just know that that tree and that cave have had a symbiotic relationship for all those years. Just behind it there is a cave gap where wolves and cavemen sheltered and my senses go into a past life there."*

Amongst other amazing archaeological finds in and around the area are bones of mammoths, wolves, bears and lions, along with prehistoric humans' flint tools, a reminder that this place has been used for shelter for thousands upon thousands of years. This is a truly ancient land and a place that many have been drawn to – where people have found shelter, safety, but also mystery and magic at various times.

It turns out that in the case of the Wookey witch, much like witches throughout the country, there's always more to the story, and often more than one witch; they need friends and allies as we all do. And when talking to Sarah I felt that at times, they even manage to transcend the constraints of historical time, bound together by their deep connections to each other and to specific places on the land. There's so much that lingers in the caves, is multiple generations of magic and belief one of those things? This thought stays with me for days after my visit to Wookey, as does that feeling of a cold chill on the back of my neck…

*

A week after my visit heavy rainfall makes the River Axe high enough to flood the Wookey caves and they are closed for the last weekend of half term. I am so glad that I got to see them and am in constant awe of the power of nature to change the world and our well-made plans.

I'm on the bus to Wells, to see the exhibitions about Wookey Hole. Daffodils have taken over the banks with pale yellow. Magnolia trees are arrayed with flowers that look like scoops of raspberry ripple ice cream, and a single and favourite tree on the route into Bath is the glorious yellow of lemon sorbet. I spot Glastonbury Tor on the horizon – an adventure for another day – but today I get off the bus in Wells and walk to the Cathedral Green. The imposing medieval cathedral is what makes Wells the country's smallest city.

I arrive at the charming coral-coloured Wells & Mendip Museum. I'm here to see the bones of the witch, in person. I learn here that experts are actually divided on whether these are the bones of a man or a woman. Some features of the mandible suggest the individual may be male, but the cranium and pelvis would be required to be confident of the sex of the individual (they are absent). Yet again, the witch defies any clear singular answer.

The witch's 'crystal ball' is here too. It's made of white calcite, a mineral common in the Mendip area – but unlike many of the natural formations we saw in the Wookey caves, this ball is hand carved calcite into an orb shape. (If I were to walk into one of the many crystal shops of nearby Glastonbury, they may mention that in modern ideas, calcite is a crystal that can improve clarity of thought and purpose.) Signs suggest that when originally fashioned, the ball would have possessed a more translucent quality than is evident today.

Herbert Balch, who carried out those early excavations at Wookey Hole Cave, also founded this museum. So many of his discoveries – a large number of Stone Age tools, Iron Age artefacts, and prehistoric – are housed here. Many of the finds from Balch's excavations suggest settled domestic life: beautiful antler and bone weaving combs, pottery, ornaments and spindle whorls for spinning wool. This cave seemed to have been a true home to perhaps many groups over many centuries. Real people lived and died in these caves.

The artefacts collectively narrate the story of Wookey Hole, its rich archaeological heritage and the legends that continue to capture the imagination. Charms and amulets that speak to us of witches and early Victorian tourist memorabilia follow its journey into a modern tourist destination. The exhibition is full of fascinating curios and artefacts. In Chris' contributions, he explores just how long people have been bewitched by the caves and the stories of the witches that may have dwelled within them.

I most enjoy reading accounts of the sounds of the caves. Michael Drayton, in his poem "Poly-Olbion" (1612), describes how "the dreadfull Caverne spake".* And the earliest account of the phenomenon in Clement of Alexandria's "Stromata" (189 CE), "In Britain is a certain cave at the side of a mountain and at the entrance a gap; when, then, the wind blows into the cave and is drawn on into the bosom of the interior, a sound is heard as of the clashing of numerous cymbals".

These caves have been speaking to people for millennia. And today, even with the neon lights and tourist parties, the caves of Wookey can still speak to us of magic.

* Part 1, Song 3 of "Poly-Olbion", Michael Drayton (1612).

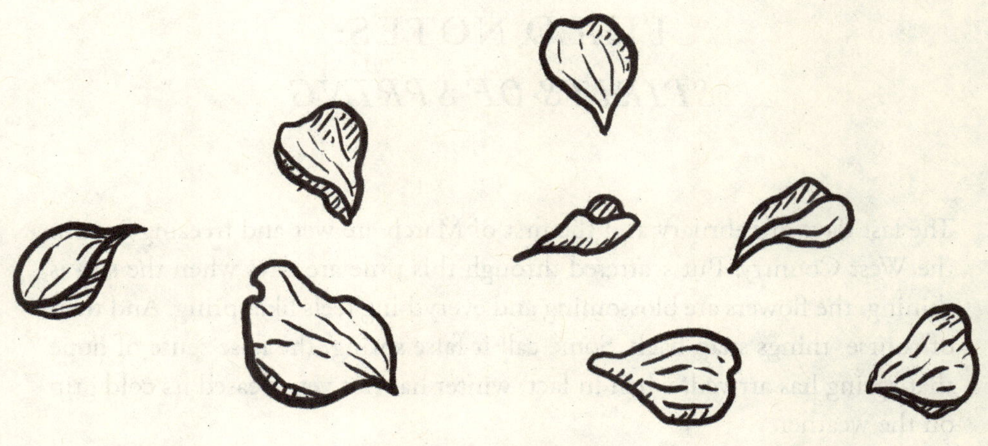

SPRING

March • April • May

Witch Hares • Wassail • Fairy Time • Spirit Nights • Sorceresses

FIELD NOTES:
SPIRITS OF SPRING

The last days of February and the first of March are wet and freezing here in the West Country. But scattered through this time are days when the sun is shining, the flowers are blossoming and everything feels like spring. And then of course, things snap back. Some call it false spring, the false sense of hope that spring has arrived, when in fact, winter has not yet released its cold grip on the weather.

Folkloric ideas of *borrowing days* scatter through February, March and April at this most anticipated of seasonal bridges, the arduous wait for warmth, and the hungry gap where the last of food stores may be running scarce. February may borrow a few sunny days from spring and the feisty nature of March is embodied in several stories of seasonal conflicts and erratic weather. March, which can be windy and stormy, is personified as reluctant to release his rule, so he borrows days from April in a last-ditch attempt to extend his influence over the spring weather before March winds finally give way to April showers.

Borrowing Days. I remember to have heard, when a child, in the north of Ireland, a far more poetical, if not a more rational, explanation of what is undoubtedly a very common interchange of character between March and April, for a few successive days towards the close of the former, and commencement of the latter, month. "Give me (says March) three days of warmth and sunshine for my poor young lambs whilst they are yet too tender to bear the roughness of my wind and rain, and you shall have them repaid when the wool is grown." An attentive observer of the weather will seldom find the recurrence of this accommodation loan to fail. This day (the 24th) and the two last days have been of a temperature very unusual so early in the year, and I have little doubt that before the 1st of May there will be a per contra of three successive days of cold and bluster carried to the credit side of April's account.

"Notes and Queries", Number 128 (1852)

The practice of borrowing days sits within the transition from winter to spring, rooted in agricultural practices and folk beliefs. I have found texts referring to borrowing days throughout Scotland, Ireland and England, observing that the weather can be unseasonably warm or cold around this time, and people might think of these fluctuations as days taken from spring to compensate for winter's harshness. A borrowed day of warmth may be 'paid back' with a cold day later, or certain days may be used to predict the weather to come. And borrowing days even held witching superstitions such as not lending or borrowing any personal items during these days…

> *Borrowing Days, the three last days of March… These days being generally stormy, our forefathers have endeavoured to account for this circumstance, by pretending that March borrowed them from April, that he might extend his power so much longer. Those who are much addicted to superstition will neither borrow nor lend on any of these days; lest the articles borrowed should be employed for the purposes of witchcraft, against the lenders.*
>
> **John Jamieson, *An Etymological Dictionary of the Scottish Language* (1818)**

*

In the Scottish folk story of *Angus and the Cailleach*, Angus borrows three days of summer to set Bride, the spirit of spring, free. The Cailleach, the crone goddess of winter, knew, as goddesses often do, that Bride was to wed her son, Angus. Afraid of losing her powers, she captured Bride in an attempt to keep her away from Angus. But Angus dreamt of Bride and sought the counsel of a wise king. He advised Angus not to rush, for the lands were still thick with snow and the Cailleach's winter reign still strong. He should wait until the first flowers bloom when her powers wane. But Angus did not want to wait, so he borrowed three days from August and the sun shone brightly that February in Scotland and Angus could set his beloved free from the now weakened grasp of the winter goddess.

Despite this bickering and borrowing between days and seasons. Light is returning to my corner of the world and the days are growing longer, minute by minute. As we step into March and April, daffodils, primroses and crocuses are all coming into golden bloom. Birch twigs begin to bud with catkins under the rare and treasured blue skies and wild garlic springs up in fresh greens and whites, scenting great swathes of woodlands. Hope is in the air and the wildwood is expanding into life.

And then, to up the ante of throwing winter days back and forth, one morning in March, we woke up to find, to our surprise that it had snowed overnight and our garden was blanketed in pillowy snowfall. I was rather delighted that the Cailleach had managed to reach out her frosty hands one last time, into our long-awaited spring, before truly bidding us farewell.

*

In the months ahead, my travels extend past the West Country and into Sussex and Wales. March is the Spring Equinox – a time when balance is a theme. I ponder if exploring the native myths and folklore of the British Isles offer us a kind of 'law' for living well on the land, in a balanced and connected way. The land you are from or live on can form part of your identity. And land has certainly influenced who we were in centuries past. So what happens when we disrespect or break that relationship? When land is destroyed, trees, plants, farmland and gardens cleared, burned or bulldozed, we lose more than a view. We may well be burning elements of our identity and our cultural roots are erased too. The loss of land or insulating ourselves so completely from nature and the seasons can cause us to lose our way, lose our balance and lose the ability to see and find meaning in nature.

In some folktales, disrespecting the natural world causes fertile land to become a barren wasteland*; in the modern world, we create wasteland ourselves via acts of disrespect and demolition, or even well-meant acts in the name of ease – like astroturf lawns, multiple cars and garden pesticides.

Barren lands, wildlands or floods can pop up as punishment for misdeeds (in both pagan and Judeo-Christian tales). A scorched earth, sweeping away of human life. I'd say, 'Be warned!' except we have been, for millennia. The consequences have long been spelt out. Perhaps balance has long been lost, ever since the wants of the wealthy or greedy outweighed the needs of the common folk.

* One such example can be seen in my book *The Witch the Wildwood*, in the story of the Green Ladies of the Hill; two brothers do not honour the land and trees and their farms fail; the brother who treats the land well finds abundant harvests.

MARCH

Wassailing and witch hares

Arundel, West Sussex

In the black furrow of a field
I saw an old witch-hare this night;
And she cocked a lissome ear,
And she eyed the moon so bright,
And she nibbled of the green;
And I whispered "Wh-s-st! witch-hare."
Away like a ghostie o'er the field She fled,
and left the moonlight there.

Walter de la Mare, *Down-Adown-Derry: A Book of Fairy Poems* (1922)

On the day of the Spring Equinox my friend Katie and I walked a loop from Avebury, a tiny and charming village in Wiltshire, home to a neolithic stone circle, the largest in the UK, and one of the largest in the world. It encompasses a massive area of stones enclosed by a henge (a bank and ditch that encircles the site). One huge stone circle runs just within the bank, and then within that circle are two more smaller circles of stone, like two great eyes on the round face of an owl. An avenue of standing stones leads out over the soft green hills towards the equally mysterious and magical Silbury Hill and West Kennet Long Barrow. We are so lucky that this place filled with ancient wonders is just a short drive away.

At Avebury one can walk amongst and touch the stones, they are rough and unhewn, each one wildly different from its neighbour, with different qualities of edges and shadows. Many cradle little offerings, like flowers, nestled in cracks.

Avebury is not just a stone circle, it is a vast sacred ancient landscape of avenues, settlements and sacred sites of burial and celebration all connected together, that include Avebury stone circle, Silbury Hill and West Kennet Long Barrow.

The sacred nature of this place means people have always gathered here and created settlements on the surrounding land. But the sacred has often struggled and jostled up against the encroachments of modern conveniences. A Saxon village was established near the henge site and as it expanded over the centuries, its buildings eventually breached the walls of the henge, and quaint cottages sidled up to standing stones. The stones suffered; some were toppled or destroyed to make way for human habitation. Today, a handful of buildings remain inside and amongst the stones, including cottages, sixteenth-century barns, and the Red Lion Pub. Less charmingly, a busy A-road cuts through the centre of the henge circle.

We walk along an avenue lined with pairs of huge stones, away from Avebury to West Kennet Long Barrow, a burial mound where people have left offerings of daffodils for the equinox – laid out in circular shapes above the barrow on the grass and individual blooms are placed between stone and ledges within the dark tunnelled interior. We walk back past Silbury Hill, a massive prehistoric man-made mound of chalk, now covered in grass. It's over a hundred feet high and strangely captivating. The hill is surrounded by a moat of water that appears when the weather has been wet – I can only imagine how beautiful it must have looked, thousands of years ago, glowing white, a chalk pyramid island. We journey back to Avebury's stone embrace and have lunch in the Red Lion pub (the only pub within a stone circle that I am aware of).

Avebury is not necessarily witchy in terms of times past, though it certainly is a place of sacred rites and rituals and was considered to be 'druidic' in books such as *Abury:** *A Temple of the British Druids* by William Stukeley in 1743. And the BBC's 'A Ghost Story for Christmas' in 1977 called *Stigma* involved a witch's curse and ancient evil reawakened in retribution for moving one of the stones. Witches and spiritually minded folk gather here regularly today; the stones are said to sing with a certain energy, and it is a very popular place to celebrate solstices and equinoxes, as is nearby (and much better known) Stonehenge.

Through the Middle Ages, when Christianity swept through England, places such as Avebury, home to vast pagan monuments, gathered associations with the devil in the popular imagination. The largest stone at the southern entrance of the stone circle is known as the Devil's Chair. It's a huge stone, like a wall of rock, one of the biggest at Avebury, with fractures that create a ledge which one may perch on, under a crooked arch and a hole that one may look up through like a little chimney. It is on the south-east side of the stone circle, looking away from the village, facing out over a mound of earth and a cluster of trees. The road is by its side. Of the many legends connected with the chair are that it was once used by the devil to survey the surrounding landscape and tempt passersby into mischief. This may be avoided if you see smoke rising from the stone chimney, which warns that the devil is holding court. This stone is also known as the guardian stone or the entrance stone, a place where one may watch and wait.

---

* This is an older spelling of Avebury.

*

Now, two days later, I am on the train to Arundel, West Sussex. I have been both anxious and excited about this trip, unsure quite what I will find.

I reflect on the train journey down to Sussex that I've learnt to tell buzzards (tail curves out) from kites (tail curves in) and hawthorn from blackthorn – blackthorn flowers before the leaf with lovely fluffy white blossoms, early in the year in February and March, whereas hawthorn blooms appear in late spring, in April and May amid bright-green leaves. This information won't be much use in the journeys of the day ahead, it turns out. But I do feel like I'm picking up snippets of nature knowledge measured in tiny blackthorn blooms. Information that will be made very clear to me, that I have not yet internalised, is to look more closely at the terrain I am planning to walk and to never entirely trust the weather forecast…

*

> *Sussex could be taken as a sample of the way in which the strange tapestry of witchcraft has been woven through the centuries. … Many ancient traditions will have lived on in its wooded glades, to form the older threads in the pattern of Sussex witch-lore.*
>
> **Doreen Valiente, *Where Witchcraft Lives* (1962)**

I was torn for some time about where to go in Sussex; should I walk out to Chanctonbury Ring, home of many a tale of spooky goings on? I discovered this place in Doreen Valiente's book, *Where Witchcraft Lives* (1962). Doreen (1922-1999), who we heard from briefly in the New Forest chapter, was a pioneering figure in Wicca, and considered the mother of modern witchcraft. Her contributions include rituals, spells and incantations that are still used today. As per her wishes, Valiente's ashes were scattered in Sussex woodland, around the roots of her favourite oak tree. She wrote that, "the traditional meeting-place of Sussex witches is Chanctonbury Ring. This is a high crest of the Downs crowned with a clump of beech trees which form a well-known landmark"*

Chanctonbury Ring is an Iron Age hill fort and circular earthwork located

---

* *Where Witchcraft Lives*, Doreen Valiente (1962)

in West Sussex. Around the eighteenth-century a ring of beech trees were planted around its perimeter. Many trees did not survive a hurricane, still known as the Great Storm of 1987, that swept through much of Britain, a storm I am just old enough to remember. But replanting continues to ensure the future of the ring of trees now considered integral to the magic of the place. The site is associated with all manner of myths, including tales of ghosts, supernatural occurrences and, of course, witches.

Or perhaps I would head to the top of Ditchling Beacon, where the tales of wisht hounds we found in Dartmoor now become "witch hounds":

> *A strange tradition attaches to Ditchling Beacon, the highest point of the Downs, 813 feet above sea-level... For centuries it has been haunted by a phantom hunt, known locally as the Witch Hounds. Listeners hear the cry of hounds, the hoofbeats of galloping horses and the call of the hunting horn...*[†]

There's also a Witch Lane and a Wych Cross, south of Ashdown Forest, which in turn is where beloved children's author, A.A. Milne, found his Hundred Acre Wood, home of Pooh Corner and Pooh Sticks Bridge. Some five miles from which is Duddleswell, where Dame Garson, a witch with the ability to shape-shift, was once said to dwell. One day in hare guise, she was chased by huntsmen and a pack of hounds, she leapt into her garden and through one of the windows, spirited safely home and those following the chase, now peering over the garden hedge, heard a triumphant voice from inside calling: *"Ah, my boys, you ain't got me yet."*[‡]

The legend of the witch hare runs from the very top of the country in the Scottish Highlands, with accounts like Isobel Gowdie's, down to where I am headed today – the warm, chalky south of England – Sussex. The witch hare has a tale, it seems, in many a county. Ambiguous identity and animal transformation figure prominently in witch stories, and witch trial records can include such tales. One example is the trial of Ann Baites of Morpeth in 1673. She was accused of riding around on wooden dishes and eggshells, dancing with the devil and turning herself into a cat, a hare, a greyhound and a bee. In the trial of the Pendle witches, James Device claimed he was accosted by a fire-breathing hare when leaving Anne Redferne's house. Perhaps one of the most well-known witch animals of all is the hare.

† *Where Witchcraft Lives*, Doreen Valiente (1962).

‡ *An Illustrated Guide to Crowborough*, Boys Firmin (1890).

When we go in the shape of a hare
We say thrice over
I shall go into a hare,
With sorrow and syt and meikle care;
And I shall go in the Devil's name,
Ay will I come home again.

Words attributed to Isobel Gowdie, recorded in Robert Pitcairn's *Ancient Criminal Trials in Scotland* Vol. 3 (1833).*

These are something close to the enchanting words of accused witch Isobel Gowdie.† No one knows what Isobel's fate was, she darted from history, like the flash of a hare dashing for cover. I hope eventually, in one way or another, she was able to stop running and find her way home.

*

In the end, Morris dancers guide me, like jingling ancestral spirit guides. To give a very short and incomplete introduction for readers not from Britain, Morris dancing is a form of folk dance performed in England by groups and sometimes, but not always, connected to other seasonal folk customs, such as 'mumming' and 'wassailing'. Dances often have themes or narratives. There is a feeling/idea that the dances have certain ritual power or bringing of fortune. Dancers often have bells fastened to the legs or body and hold sticks that are struck on the ground or with other dancers or handkerchiefs for waving about. You also get ribbons, top hats, waistcoats and tattercoats. As a former Morris dancer, I had a tatter coat: an old shirt of my dad's made into a jacket of yellow and green rags, which was, looking back, rather Green Man-esque.

* Translated into modern English using Pitcairn's footnotes.

† Records and interpretations vary. When researching her book, *The Visions of Isobel Gowdie,* author, Emma Wilby, found the original transcripts of Isobel Gowdie's trial, long thought lost, a much more ragged, wild text than Pitcairn's neatly laid out account, including words can no longer be made out. Texts like this are so very precious because they are about as close as we can ever come to the real words of those accused and those who suffered during the witch trials. This is the original text, as Wilby shared:

"Qwhen we goe in the shape ofan haire, we say thryse ower I sall gow intill a haire wlith sorrow and syt and meikle caire and I sall goe in che divellis nam ay whill com hom (damaged – words missing) Ga?"

I follow the website of Sompting Village Morris side, as their events, like many Morris sides, correspond with what we may call the pagan festivals – equinoxes, solstices, May Day and wassailing. I spotted that they would be dancing in March, at a community orchard in the town of Arundel to see in the spring, a most auspicious time for me to seek March hares as well I hoped.

But I also considered this practice of dancing at the equinoxes and solstices and how this connects to the many stones said to once have been women who danced on the Sabbath or holy days – like the Nine Maidens in Dartmoor. So, I thought it symbolic on this journey to go and support the women and men, who dance on sacred days nowadays and (all being well!) remain flesh and blood.

I catch the train to Arundel. It is a very beautiful town, watched over by the twin striking structures of Arundel Castle and Cathedral. I plan to head to the community orchard to celebrate the spring equinox before heading out to walk a route, called the Hare Loop, that runs out to the west of Arundel and loop back to the town to get a late train home.

As I shuttle along by rail into Sussex seeking witch hares, I consider another sign of the witch, known in Sussex is as the "hag-track". Some texts liken them to "fairy rings" of mushrooms. In the *Eastbourne Gazette,* April 1895, a wonderful article called "The Down Country" shares:

> *Rings on the dark, green grass are called " hag-tracks" or "fairy-rings." Until quite recent times Sussex country folk believed that pixies here did dance on ringlets to the whistling wind, or in the quiet of the broad moonlight. These "fairy-rings" are often formed in a single night and they will disappear as suddenly as they came. They are softer and of a deeper green than the surrounding grass. There in no doubt that they are formed by the little buff fungus, Champignon – a good edible fungus, although few know it. Some of the country people use it in soup, or dry it and string it up for winter use. The rings it forms sometimes measure many hundred feet in diameter, but the majority are much smaller. They are caused by the spores being thrown outward.*
>
> **Also in *Plant Lore, Legends and Lyrics*, Richard Folkard (1884)**

These rings, often found on the Sussex Downs, are called hag-tracks because they are thought to be caused by hags and witches who dance there at night.

Whilst spring is a great time for spotting hares, I don't know if autumn might be more appropriate for the mushrooms. But I enjoy reading about these hag-tracks all the same. And like the hag stone, the word hag is used to mean a magical phenomenon or item. Depending on which region of the country you are in, a stone with a naturally occurring hole in the centre may be called a hag stone, adder stone, fairy stone, holey stone, or witch stone. As the names suggest, there is more than a passing association with the supernatural. And stones like these have long been used as charms, carried in pockets or hung in windows. One may use it as a lucky charm to keep witches at bay, ward off diseases and prevent nightmares – but if women with certain skills looked through holed stones they may see the fate-hags spinning…

Haws, hags & hedge witches

When I started scouring maps for possible sites for this book's journey, I searched first, obviously for the word 'witch', which showed me sites such as *Witch Hill* and *Witch Wood*. But then I moved on to 'hag' – another word synonymous with magical (and often malevolent) women and found a number of *Hag Wood*s and *Hag Hill*s. Something quite similar happens when I am trawling through online texts looking for witch stories; if no result comes up for 'witch', I then try 'hag' and 'crone' and often just the word 'woman' or 'old woman' – often they all lead to the same place: to witches and their stories. Funny that, to some folk, woman is just another word for witch, and vice versa.

The word hag is deeply interwoven with women and the land, with both the natural world and witches.

In Old English *haga* means 'hedge', a boundary to an inclosure. In old Scots *hag* might also be a clump of earth or peat. But, *haga* as a root word for hedge also gives us the word 'hag' – a name often used to denote a witch. Somewhere around the thirteenth century, in Middle English, the word *hag/hagge* was used to describe a demon and/or an old woman. This is one of a few German words that denotes a witch: *hag, hagazussa, hagtesse, hex*. All are drawn from the same root words for hedge. In English this connection is reflected in the folk names of one of our most common hedgerow plants: hawthorn, often known as hagthorn and hedgethorn. The shared words of 'hag' and 'hex' in English and German indicates our united history. It's a jumbled but fascinating journey through the roots of these words. It's a tanglewood of words that all lead us back to the hag being a wily-wild-woman-thing.

'Hag' is all at once witch, hedge and earth. Further proof, if it was needed, that the witch is inseparable from the landscape she haunts.

And here I try to drag us from careering, hag-ridden, too far off the path and back, to Sussex and our hag-tracks and witch hares…

*

January and February have been intensely wet this year; it feels like March is only just ruffling its wings and drying out now nearing the end of the month. From the train, I watch the countryside roll by. Pom-pom baubles of mistletoe sit in bare-branched trees and hawthorn and blackthorn fill out the hedgerows with bright white and fresh green.

Departing the train at Arundel, I watch hailstones cascade off the station awning, hoping it will pass and cursing myself for not bringing a raincover for my rucksack or waterproof trousers. On the journey here, I have watched whipping winds, glorious sunshine and torrential rain, arrive and depart in relatively quick succession. And now, not mentioned on any forecast – ferocious hailstones. It does eventually pass, and I power-walk to Arundel community orchard, concerned I will be late (I hate being late), but they too, have been waiting for the weather to ease and the sun is shining when I arrive.

Wildings, witches & wassailing

The custom of wassailing used to be observed on the eve of the Epiphany, when the people went to the orchards and there, encircling one of the best bearing trees, drank the following toast:

Here's to thee, old apple tree,
May'st thon hnd,. niay'st thou blow,
May'st thou bear apples enow!
Hats full! caps full! Bushel, bushel, sacks full!
And my pockets full, too! Huzza!

Sussex Archaeological Society, *Sussex Archaeological Collections Relating to the History and Antiquities of The County* (1848)

Wassailing is rooted in traditions branching out for over a millennium, bringing merriment and mischief to, usually, the dark days of midwinter. I am thrilled that a wassail will be bringing merriment to this rainy day in early spring. The word "wassail" comes from the Anglo-Saxon *waes hael*, meaning "be well" or "be in good health." In the poem "Beowulf" (circa 1000 CE), it appears as a salute to warriors. By around 1135, Geoffrey of Monmouth recounted the tale of Saxon princess Rowena, who presented King Vortigern with spiced wine, saluting him with *"Wass-heil!"* to which he replied, *"Drinc heile!"* Captivated by her charm, he later married her.

There is no definitive recipe for the wassail drink, varying by county and local ingredients, but typically it includes plentiful apples. Wassail has been made from warm beer, ale, or cider, cloves, ginger, nutmeg and sugar, often with bread, cake, or sliced apples floating in it and pulped roasted apples known as "Lamb's Wool." It may also be fortified by wine, brandy, whisky, rum, or any other alcoholic liquid. The mixture is sweet, hot and boozy, with warming and healing herbs or spices.

The wassail drink may be carried around villages in special bowls to share in imbibing and end up at the local orchard for the wassailing ritual of blessing the trees. Taking the wassail to local orchards was meant to ensure an abundant apple harvest and wish good health to the community. This included scaring away evil spirits from the branches, sometimes by firing guns or banging on pots and pans. Toast or cake might be hung in the trees, literally 'raising a toast' to feed and thank the trees. Wassailers might make rounds of their village, fields, livestock and even visit beehives to declare *"Waes Hael!"* to the bees, assuring abundance for the coming year. This ritual is still prevalent in areas of Somerset, Wiltshire and Sussex and places known for their apple orchards.

Of Poisoned Apples

Throughout fairytale and myth, apples are often connected to magic. Who doesn't know the image of the witch with the apple, such as in the tale of Snow White who is offered a shining but poisoned apple?

My home counties (Somerset and Wiltshire) are famously home to apple trees, including those of Avalon (Glastonbury). Once we had just the crab apple *(Malus sylvestris)*, the wild counterpart to the cultivated apple tree *(Malus domestica)* and signs of crab apple fruits have been found in burials dating back to the Neolithic Age. Wild crab apples, sometimes known as "wildings", may have been foraged, but in time, apples were cultivated – with the help of the Romans – to create the many domestic varieties we know today. Witches and cunning women were said to use apple skin and seed for divination. And the most skilled witches were able to conceal their poisons or bewitchment within the fruits, which they offered to poor villagers – accused witches in my local area were tried for doing precisely this…

Accounts of my local witches at the Somerset witch trials around the 1660s can be found in a book called *Saducismus Triumphatus** by Joseph Glanvill, a writer, clergyman and rector of Bath Abbey. The trials of accused witches, including Elizabeth Style and Jane Brooks, who gave apples to people who would later accuse them of maleficium, have more than a whisper of fairy tale about them. Elizabeth Style, in one account, brings two apples to the house of a woman called Agnes and offers up "one of them a very fair red Apple, which Style desired her to eat, which she did and in a few hours was taken ill and worse than ever she had been before…" Agnes claimed herself "be-witched" and died not long after. Jane Brooks offered apples to a boy in return for bread, after he takes the apple he falls ill, but he survived the ordeal.

* Its English title was *Full and Plain Evidence Concerning Witches and Apparitions.* The book was published posthumously in 1681 and was based on original records made by magistrate Robert Hunt and a collection of earlier works by Glanvill.

With both apples and apple trees able to hold certain magics, offering blessings to the tree was thought prudent. And the practice of wassailing is still enjoyed to encourage a good crop. The Apple Tree Man is the name that folklorist Ruth L. Tongue said was given to the oldest apple tree in the orchard; within this tree a spirit resides, and the yield of the orchard is under his control. The last apple of the season may be gifted to him to further ensure a good crop. I admire the trees of the orchard, including the Apple Tree Man. He has been dressed for the occasion today: his branches hold red-trimmed paper ribbons that display the words the wassail song, he is looking dapper indeed.

The Morris dancers circle the orchard in a slow jingling procession with musical accompaniment, making their way to the Apple Tree Man and the drinking of warmed cider begins. Toast is hung in the branches of the tree adorned with the wassailing words, and finally, the cider is poured on its roots. We all sing the wassail song together. It has started raining heavily again, so cakes and cider are consumed quickly before we dash off and seek shelter. Or that's what many people do – I don't have time, I leave the orchard to start my walk out to the Hare Loop…or that's what I was intending. But the path along the River Arun is slick and sticky with mud. A rabbit flashes through scrubland and I think that it has to be a good sign.

I have never seen a hare in England; up until last year, I had not ever seen one in the wild at all. But for my fortieth birthday, Dan took me to the Faroe Islands far off the northern coast of Scotland. On our first day there, we were walking in an impossibly atmospheric mist around a lake known as "the lake above the ocean" (that, as the name suggests, sits on cliffs above the ocean). After passing the swirling cauldron of salt spray around the looming ocean cliffs, I spot a hare! And a very beautiful one at that. I stop. He stops. I make a squawking sound to Dan, trying to alert him whilst not moving, trying not to spook the hare. Dan stops and follows my eyeline, neither of us daring to move. The hares of Faroe are not the honey-hued brown hares *(Lepus europaeus)* of amber eyes, who blend with warm-toned corn fields and bracken of Britain. This was *Lepus Timidus* – the mountain or blue hare – that I often call the blue mountain hare, which is not quite right, but I like it. The blue mountain hare is grey to blend in with the mist and granite and grey skies of the Faroe Islands (they can also be spotted in northern Britain and Scotland). Their eyes are large and dark and their feet and soft underbellies are cotton-wool white, like their tails. I was lucky to spot him emerging from a large stone, just uphill from our path. He sits now, nose twitching. He's round of body, more *bunny-shaped* than the long, lean, angular brown hare. And I was close enough to see he had a puff of fluff stuck on the end of his nose – so cute! The difference is evident when he stands up: his legs extend in an inexplicable concertina of folded limbs that bring him to grow upwards by at least three times his height, to my eye. And in a blink, it's a rising of long white legs and away… He is bounding uphill through the rocks and mist, vanished, with wolfing speed.

*

The weather today in Sussex is a layer cake, lemon drizzle. Bands of colour striated before me from brown murky river, gold river bank reeds that line up below a strip of blue sky weighed down by the thick heavy cream frosting of rain-laden clouds. Sugared with raindrops, of course. I find myself disorientated and disheartened, my confidence well and truly dampened amongst the thick layers of buttery mud that slow down my progress. I am truly walking between worlds, layers and veils. My sense of direction disintegrating away into soggy crumbs.

I cross over a railway bridge and in another torrential downpour I misread the map, I am trying to follow the Monarch's Way up to Wepham, but instead find myself walking round the edge of a field that rises up a hill. Along the tree line, families of pheasants scurry back and forth, I see burrows and freshly dug holes, a clear deer hoofprint in the mud.

As I approach the top of the sloping field, the rain stops and suddenly, the late afternoon is soaked through with lemon sunlight, seeping light onto sodden fields. A flit of movement catches my eye in the light. I think it's a hare. There is a cluster of old corn, yellow and brown, they are perfectly camouflaged. I move closer. It dashes to the tree line. And another skims across between corn rows. And just like that they are gone. Witch hares, scarcely a glimpse. But see, I am in amongst the corn now, rocky ground, very 'harvest goddess'. I think what a great place this would be to find a holed 'hag' stone, but of course, such treasure is not so easily found. I find a flinty stone with a circular quartz centre that looks like an eye. This will do, I think.

As I walk to the end of the field, I see a glaring red sign that reads, "Strictly no trespassing." Shit! Where am I? Another sign nearby says I am on the Angmering Estate, but there is a public footpath sign as well peeling off from the top of the field. After a minute of walking through thick mud steeply downhill, I know I'm not going to make it down this path. So, I retrace my steps, trespassing a second time and see a rabbit on the way down. I'm not going to make the Hare Loop, I've barely made it to the edges of Warningcamp and I'm frustrated by my slow progress. I'll also not make it to the woodlands, where I might have had a better chance to see hag-tracks. My mood is drizzly and defeated as I stumble back along muddy, rocky tracks.

*

I could fill a book, several probably, with stories from the British Isles of witch hares, one of the most common stories being of men hunting in fields. They shoot a hare, or their dogs catch one in their jaws for a moment before it escapes and flees, bleeding. Through the fields the hare runs and to a cottage, perhaps the tumbledown one on the edge of the village, standing between wildwood and civilisation. The hare disappears somewhere in the cottage garden of this little place, only for a woman to appear at the door a moment later. The hunters see her. She is bleeding, bruised or has a limp. *She was the hare,* they cry; *she is a witch,* they accuse. To my mind, this always sounded an awful lot like a folkloric spin on domestic abuse, and at the very least, mirrors the inhumane treatment of both hares and those people considered to be witches.

> *My mates and me was resting under a hedge nigh Up Waltham, 'aving our dinner, when a hare comes lopping along… "That bain't a hare, that's that old 'ooman down along under,' (speaking of a village where we was lodging). I takes up a stone and throws it and catches that hare. She didn't half holler, letting out a screech just like an ol' 'ooman; an' then she goes limping away. That night, when we was down in village, ol' Sary Weaver, wot people said could make a cow run dry by lookin' at her – folks said she were a witch – comes 'obbling outer 'er cottage. When she sees we, she lets out a screech, same as hare did, an' goes a-limping off, for all the world as if she were that there hare. She were lame in the same leg wot the hare was, but she 'adn't been afore!*
>
> **From a 'countryman' source in *The Folklore of Sussex*, Jacqueline Simpson (1973)**

*

I make my way to the train station, it's 6pm now, and the sun is low in the sky. Dusk settles softly as rabbits fur over Arundel, the sky is clear now, silhouetting the great castle and cathedral. The train pulls away from the station and I head for home. The lights of the train feel brighter as it gets darker outside. As the hour latens and darkness falls in earnest on Saturday night, revellers begin to fill the carriage. Girls doing their make-up and sipping from berry-coloured drinks in Evian bottles. Groups celebrating birthdays and greeting the ticket conductor by name. As I journey back through the counties of Sussex, Hampshire, Wiltshire and Somerset, I think of my favourite witch hare folktale as the hubbub of merriment grows. It's from Devon and Dartmoor and is quite different to the usual theme of injury to the hare resulting in injury to the witch. Instead, two women come together to look out for each other in a dark and devilish world.

An old woman was walking country lanes at midnight, some stories suggest she was confused, I'd wager she was too wise for that and knew exactly what she was about. Somewhere skirting along the edges the moors, under the light of the moon she saw a white hare race out and into the old woman's path. The old woman could see the fear in the creature's eyes and she understood why when she heard the unmistakable cries of the wild hunt; the raucous band of demons and dark spirits. The old woman bent down and gathered up the creature and hid it in her basket under scraps of cloth. Not moments after, the devil himself appeared in the form of a black-clad horseman; he rode a headless horse.

The old woman stood her ground. The devil growled and demanded to know if she had seen the hare, she replied simply, 'No.'

*He passed with his retinue of demons trailing behind and when all was peaceful once more, the old woman released the hare, placing it gently back onto the earth. The hare transformed into a lady, one, it was clear to the old woman, that was not quite of this world. In return for the old woman's bravery and help, the lady promised her, as a reward, that her hens would forevermore lay two eggs instead of one, her cows would yield milk all the year round and that she would be able to talk twice as much as before and her husband would always listen and obey her! With this, the lady vanished. And it is said that from then on, the affairs of the old woman prospered and she found the best possible luck for the rest of her days.**

A few days after this ill-fated trip, I looked back over a short film I took of the cornfield. Now I think perhaps that the two creatures I thought were hares were actually rabbits, I can't say for sure. This surely is the way of hares and their witching nature. In the hares that became witches, people saw what they wanted to see, maybe that's what I did in Sussex, so keen was I to spot the magical hares. The nature of the witch hare perhaps is to always keep us guessing…

* You'll find versions of this story in *The Folklore of Devon*, Ralph Whitlock (1977) and *Folk-lore and Legends: English*, Charles John Tibbits (1891).

APRIL

Fairy Time

Vale of Glamorgan, Wales

May Eve is a very fairy-time and precautions must be taken against their wiles. Where the fairies are busy, there also the witches are sure to be about.
Eleanor Hull, *Folklore of the British Isles* (1928)

It is May Eve, the day has started with a misty curtain of rain. I watch the trails of droplets scatter on the train windows. I feel like it has rained every day since my last expedition in Sussex in March and authoritative sources agree that these first months of the year have been some of the wettest on record. I am delighted then that during the train journey into Wales, the rain stops and blue skies and sunshine appear. Although, the mist and rains may well have been more appropriate; mists are woven around the lore of witches all through Europe and very much here in Wales.

Mist & magic

Gwrach-y-Rhibyn, in English, the Witch of Rhibyn or the Hag of the Mist is a Welsh spirit who appears in a monstrous form. Like a harpy or vampire she is wizened, withered and bony with leathery wings, long black teeth, a blood-stained mouth and trailing black hair and robes. Considered, among other things, a night hag and a witch of death – not dissimilar to the Irish banshee or Scottish *baobhan sithe*[*]. The person who sees her is being warned of their imminent death or that of someone close to them. To hear her shriek is a portent of death or misfortune. However, some say she only appears before the death of a person who lived a wicked life. One might be unlucky enough to see her silently glaring at a crossroads or a stream when the mist rises, washing or wringing her hands in despair. The Gwrach-y-Rhibyn can be silent, stalking through shrouds of mist, watching until it is time to reveal herself with a wail and shriek. If you were lying in bed waiting for death, her dark shape might appear at your window, and you would know that the death witch had come for you.

Some of the stories of the Gwrach-y-Rhibyn place her at specific sites. One lived in the Caerphilly swamp in the late 1700s, through which the Nant-Gledyr river flows. After the swamp flooded, she moved into the town and

* Pronounced *bavan shee.*

occasionally, she flies low down along watercourses or around crumbling mansions or castles. Stories abound of her appearing at the windows of castles, flapping her bat-like wings in the twilight and rattling her talons upon window panes.* At Pennard Castle, which, as the old story goes, was built in a single night by a Welsh sorcerer, her wandering form could be both seen and heard by anybody who slept amongst the ruins of the castle, and she would descend to bewitch or devour them. Or she may lurk at boundary edges, accompanied by black hounds or weave through swamps, rivers, lakes and marshy ground. Through the shrouds of rain and mists, Gwrach-y-Rhibyn might rise, wings, hair and talon-like fingers all sparkling with water droplets in the darkling twilight.

Creatures of kin to Gwrach-y-Rhibyn include the ever-popular large spectral black dogs, or hellhounds *(Cwn Annwn)*, almost universally regarded as evil. They were said to prowl alone or in packs, led out at night by various masters and mistresses to hunt the souls of the damned. The legend of the Gwrach-y-Rhibyn is sometimes blended with tales of the *Cyhyraeth*, a ghostly spirit who may moan before a person's death, calling a threefold warning before the person expires.

Another fearsome hag of legend is called *Mallt-y-Nos*, Matilda of the Night. Mallt-y-Nos shrieks and wails and drives her hounds. She was once a beautiful woman with such a love of hunting she declared, "If there is no hunting in heaven, I would rather not go!" Her wish was granted as she now hunts forever in the night sky (whether or not this is a misfortune may be open to debate). Then there is the *Gwyllion*, a female fairy you wouldn't wish to meet on a dark spirit night, or any night. Fond of dark mountain tops, she haunts the lonely paths. The Welsh word *gwyll* describes a spirit of nightfall and gloaming, but they may be seen as hags or witches.† Those that hear her cries on a murky night may follow the cries unaware that they were being led purposefully astray and only once thoroughly lost may the victim hear the cry turn to a cackle…

Mist is a natural phenomenon, but it is also seemingly evocative of feelings of great magic. From the various creatures of the mist in Wales to Vixana from Dartmoor, using mists to lure men to their deaths is commonplace in folklore.

---

* Such as in *Folk-lore and folk-stories of Wales*, Marie Trevelyan (1909).

† As suggested in *British Goblins: Welsh Folklore, Fairy Mythology, Legends and Traditions*, Wirt Sikes (1880).

Throughout Europe, morning mists are delightfully attributed in folk tales to hares, foxes or witches brewing coffee. These are, in fact, my all-time favourite folktales (I'm easily enchanted by caffeine). In German, the mist that hangs over forests and trees in the early morning air may be caused by *"Die Füchse kuchen Kaffee"* – "the foxes making coffee."[‡] Other variations of this saying include "the witches are making coffee", "the hares are making coffee" and *"Hexenküche"* the witch's kitchen (where all manner of magic may be cooking…). The Danish also use similar inspiration, connecting brewing and morning mists: *"Mosekonen brygger"*, roughly translates to "the bog woman/the witch is brewing." It seems in many lands that mists, witches, hares and foxes all speak of magic and hint at the charm of natural wonders.

Maybe it happens that tales of the Otherworld speak of veils and the hidden occult and the closest to seeing this in the material world is mists in their myriad forms. Or times of dawn, dusk and poor weather, where one's world becomes changed, half-hidden and indistinct around the edges.

The mists of Cumbria (where we'll meet Long Meg in August) may be called "haut" or "haunt", suggestive of a more eerie or terrifying nature than just low cloud.[§] The Green Mist is something else again, seemingly contained within fenland folklore[¶] of the east of England. Amongst the wet meadowlands and fertile farmland of East Anglia, in spring, it's said, the fairies stir from their hidden hollows to cast their spells of revival, awakening the earth and the wild world. Their seelie[**] seasonal magic is hidden from view within a verdant veil that rises with the temperatures, known as the Green Mist, which holds a certain magic of its own.[††]

> *But in the Spring they went – the folk did as believed in the old ways – to every field in turn and lifted a spud of earth from the mools; and they said strange and queer words, as they couldn't scarce understand themselves, but the same as had been said for hundreds of years. And every morning at the first dawn, they stood on the door sill, with salt and bread in their hands, watching and waiting for the green mist as rose from the fields and told that*

---

‡ You can read my retelling of this magical story in my book *Kitchen Witch*.

§ *Bygone Cumberland & Westmorland*, Daniel Scott (1899).

¶ The Fens is an area that was once largely wetlands that ran down the eastern spine of Britain; through the counties of Lincolnshire and Cambridgeshire and parts of Norfolk and Suffolk. Most of the fens were drained centuries ago, to create flat, dry land for agriculture.

** *Seelie* is a term for fairies in Scottish folklore.

†† *Telling the Seasons: Stories, Celebrations and Folklore around the Year*, Martin Maudsley (2022).

the earth were awake again; and the life were coming to the trees and the plants and the seeds were bursting with the beginning of the Spring.

Alan Garner, *Complete Folk Tales* (2011)

*

When planning where I would visit in Wales, I knew from the start *when* I would come – one of the *Teir nos Ysbrydnos* (Three Nights for Spirits) "upon which elves and goblins and all sorts of sprites are fonder than usual of Welsh company and frequent every merry circle and may be wrought upon, by proper enchantments, to give an insight into futurity."*

Wales is both a Celtic and a Brythonic nation. Brythonic (anglicised it's Brittonic, so that's another spelling you may know) refers to the southern group of Celtic languages and lore originating from ancient Britain; including Welsh, Cornish and Breton (of Brittany, France). These Celtic languages were spoken in Britain before the arrival of the Anglo-Saxons. This Brythonic connection contributes to the unique lore surrounding Tinkinswood and to many Welsh festivals that, whilst similar to celebrations in England, are distinct to Wales (you'll find a very close connection to festivals in Cornwall and Brittany, though).

The first of these Three Spirit Nights is *Nos Galan Haf* – April 30th; the last day of spring, the eve of May 1st *(Calan Mai/Calan Haf)*, known in other realms of the British Isles as May Day and Beltane. The other two spirit nights are *Nos Gwyl Ifan* (the eve of Summer/Midsummer in June) and *Nos Galan Gaeaf* on October 31st (the eve of *Calan Gaeaf,* Halloween or Samhain).

On spirit nights people may build bonfires to protect themselves from evil spirits and offer rituals to bring luck for the rest of the year. They may leap over the flames, drive cattle between fires and use the ash as a warding charm. *Calan Mai* is seen as the start of summer and after the challenges of winter, it was greeted with *dawnsio haf* (summer dancing) and *carolau mai* (May carols). People would decorate the outside of their homes with hawthorn branches to symbolise growth and fertility and they'd turn their herds out to pasture.

Summer solstice, the longest day of the year was welcomed, as was wide-

* *The Vale of Glamorgan: Scenes and Tales Among the Welsh*, Charles Redwood (1839).

spread through England and Europe, with dancing, merriment and the lighting of bonfires – all celebrations that were seen as essential to producing a bountiful crop. On Midsummer Eve, known as Gathering Day, medicinal plants may be harvested. To Druids, mistletoe in particular was thought a cure-all, cut with a golden scythe and caught in a cloth so as to never touch the ground.

Finally, *Nos Calan Gaeaf,* marks the end of harvest and the start of winter. On this night, villagers would gather around bonfires once more before seeking home and safety from fearsome spirits or creatures of the night. The winter solstice was sometimes also seen as a spirit night where ghosts and spirits may roam.

To Tinkinswood...

The draw of many spirits led me to a stone site known as the Tinkinswood Chambered Tomb in the lush green Vale of Glamorgan in Wales, a short bus ride from the Welsh capital of Cardiff. A place whose very name rings like it will be filled with fairy mischief. Tinkinswood is a collection of stones called a *dolmen* or the more magical sounding *portal tomb* – which looks like a stone table, with two or more upright stones, supporting a flat capstone. *Cromlech* is another word used to describe it, often used interchangeably with dolmen, which is true in some of the texts I cite.

It is said that if you were to spend the night at Tinkinswood burial chamber on the *Ysbrydnos* spirit nights you'll either die, go insane, or gain the gift of poetry.

I am here because, albeit briefly, Tinkinswood was called The Witch's Castle – I've read it named such in a few scraps of text and, more recently, heard it mentioned in a podcast I was listening to whilst waiting in a café in Southampton train station, on the way back from Manningtree. This is how my travel plans for April were inspired, but I know little more than that, it's not much to go on, but I'm keen to explore it, nonetheless. And because today is the eve of May Day and a spirit night. More than one person I told this story to suggested that I definitely should sleep here tonight. The answer was a firm no, I am not a fan of camping at the best of times, I'm certainly not going to risk any kind of fairy wrath by changing my habits tonight. So, I'm here in the daytime on April 30th. After the lost adventures of March in Sussex, my journey in the Vale of Glamorgan is very civilised: a walking loop of a mile or so from The Witch's Castle to St Lythans burial dolmen via a pitstop for tea and cake. This is a very genteel adventure, and I'm excited (naively perhaps, I think I won't get lost, and while I manage to follow the trails, I sure do get lost in the folklore and superstitions). I did spend many hours scouring the internet for some kind of organised events on the spirit nights in Wales – but was unsuccessful. This is no criticism. It's very possible the pagans of Wales don't wish grockles* like me to crash their special festivities. I get a strong feeling that the rituals and folk customs of Wales are not showy for the sake of tourists, but rather a sacred and serious business of preserving history, like their passionate dedication to keeping the Welsh language alive.

I take the train to Cardiff and then a bus through the suburbs. I get off the bus at the white houses, black slate roofs and stone walls of St Nicholas. A nice big sign points me towards a list of delights: Tinkinswood, St Lythans burial chambers and Dyffryn Gardens, a National Trust house and gardens. I walk down a lane lined with low stone walls and beautiful houses. It's not long before the houses thin, revealing flourishing green fields ahead. I take a right over a stone stile and walk through the fields for half a mile to arrive at Tinkinswood, my first stop and primary point for this visit to Wales.

The sun is shining brightly as I walk over the fields and I am feeling sweaty as I peel off the layers, tying the jumper under my waterproof jacket around my waist. There are glaring signs of human life: neon orange bollards and a path for construction vehicles (I find out later this is connected to sewage works in the area) and huge pylons tower over the burial site. But the stone still cuts a dramatic figure, and it's easy to spot: it's huge. Tinkinswood was once a village but now all that remains to hold the name is this burial chamber – a raised ridge of earth topped now with grass and stone, and the dolmen stone with its hulking capstone that stands before it, like a grand gatehouse: a vast relic of a prehistoric funerary and ritual landscape.

I arrive at the welcoming visitor sign which reads:

> *The restless dead – weighed down by the largest capstone in Wales. This chambered tomb has stood here for 6000 years: still and immovable. Not so*

* A West country term for tourist/someone not local. I had never before looked up its meaning. I am utterly thrilled to find out a grockle is a magical dragon-like creature in several comic strips of the 1950s which may or may not have hatched this common term for tourist.

the fifty people housed inside! Their bones may have been moved by their own Neolithic relatives many times. Skeletons of men, women and children found inside the burial chamber had bits missing. It is thought that they were not left to rest in peace but were taken out into the light for some special ritual. Over time fewer bones survived the trip. Rituals may have taken place in front of the burial chamber.

Over thousands of years, the tomb was still respected as a sacred place by people who had no memory of its Neolithic builders. Bronze Age people brought their own burial practices, mingling the bones of their dead with those of domestic animals. Neolithic bones were found within the stone dolmen, Bronze Age ones in a burial pit further back on the burial mound.

The dolmen faces east, and extending out from either side are walls that curve out like projecting wings, that have been rebuilt and restored as herringbone stone walls, as if to gather up the rays of the sun at each new dawn. (The Belas Knap Neolithic barrow in Gloucestershire has similar sweeping walls that guide one to a false entrance, thought by prehistorians to be a 'spirit door', to allow the dead to come and go. So perhaps these winged walls of Tinkinswood are seeking to guide spirits and well as sunlight.)

There is a cluster of stones just to the west of the stone table, on top of the burial mound, in a huddled circle, in front of a shallow circle of what was once a round burial pit; some say these are the women/witches petrified for dancing on top of the tomb on the Sabbath. There are more stones scattered to the south of the chamber and in a nearby field, also said to be dancing/petrified women. I imagine the story may well be applied to any proximate stones.

There is not much inside the Dolmen, just a pool of green water, a reminder of all the rain we've had so far this year and a modern brick column providing additional support to the capstone and noting the site's excavation in 1914. To the right, the inside of the ancient stone is scratched, scarred and lined.

The signage also says: "Tinkinswood still holds a spiritual fascination for us today. It is said that it has the power to change you forever." It repeats a similar story of being here on notable spirit nights, though on the sign, it's May Day, Midsummer, or Midwinter rather than Halloween. I am here, of course, in daylight and the 'crossing over' for my journey seems to have happened from the wild rain of the morning to the present moment. Now the sun is out, suddenly it feels like a new season, as though summer has just appeared in a sigh of sunlight. I sit and soak up the sunshine. I can hear birdsong and traffic, wind in the trees and the occasional bark, no one else comes to the burial site in the short time I am there.

This gives me a chance to arrange my thoughts, which are whirling in a *merry circle* indeed. Here's what I know; Tinkinswood has been called many names over the centuries and is connected to various myths. One such name is *Castell Carreg,* meaning Stone Castle in Welsh – which is a fact I try to hold onto as a spiralling jumble of other words, glide around this place and its stories.

Stones and burial chambers, such as Tinkinswood, were seen by later cultures as portals to the Otherworld, where supernatural beings may appear at certain times. And it's exploring these supernatural presences here, probably appropriately so, where things get muddled, and fairy-led in my research.

In 1880, American author Wirt Sikes (who lived in Wales for seven years) connected the burial chamber with specific fairy folk. He said that Castell Carreg, which he spelled "Castle *Correg*" struck an observer as like "The korreds and korregs of Brittany closely resemble the Welsh fairies in numberless details. The korreds are supposed to live in the cromlechs, of which they are believed to have been the builders. They dance around them at night, and woe betide the unhappy peasant who joins them in their roundels." Squiffy spelling aside, Sikes connects to this idea of long-held lore that spirits dwell around ancient sacred stones and burial places.

I believe what Sikes is speaking of is a creation of Breton folklore, called korrigans/corrigans: a fairy or dwarf-like spirit, fond of dancing around dolmens and crossroads, where they may also dwell. Corrigans may be described as mischievous (though I'd say they veer into terrifying), dressed in white linen or veils, and may be seen and heard at dusk or on clear moonlit nights. And maybe, in Wales where witches and fairies seem closely linked, that brings us to a present-day where, to some, fairies have become witches.

The book that perhaps goes into the most detail of corrigans, was by another American, Walter Yeeling (W.Y.) Evans-Wentz, who in 1911 wrote *The Fairy-Faith in Celtic Countries,* in which he speaks of corrigans hosting sabbaths, troubling horses at night, as witches were famed to do in superstition:

> *The corrigans were the terror of the country-folk, especially in Finistère, in the Morbihan, and throughout the Côtes-du-Nord. They were believed to be souls in pain condemned to wander at night in waste lands and marshes. Sometimes they were seen as dwarfs; and often they were not seen at all, but were heard in houses making an infernal noise. Unlike the lavandières de*

nuits (phantom washerwomen of the night), they were heard only in summer, never in winter.

Put that account next to Dr James MacKillop's, in his 1998 *Dictionary of Celtic Mythology,* who sees them as:

Wanton, impish, sprightly female fairy of Breton folklore who desires sexual union with humans. Thought to be descended from ancient Druidesses, Korrigans are especially malicious towards celibate Catholic priests. Each Korrigan has the power to enmesh the heart of the most constant swain (country youth, lover or suitor) and doom him to perish for love of her.

And we can see whispers of where the corrigan is considered a wanton and frightening female spirit, a little closer to an image the English may call a witch. Luring humans with their deadly wiles. We do eventually arrive at more direct references to witches, but in text form this seems a very recent development as far as I can find, a small article in *Wales Online* from July 2020 "Tinkinswood has had a number of names and was once known as Castell Carrigan, meaning the Witches Castle." And according to stone-circles.org.uk, in 2024: "Tinkinswood was formerly known as Castell Carrigan, meaning the Witches Castle and according to legend it represents a group of women turned to stone for dancing on the Sabbath – a common piece of folklore attached to many ancient sites, particularly stone circles."

I cannot for the life of me figure out how we got to Carrigan, or what that word even means. My best guess is that *carreg* – stone – and corrigan/korrigan – spirit – have been spliced together. You'll see a variety of spellings of the spirit creations in these excerpts of texts I've found. So, as far as I can tell, Castell Carrigan – does not mean, literally, Witch's Castle, even though the spirits around the site may have imbued that name upon it. It has entered the folkloric discourse somehow, but it would take someone more expert than me to pull all the threads apart to how we got here. It's entirely possible I've missed some key text in Welsh that could unravel this whole mystery. Like in Dartmoor, names can be changed and crafted to create new ones – when Maen (stone) and Var Maen (Great Stone) may have become maiden and Bowerman, respectively.

This is folklore in action: the many myths and history that dance around this place and we gather what we can. The archaeologists find part of the story, the folklorists another and countless other walkers, farmers, everyday folk add their own – the spirits felt, the bones found, the sense of sacred connected to, stories added, and the connections made. I haven't quite managed to piece it all together yet. And maybe that's a good thing. Wales, Tinkinswood and St Lythans were never going to reveal all their secrets on one visit. I may feel a bit fairy-led by all of this, but I'm not disappointed by this revelation that I can't really document the history of this place being called The Witch's Castle. As I sit in the sun, butterflies flutter around me, between the stones that may have been dancing women, fairies or witches and the entrance to a place that really was sacred, sitting somewhere between history, folklore and the fairies. I am reminded that a site's history and its folklore does not end, it is always dancing, moving forward as we do. Tinkinswood's history began with the ancient communities that used it, and as centuries rolled past it, new stories emerged and will continue to do so.

Maybe the Witches Castle refers to the stones haunted by remnants of Celtic pasts or places haunted by the Gwrach-y-Rhibyn, and I so loved the idea of the grand dolmen being a place of festivities, the great capstone set like a table for a feast, where the witches gather with fairy folk who float in through spirit doors from across the land to savour cake and golden drams, toasting the sun's cycle, dancing and singing on top of the burial chamber before turning once more to stone.

In sun, in wind, in storm, in thick mist… Let him sit for hours musing amid cromlechs and dolmens, and beside menhirs, and at holy wells. Let him marvel at the mightiest of menhirs now broken and prostrate… let him wander in footpaths with the Breton peasant through fields where good dames sit on the sunny side of a bush or wall, knitting stockings, where there are long hedges of furze, golden-yellow with bloom – even in January – and listen to stories about corrigans, and about the dead who mingle here with the living.

W.Y. Evans-Wentz, *The Fairy-Faith in Celtic Countries* (1911)

Dryffyn Gardens

In many parts of Wales where lie rude heaps of stones, the peasantry say they were carried there by a witch in her apron.

Wirt Sikes, *British Goblins: Welsh Folk-lore, Fairy Mythology, Legends and Traditions* (1880)

St Lythans is another chambered tomb I intend to visit today, which lies about a mile from Tinkinswood. But I'm going to make a stop before I head there. St Lythan seems to be a saint for whom a church and parish were named but I can find little else on their story; if I'm honest I don't look too hard, I've got enough tales and fairies, stones and witches to fill my head as it is. I take a different path to bring me out onto the lane to Dryffyn Gardens. It has absolutely nothing to do with witches that I know of, but it is a sunny day and I have a National Trust membership card, so I head in for a fortifying slice of cake. I watch a coal tit, blue tit and robin eat seed from a little feeder in the shape of a miniature picnic bench with seed feeder attached: it's adorable. I have a wee and a wander around the very lovely gardens and find myself spotting dragons everywhere – I see them as stickers on cars, Welsh flags and some very beautiful Chinese dragons adorn this garden. This is a land where mythical beings – dragons and fairies fascinate but where witches too, live more in the realm of the otherworldly.

Welsh witches

When the English concept of the *witch* was first introduced into the English-run court system in Wales, it was a foreign notion and not a word that existed in the Welsh language, so they were forced to borrow the English one.

The modern Welsh term *gwrach* (witch), leans into the fairytale-style hag witch, rather than the neighbourhood crone. Modern workers of magic in Wales may well call themselves Welsh witches rather than *gwrach* – as *gwrach* is a creature of fantasy, a term that may be used as an insult, similar to how we use terms like hag or crone, or applied to personifications of death, illness and disease like *Cyhyraeth* and *Gwrach-y-Rhibyn*, rather than someone who practices magic. Modern day magic workers may call themselves *swynraig* (charm woman or folk healer), *hudwr* (enchanter) or *brudiwr* (soothsayer, diviner).

The term *gwrach*, used for witch, can be found in a few spots in the Welsh landscape – Pwll y Wrach waterfall near Talgarth (Witches Pool), the villages of Cwmgwrach (Valley of the Witches) and Blaengwrach (meaning Upper Reaches of the Witch's Stream) in the Neath Valley, implying that witches and witchcraft have played a part in the area's history.

Wales seems overall to have been far kinder to its witches, despite the horrifying figures they cut in Welsh folklore. Or perhaps with their interchangeability with fairies and their fondness for shapeshifting (as we'll see in Cerridwen's story shortly) witches in Wales are just all round harder to find. During the witch trials in England, witches' powers were feared because they were gifted by the devil. Witches were more often considered in league with fairy folk in Wales and so, perhaps, were less feared. In folk tales like "Fairy of the Dell" and "The Two Cat Witches"* witches can come by their powers directly from the fairies. In the case of the cat witches, fairies gift two sisters the power to transform into cats.

With the rough numbers, we have about two and a half thousand people who met their death as witches in Scotland and a thousand in England. There were around forty-two prosecutions for witchcraft in Wales, eight were found guilty and just five were hanged for witchcraft. Theories for this low number include the Welsh language – very few examiners or judges spoke Welsh and many sensational witch pamphlets that circulated England would not have been translated into Welsh. And many of Wales' small, rural communities would have been reliant on their local wise women and healers for their potions, salves and charms.

Wales seems to me, a place that tries to hold strongly onto its roots and rites, which is perhaps how the people of Wales did not lose their heads to the 'witch craze' that swept through much of the rest of the British Isles. Perhaps Wales is a place that respects its magic and does not seek the impossible task of stamping it out as other corners of Britain did, embracing the magical side of the world alongside religions.

The 5...

Gwen ferch Ellis (a surname meaning Daughter of Ellis) was a linen-maker by profession, but she also had a reputation for being a folk healer, treating the sick of the community. Invited to tend to a sick man, who died shortly after her arrival, Gwen was blamed for causing his death. At her trial Gwen was asked if she practised or used witchcraft in order to help or harm, she responded, "I hereby hath helpen some diseased children and also beasts as

* In *Welsh Fairy Tales*, William Elliot Griffis (1921).

well as by the same charming as also by salves, drinke and plasters." In 1594, Gwen was hanged. Almost three decades later, in 1622, three accused witches from the same family were found guilty and killed: Rhydderch ap Evan, a yeoman (what we might call a smallholder today) and his sisters Lowri and Agnes. Here, the main issue was the death of the wife of one of the local gentry and accusations of bewitchment of the man's daughter. But even so, many magistrates were unsure as to the correct path of action when otherworldly forces were involved. A letter reveals how they said: "we do not know how to meddle in this business."†

The last person to be hanged in Wales as an accused witch was in 1655, Margaret ferch Richard was convicted of fatally cursing her neighbour. That same year; in one more case of an accused witch I'd like to share with you, in Flintshire, Dorothy Griffith was accused of bewitching a travelling seaman, William Griffith (no relation as far as we know). William claimed to have seen Dorothy with lantern lights hovering around her, that led him to an ale house. Apparently, William arrived in the ale house looking wild and affrighted and when the landlords wife entered the room carrying a candle, well that was one damn light too many and William fell into a swoon. Between bouts of fainting, he said that Dorothy Griffith had come towards him surrounded by lanterns and had led him to the ale house and the marsh was so covered in flames that one could have gathered needles, the light was so bright.

He may have thought these lights to be 'corpse candles' – thought to be seen around watery lands. Similar to will-o'-the-wisps, a mischievous spirit that tried to lead travellers astray, in Wales they were specifically an omen of death. People believed these corpse candles appeared on the night before death and may trace the paths between homes and cemeteries. Hence William's intense fear in seeing them.

"They [corpse-candles] foreshadow deaths, don't they?"
To which the shepherd replied: "They do, sir, but that's not all the harm they do. They are very dangerous for anybody to meet with. If they come bump up against you when you are walking carelessly, its generally all over with you in this world."

Mary L. Lewes (Scholar of Welsh folklore) *Stranger than Fiction* (1911)

Dorothy Griffith was sent for. She protested and said a prayer on her arrival,

† Drawn from the letter by Sir Thomas Middleton and Sir Roger Mostyn, 1656, referenced in *Witchcraft and Magic in Wales*, Richard Suggett (2008).

possibly for patience – as the only outcome from William's ordeal seems that he had made his way to a pub and passed out, something she may well have witnessed many times before. What happened next was that William recovered and went home and Dorothy was detained for seven weeks. Luckily, she had the support of the community and was able to gather signatures from local people stating they had no reason to believe there was any relationship between Dorothy and witchcraft. Other reasons such as a tense relationship between the two families and that William had been ill (or drunk one may speculate, or both) were suggested. The support of her community was invaluable to Dorothy – and a rarity in many of the witch trial cases we have explored. Dorothy appeared at trial, but she was never sentenced, suggesting that the trial was dismissed. The case of Dorothy Griffith is one of many cases that were acquitted and while Dorothy was not subjected as far as we know to the witch-pricker, sleep deprivation or starvation as used in England and Scotland, she still went through quite the ordeal to return to her freedom.

St Lythans

Folk-lore is the story of the soul of a people… Mystery, which has still, I think, some attraction for the Ordinary Person. For, chained as most of us are through force of circumstance to the matter-of-fact and material side of life, one has yet occasional hankerings after the mysterious and inexplicable. There are hours when we like to listen to a "creepy" ghost story, heedless of its evidential value; to rake amongst half-forgotten country-lore for treasures of ancient custom and belief… considering Nature and her ways and our kinship, not only with other human beings, but with the whole Universe and its innumerable aspects of existence. In short, it is pleasant at times to avoid the obvious and let our thoughts dwell a little on the 'Queer Side of Things'.

Mary L. Lewes, *The Queer Side of Things* (1923)

I walk to St Lythans next. The burial chamber has a number of different names associated with it, such as *Gwâl y Filiast*, which translates to The Greyhound Kennel/Lair, specifically a female greyhound, and the surrounding area is *Maes y Felin* (The Mill Field). It spots with rain seemingly from nowhere on my walk there, the sky is still blue, but scattered with clouds. It feels, as is probably always the way, we were all of us very ready for more light and warmth and today has in parts, even with scattered rain begun to deliver on the promise of spring. Blossoms scatter in soft pink drifts along the road and very soft young green beech leaves spread out from hedgerows. I pass several groups of hikers and several fenceposts spotted with the coloured arrows of named footpaths.

I pass through the metal kissing gate and am immediately met by a welcome party of ten young dairy cows, peering over the fence as if they had been waiting for my arrival. They step back just enough as I approach for me to get in. I walk slowly and calmly around them, I know herds of cattle do hold potential to be dangerous, but these beauties all seem to be young and kindly in their inquisitiveness. They follow me on my short quest from kissing gate to St Lythans dolmen.

There is a story of St Columba, said to be the builder of the abbey on the Scottish island of Iona. Part of the wide-ranging lore written of him includes that he banished women and cows from Iona, claiming that "where there is a cow there is a woman and where there is a woman there is mischief." So both cows and women were outcast to a nearby island. I'm very glad I remember this tale, I don't know if any Welsh saints have said something similar, but it's a reminder that sometimes, as a woman, you just can't win; even the mundane act of hanging out with cows can land you on a banished island (imagine a Scottish island tended by women and roaming cows… I mean, it sounds alright to me!). This makes my run-in with the cows at St Lythans all the more delightful. And I'm enchanted to be here for all cows, women and mischief that may be encountered.

One cow follows me into the small dolmen, intrigued also perhaps to see what I am looking for and I tell her (as you'll know by now, I'm quite happy to speak to animals when the occasion arises). This structure is known as a dolmen and it's made of limestone. The stones have some small, pocked holes in them. Three flat-ish standing stones support one large capstone and the rear standing stone has a hole in it, through which I can see the sky, like a giant hagstone, I point this out to my bovine assistant but it's a little high for her to see through. So, I place a hand on her soft wide forehead instead, and she tries to lick my hand, obviously hoping for snacks rather than these tiresome historical titbits. She settles herself into giving my jumper a good lick before continuing her own surveying of the ancient site. Part of the lore of this land is that the stones stand on an "Accursed Field", so called due to its supposed infertility. The ground looks very lush grass for the cows grazing, but maybe grass doesn't count, I don't know how other crops fair.

The information sign here reads:

> *LLWANELIDDON. St Lythans.* Yn wyneb haul, llygad goleuni – *House of the Rising Sun – Six thousand years ago the first farmers in Wales built a house for the dead on this low hill. Protected by a vast mound of earth, it faced east so that those within could be warmed by the reviving force of the rising sun, forever. Only the stone skeleton of the tomb survives today; a glimpse of a lost people's hope of eternal life…*

Folklore always enjoys filling in the gaps or embellishing history – like the tomb's local name, *Gwâl y Filiast* (Kennel of the Greyhound).

The spirit night where this dolmen really comes into its own is Nos Gwyl Ifan, the eve of Midsummer, when apparently the capstone spins round three times and the stones go down to the river to wash. And Nos Galan Gaeaf, Halloween, when wishes whispered into the tomb will be granted.

Last month I got lost in Sussex, this month I feel like I've got lost in the lore. I am nonetheless happy to be here with the gentle magic of sunshine and cow friends. And I feel content, even if I did not find quite what I was expecting, the links to witches here were grasping at fairies, as I make my walk back to the bus stop, re-treading my steps from St. Lythans, past Dryffyn Gardens and past Tinkinswood signs. Ready to leap into Beltane tomorrow and May. The full round-trip walk is about five miles. Rain gathers in on my journey home, the mists and witches are still here then.

The eve of May is when we descend into the first spirit night of the year, but yesterday, April 29th, is another notable date of Welsh myth, the 29th is noted as the birthday of Taliesin, the renowned bard. And at least one story of his birth involves the famed sorceress and cauldron bearer, Cerridwen, who transformed into many animals, including a greyhound. Did she perhaps come to rest at St Lythans? Here is yet another whisper of a witch…

Cerridwen's story

From the Mabinogion *by Lady Charlotte Guest, an English translator of texts. Lady Charlotte Guest, published her translations of eleven medieval Welsh folk tales in seven volumes between 1838 and 1845. Many of the tales are much older in origin and drawn from texts such as the* White Book of Rhydderch *(1300-1325) and the* Red Book of Hergest *(1375-1425) and texts attributed to Taliesin – the Welsh bard.*

Cerridwen, a skilled sorceress, decided that she would produce a potion to make her son Morfran more beautiful and wise. She prepared a cauldron of *Awen a Gwybodau* (Inspiration and Knowledge). The cauldron had to be boiled for a year and a day. Gwion Bach, a servant boy, was given the task of stirring the potion and keeping the fire burning. But just as the potion was ready, three drops splashed onto Gwion's finger. They were so hot that he put his finger in his mouth. When he did so, he came to know everything. Cerridwen was not best pleased and a chase ensued – Gwion turned himself into a hare to flee from Cerridwen, but she turned herself into a greyhound to outpace him. Gwion then turned himself into a fish and he jumped into the river, but Cerridwen turned into an otter and swam after him. Cerridwen had nearly caught Gwion when he turned into a bird and flew into the air, but Cerridwen turned into a hawk and edged closer and closer. Gwion turned into a grain of corn and jumped into the pile of the grain to hide, but Cerridwen turned into a hen and ate all of the corn, including Gwion.

But in consuming him, Cerridwen became pregnant; the baby inside her was Gwion. When he was born, she could not kill this beautiful baby, so she wrapped him in a bag and cast him to the mercy of the sea. On the twenty-ninth day of April (according to some versions of the tale), he was found by Elphin, the son of the local lord. He lifted the baby boy in his arms, and the baby spoke in beautiful poetry to Elphin. The baby was named Taliesin – meaning 'radiant brow'.

There are more mists to come, as we journey into May with sorcery, springs and the mists of Avalon to meet a few more fairy folk…

MAY

Avalon Underland

Glastonbury, Somerset

Glastonbury is a place in Britain that holds magic in its own unique way – home to many alternative cultures, in this historic West Country town Druids rub shoulders with priestesses, Ufologists and Green campaigners. And something that happens whenever I go to Glastonbury, is that I get lost. Almost every time I visit. I go to the wrong venues for workshops, I can't find places on the map, I get confused about time. Now, we know from March that I'm no expert in map-reading, but Glastonbury town is not a huge place. And I've been here often; it's about an hour's drive from Bath. I've done the journey for magical happenings, meditation journeys, dark moon rituals, meeting priestesses in the Goddess House and plenty of shopping for incense and lunch in cafés. But something seems to happen every time I go, something that seems to throw me and often, the people I'm with, softly off-kilter in some way. This isn't really the point of this month's story, but maybe a setting of Glastonbury as a weird and magical place. And one that I still haven't quite got to grips with.

Maybe this is echoed with my own uncertainty around whether I should include Glastonbury and the magical figure I face in May – Morgan le Fay, who is both fairy and witch and many things in-between. She is very much the shape-shifter, hard to outline and pin down. And even in Glastonbury, where she seems to be very well loved, it's hard to define her presence here with any certainty.

Stories of King Arthur are popular in England; they have been for centuries. And these Arthurian tales often focus on the bravery and battle-worthy-ness of the male characters. We do also have recurring female characters though: Guinevere – the alluring and beautiful wife; the enigmatic Lady of the Lake, Nimue, who may or may not hold a sword and Morgan le Fay*, a powerful enchantress, who, is often, but not always, portrayed as a villain, rarely successful in any of her plots that are usually foiled by a hero character who may or may not be connected to the wizard, Merlin, King Arthur and the Round Table Knights. In various works and at points in history, she seems to have been a kind of medieval symbol of the potential danger of uncontrolled female power. Seductive and power-hungry, wishing to rule Camelot and overthrow Arthur, she is, at times, a hybrid of all the many patriarchal nightmare-women of literature. But in diving deeper into texts, I find that things

* There are many ways to spell her name including Morgain le Fee, Morgan le Fey, Morgne la Faye, *Morganda Fatata* but I'm going to stick with the most common modern version, Morgan le Fay, for ease's sake.

are a little more nuanced and stories of her explore that murky, complicated matter of demonising women and 'otherly' characters, especially those outrageous enough to have a duality of personality and be complicated.

While many works make Morgan human, she almost always has magical powers of some kind, that are used for good as well as mischief. We could contrast, for example, Gerald of Wales' *De Instructione Principis* in 1190, where she is a noblewoman and close relative of Arthur, with Gervase of Tilbury's *Otia Imperialia*, written around the thirteenth century, where she is *Morganda Fatata* (Morganda the Fairy). Morgan, as a character, regularly flutters in stories between sorceress, fairy, woman, witch, goddess and priestess and here in Glastonbury especially, she is celebrated in her goddess status.

And it's with this in mind that my friend Trish drives us to Glastonbury on a Wednesday at the beginning of May. Beltane passed just a few days ago. And before us, the Tor is rising, as it so often does, out of shrouded mists. Mists frequently lie settled on the low land of the Somerset Levels surrounding the Tor, as does water, when the Levels flood. This happens more often than residents would like I am sure, but the shimmering tides turn it briefly back into the *Isle of Glass,* one of the many enchanting names for Glastonbury, along with Avalon, the Holy Isle and the Isle of Apples. The Levels are unusually flat coastal plain and wetland area of Somerset, stretching for miles from the Mendip Hills to the Blackdown Hills. Glastonbury Tor rises as the highest point for many miles around, topped by St Michael's Tower, like a lighthouse on an island.

I almost didn't include Glastonbury in my list of places to seek witches, as I am aware that this book is already biased towards West Country locations. And Glastonbury is already such a well-known and well-written of place. I wasn't sure I had anything new to add to the beautiful collection of magical writing that already exists. But, when seeking a present for Trish's birthday, I found a day retreat hosted by a modern-day priestess to explore Chalice Well gardens and, perhaps most appealingly, bathe in the waters of the White Spring, something we've both wanted to do for many years. So, I bought us tickets and today we are driving through the mists, hoping that we have packed enough warm layers (the White Spring is famously nippy). Morgan is connected to both Glastonbury Tor, the earth underneath it and to the element of water – so the springs of Glastonbury seemed about as close to her presence in a physical sense as I could hope for.

King Arthur in Wales and the West Country

The myth of folk hero King Arthur seems almost omnipresent here in Britain, and in Europe – even in death, he is still present. Arthurian legends seem to have particularly deep ties to both Wales and its close geographical neighbours in the West Country, particularly Cornwall, Somerset, and Glastonbury. Cornwall and Tintagel Castle are often cited as his birthplace; Glastonbury, and the Isle of Avalon where Arthur was taken after his final battle, and amongst the ruins of Glastonbury Abbey a sign suggests that this may have been his final resting place, alongside his Queen Guinevere.

Like all things Arthur, debates still rage. Some suggest the earliest stories of Arthur originated from Wales, when a Welsh monk Nennius wrote of a hero named Arthur in the ninth century, and Geoffrey of Monmouth (on the Welsh–English border) created the Arthur we know today. Maybe the impact of some foundational texts, such as those by Geoffrey of Monmouth and Gerald of Wales, proved useful to tie this area into the foundations of these myths. They may well have been influenced by local folklore, intertwining the mystical qualities of Wales and the West Country's geography – rugged coastlines, misty moors, and ancient woodlands – with the stories of Arthur. (But stories of King Arthur are everywhere; from the south, in Cornwall all the way up north to Arthur's Seat in Edinburgh.)

One popular myth suggests Arthur is sleeping under Cadbury Hillfort in Somerset, along with his knights. Ready to rise again should England need them. On Midsummer's Eve, visions of King Arthur may be seen to lead the knights down the hill's slopes for a yearly jaunt.

Gerald of Wales wrote of Arthur as a hero of the Welsh. But he also claimed King Arthur's tomb and remains were at Glastonbury in his work *De Principis Instructione*, written around 1190 (this extract is a translation of the text by John William Sutton for The Camelot Project, a database of Arthurian texts):

> *Tales are regularly reported and fabricated about King Arthur and his uncertain end, with the British peoples even now contending foolishly that he is still alive…the truth about this matter should be revealed plainly, so here I have endeavored to add something to the indisputable facts that have been disclosed.*
>
> *After the Battle of Camlann … after Arthur had been mortally wounded there, his body was taken to the Isle of Avalon, which is now called Glastonbury, by a noble matron and kinswoman named Morgan; afterwards the remains were buried, according to her direction, in the holy burial-ground. As*

> *a result of this, the Britons and their poets have been concocting legends that a certain fantastic goddess, also called Morgan, carried off the body of Arthur to the Isle of Avalon for the healing of his wounds. When his wounds have healed, the strong and powerful king will return to rule the Britons (or so the Britons suppose), as he did before. Thus they still await him.*

Gerald gets a good dig in at foolish old English folks, but there are similar Welsh legends that suggest that King Arthur, if not still alive, is capable of rising in some way. Craig y Ddinas/Dinas Rock at the bottom of Bannau Brycheiniog National Park in Wales (also known as the Brecon Beacons) is another place that lays claim to being King Arthur's resting place. The rock is a vast expanse of limestone topped by an Iron Age hillfort, and the legend states that there lies a cavern below its base, where a sleeping King Arthur and his army wait for the day when they can rise again. An addition to this Welsh version of the myth is that they guard piles of gold and silver, but should any would-be thieves approach, bells of warning would ring and wake the men.

*

So that's Arthur, who might be underground in and around Somerset, either buried or waiting to rise again. But at Glastonbury Tor, it's Morgan le Fay who resides under the hill and she's not alone…

It's another common myth that mountains and hills may hold a presence, slumbering at their centre, offering quiet hope or doom, reflecting perhaps a desire to add to the realms of the unseen, under, out of sight. One more way to capture that feeling of walking the land, that you are never *just* walking the land. But engaging the senses, journeying over ancient places and old ways, remembering and treading, as W.B. Yeats puts it, *on dreams*, as well as stories, lives and memories (*so tread softly,* he cautions). Exploring what else walks beside you, watches over you (or up at you), may touch on what we long for in each day, what we walk to and walk with. This idea fascinates me and I walk with this awareness of the many layers of the landscape.

*

Vita Merlini by Geoffrey of Monmouth, written around 1150, introduces the magical realm and the Ninefold Sisterhood on the Fortunate Isle (another fine name attributed to Glastonbury) – an abundant realm filled with apple orchards. Merlin takes Arthur there so that Morgan, the leader of the Sisterhood, can treat his battle wounds. She is a healer, winged fay creature and shapeshifter. Her eight sisters are similarly introduced as healers, sorceresses and magic workers. We meet Morgan le Fay, the eldest and her sisters: Moronoe, Mazoe, Gliten, Glitonea, Gliton, Tyronoe, Thiten and Thiton. The sisters receive the dying Arthur in the hope they can revive him. And in many later tales of Arthurian tradition, the dying Arthur is returned to Glastonbury/Avalon as his final resting place/place of healing.

So, these are pretty positive beginnings, but Morgan is also regularly portrayed as both a healer and a manipulator, blurring the lines between good and evil – and this a theme that is almost always brought up about her – I rarely read about Arthur, Merlin or any of the knights being of dual character. Although all of them, at some point in medieval texts, behave like villains, I'd say. Morgan, however, seems a novelty because complex female characters are a novelty – she challenges traditional notions of women in medieval literature, defying easy categorisation as either a benevolent healer or a malevolent enchantress. Maybe this is how Morgan has enchanted us for over eight hundred years and continues to do so.

When I started this Avalon journey, I assumed that Morgan was always portrayed as a bit of a villain. Now, I'm less sure. She has certainly been largely portrayed as complicated. Medieval literature of England and Europe included a wealth of stories of Arthur and, more specifically for my purposes, Morgan and her character goes on quite a journey. After *Vita Merlini*, German writer Hartman von Aue created a poetic adaptation of a French chivalric romance, which is considered the first Arthurian Romance in German.* He said of Morgan, that she was a goddess who could fly and magically live on earth, in water and in fire. She could also change men into animals, command wild animals, dragons and demons, and was kin to devils. But she was also very knowledgeable in the use of all herbs and offered healing to the injured. So, there is a malevolence and echoes of witchlore creeping in…but not entirely so. And then, through the 1200s, she becomes – in varied collections of tales†: a bastard daughter, half-sister to Arthur and student of Merlin, pitted against Guinevere. Lustful and power-hungry, she hates Arthur and seeks to kill him and steal or destroy his kingdom. And in one story Morgan le Fay uses her

* *Erec*, written around 118

† Namely in the collections of French prose stories known as the in the *Vulgate* and *Post-Vulgate* collections/cycles (vulgate meaning written in the common tongue.)

magical powers to transform herself and her companions into stone to escape danger, themes and stories that will stay with the character and that you may well still recognise today.

In one of England's most popular Arthurian tales, that we know as "Sir Gawain and the Green Knight", Morgan is responsible for the whole conflict, sending the Green Knight to challenge Sir Gawain (one of King Arthur's knights). In the story, she is called both "Morgne la Faye" and "goddess" perfectly capable of being both fairy, goddess and trickster. And this is also a reminder that she's been considered a goddess long before contemporary Glastonbury priestesses named her so. Then, in the late 1400s, we arrive at the Morgan of *Le Morte D'Arthur* by Thomas Malory, who is largely depicted as evil and plotting, seeking to kill Arthur. Despite, or perhaps because of, such varied depictions, she has endured into the modern day as a revered goddess figure in Glastonbury.

*

Variants of the popular Nine Maidens theme can be found throughout British myth (we met another group of Nine Maidens, the ones made of stone in Dartmoor). And a few are tied up with King Arthur – perhaps this is how the ideas of the Nine Morgans arose, particularly around the west of Britain: Wales, Cornwall and West England.

In the *Mabinogion* in Peredur's story, we meet the Nine Witches, maiden-hags of Caer Lloyw, also known as the Nine Sorceresses of Gloucester, who are fearsome black-clad war-mongers who terrorise Britain. Peredur, with the help of King Arthur, slays them all. And in "Preiddeu Annwfn" (The Spoils of Annwfn), a poem from the fourteenth century *Book of Taliesin*, we meet the nine priestesses of Annwfn (the Otherworld) who dwell in a fairy fortress and guard a dark, pearl-encrusted magic cauldron, which they warm with their breath. King Arthur sets out to this otherworldly realm, but it's not clear to me what actually happens as a result of this raid, though if they set out seeking 'spoils' one can imagine where this is going.

My poetry, from the cauldron it was uttered
From the breath of nine maidens it was kindled,
the cauldron of the chief of Annwfn.

"Preiddeu Annwfn"

*

Glastonbury is a place where wisps of lore have been gathered up and made into new traditions of priestesses and some very place-specific lore. It's fascinating to delve into it, as stories and myths move through generations and new spiritual practices are born. Within the Glastonbury Goddess Temple, a room above shops in a small courtyard at the bottom of Glastonbury High Street, many priestesses are trained. The purple-carpeted temple space is decorated with red for Beltane and maypole-like ribbons. The Temple also holds a large 'Morgan Circle' of nine wicker figures with their arms outstretched, a circular hug of held space. Each of these nine morgans/morgens is named very similarly to the sisters mentioned in *Vita Merlini*. Each has her own element: a different aspect of being, a combination of virtues and energies. I don't know if this is based on texts (I couldn't find any that referred to this) or created anew for the Goddess Temple. Here the Nine Morgans are: Cliton (fire and transformation); Thetis (love); Gliten (water); Moronoe (earth); Tyrone (air); Thitis (maiden); Glitonea (mother); Mazoe (crone); Morgan le Fay (heart).

When we visit, the temple is honouring Thetis, Morgan of Love and by connection the Morgan of Beltane. Each Morgan can be applied to the eight festivals in the Wheel of the Year, with Morgan le Fay at its centre. "As the wheel of the year turns and the earth blooms with vibrant colours, we find ourselves immersed in the enchanting embrace of Beltane. In the Avalonian Tradition, this is the time of the year when we meet the Lady of Avalon in her aspect of Lover as well as Morgen Thetis."* Morgan and her sisters are clearly seen with fondness in Glastonbury, particularly by the priestesses to the Goddess Temple.

*

After arriving in Glastonbury, Trish and I started with coffee in one of the many colourful cafés on Glastonbury High Street before heading to Chalice Well Gardens, a sanctuary of springs and plants at the base of the Tor. Morgan, at least in some tales, is said to dwell on this earth under the Tor, so this seemed a good place to start. We are enjoying our coffee so much we are late. But we settle quickly with apologies and we start the retreat at Chalice Well

* From the *Glastonbury Goddess House Newsletter*.

in a room of women gathered in a circle. The event is hosted by a warm and welcoming priestess called Christine. Priestess is one of the roles Morgan has held. One can train to be a priestess here in Glastonbury, learning to host events, hold circles and officiate such ceremonies as handfasting and funerals. It is possible to make a career of being a priestess and, from our regular trips to Glastonbury, Trish and I know a few.

Our priestess and guide for the day tells us of the most well-known story of Morgan and Glastonbury: that Morgan and her sisters dwell under the Tor. The Nine Morgans reside under the earth of the Tor, tending the springs that run from it, perhaps imbuing them with curative magic continuing their long history of being healers. The Nine Morgans are connected to the trees as well, our priestess tells us, as animals and birds, most notably as nine crows that may be seen circling the land. Their presence is also noted in the variety of natural elements of weather upon the landscape: clouds, sunshine, wind, rain, ice and snow. Morgan and her sisters are, it seems, everywhere all at once in Glastonbury.

*

The Isle of Avalon is home to two different healing springs, one red with iron and one white with calcite and they bubble through the earth from the caverns beneath Glastonbury Tor.

The Chalice Well surrounds one of Glastonbury's most famous natural water sources: the Red Spring, so called for the iron oxide it deposits in its basin. On our walk around Chalice Well gardens, Trish and I sit on soft grass by the rosy-hued circular pools created for this spring. Flowers surround the circular lawns and various water pools. The sun has broken through the mists and is shining with May warmth. A young man sits on a bench and plays the guitar. There is a low hum of chatter as small groups wander and sit to soak up the sun. It is heavenly.

And the time soon comes to visit the second great spring of Glastonbury. Down a little lane at the foot of Glastonbury Tor lies the White Spring. Housed within an old Victorian red brick pump house, now converted into the White Spring Temple. Originally, the White Spring was in a wooded glade, until it was turned into a reservoir and a Well House was built by the Victorians in 1872, to bring clean water into Glastonbury. But the water pipes calcified and blocked and it fell into disuse. It was reawakened in the twentieth century in its new role as a sacred space.

We take the short walk in the sunshine from the Chalice Well garden entrance, around the corner and up a gently sloping road. A few people are sitting outside the Well House in the sunshine which is tucked away beside sloping ground of the Tor's base, nestled in trees. Brambles, ferns and mosses grow over the building, softening its corners a little. A paved stream and splashing bowls in the courtyard entrance mean people can sample the waters outside the Well House as well. Another young man provides musical accompaniment, this one sits in a van with the back doors flung open and plays a small tin drum.

Our priestess goes on ahead to make sure all was set up in the space and on our group's arrival, the gates clank open for us to enter. At the iron gates a sign reads: "CAUTION, NAKED FLAMES, DEEP WATER, FAERIE PORTALS… ENTER AT YOUR OWN RISK."

Candles flicker as we navigate steep steps to the ground in the Well House. Our host is playing a crystal bowl and singing; it reverberates around the moist red brick walls, along with the sound of the running spring water and the wind whistling through the space. Altars for the Goddess/ Earth Mother and the Lord of the Wildwood sit in opposite corners and a huge pool of water is in the centre with knee-deep wading water within. The space is a constant temperature. And that temperature is cold. I sense this as I take my shoes off to feel the water streaming over the floor.

The Well House is a cavernous space, echoing the sounds of splashing spring water. There are old skylights, just squares in the brick roof that let in a little light, and the rest is from candles. The high ceiling arcs in waves of three domed vaults creating a cavernous space like railway arches. The brick floors are gently bowed, mirroring the ceiling; they channel the spring waters into shallow snakes of flowing water "like the hull of a boat moored at the portal to the Otherworld."* And, I think, like the boat that took Arthur to be healed in Avalon by Morgan. Many people hope to journey to healing here in this place.

The calcite in the water that forms the calcite crystals is thought to have healing properties. Calcite crystals, that one can buy in many Glastonbury shops, are said to promote calm and clarity.

A series of pools have been built within the Well House – one large round and shallow pool at the centre of the space, with three stepping pools leading

* A description from The White Spring website.

up to a deep plunge pool in the corner – built according to the principles of sacred geometry. We are told that the Ley line known as the St Michael Line, flows through this place, a line that journeys through sites such as Avebury, Dartmoor and Silbury Hill on its way to St Michael's Mount in Cornwall.* Deities are mentioned too: Brigid, a Celtic fire goddess and guardian of sacred springs and Our Lady of Avalon, who sits beside the healing pools. But no mention of Morgan le Fay. If these waters come from under the Tor, that would be the place she resides, with or without her sisters.

Walking from the entrance, I start in the far-left corner, where the stepped pools bring you up to a small, deep, plunge pool. I lay my bag and clothes on one of many tree trunks turned into benches, and take my time to shuffle on my bum up the three-stepped pools, not wishing to slip on the smooth stone pool floor. I slide into the top and deepest pool, first to the waist, holding on to the edge, feeling with my feet where a dark, invisible step in the water drops away into deeper waters. Staying clear of the deeper drop, I dunk myself in very cold water for just a moment. My breath comes out in plumes in the damp air as I surface. I descend the stepped pools as I went up them, careful bum shuffling and kneel in the wading water of the large central pool before one more dunk in the deep pool.

Feeling that I have dunked myself in all the places one may dunk, I make a quick change back into dry clothes and sit at the wildwood altar in the other far right corner, along the back wall. The music of our host priestess still echoes around us. A ceramic antlered man sits at the centre of the altar, amongst bones and wood. I head over to the Goddess altar to the left of the entrance. Here I enter a bower, a wicker woven tunnel adorned with clooties that remind me of the witch trees and wishes of Grovely Woods. At the centre of this altar is a dark-hued painting of a shrouded woman with a radiant heart and flames in her hands. Wishing to make the most of my time here, I try to sit in every spot and dip in every pool. I'm not quite sure what I am looking for or think I may experience. So I try to simply take it all in for now.

*

* Ley lines are tracks of alignments of landmarks, religious sites and man-made structures. Alfred Watkins popularised the idea of these lines as energetic maps or meridians in the 1920s after he noticed that ancient sites in Britain appeared to be aligned in straight tracks. He proposed that these lines may represent ancient trade routes or pathways. Some believe they hold spiritual energy in their connection to various sacred sites.

This is as about as close as one can get to being under the Tor where the Morgans live and something close to worshipping in a pagan temple. I think of my hometown of Bath and the sacred spring of Sulis, another pagan temple of sorts and special relic of goddess worship dating back to the ancient Roman occupation of the town of Bath when it was Aquae Sulis, a town named for a goddess.

I think of the Morgans and their connection with water, which is a wonderful whirlpool of possible root words and confluence of myths. In Welsh and Breton folklore, water spirits can be called Morgens, Morgans and Mari-Morgans and in Irish lore, the Merrow. All, like sirens, are notorious for drowning men at sea. But these myths don't appear in print until around the 1800s[†] long after Morgan is first mentioned by Geoffrey of Monmouth. Ancient carvings and medieval texts can take us back further to speak of goddesses that may or may not be connected to Morgan: the Irish Morrigan, the Welsh Modron and Celtic Matrona/Matronae, deities of war and fate, fertility and motherhood and earth and fertility respectively.

The oldest occurrence of the Morgan character as we know her in print is actually in the *Vita Merlini*, when Geoffrey of Monmouth named Avalon's ruler Morgan: did he intend to evoke water spirits? Was he drawing from oral myths? Was he hinting at the power of healing waters? The origin of Morgan may be connected to watery myths or the other way around. The medievalist Lucy Allen Paton argues that Morgan le Fay was not associated with the sea until later literature. But Morgan has long dwelled on islands surrounded by water. Connections between Morgan and water certainly do emerge in later literature and folklore.

In the *Dictionary of Folklore Mythology and Legend* (1949), American folklorist Maria Leach has thoughts on Morgans flitting between witch and fairy and the corrigans we met in Wales last month. The lore between Wales, Somerset, Arthur and Avalon is tightly woven and the fact that I visited these places consecutively seems very appropriate.

> *The sirens of the western seaboard and islands were known as Morgan or Mari Morgan and had male counterparts. There were also the ghostly cannered noz (washerwomen of the night), who were supposed to be thrashing their shrouds as a penance and could be heard about midnight beating their linen on the banks of pools or streams. The male dwarfs were usually called*

† Such as in the *Fairy Mythology*, Thomas Keightley (1850); *Le Foyer Breton (The Breton Fireside)*, Émile Souvestre (1844) and *Fairy Legends and Traditions of the South of Ireland*, Thomas Crofton Croker (1828).

Corrigans and were the subject of the usual superstitions; they guarded treasure, helped in the housework, danced on moonlight nights among the menhirs and dolmens, led travelers astray with a torch, could transform themselves into black horses or gnats. A mortal who found himself in the midst of a Corrigan dance was likely to hear them repeating in chorus "Monday, Tuesday, Wednesday," and if he could complete the list would win their favor. A child suspected of being a changeling was called "Little Corrigan."

It feels as though Morgan was destined to be a fluctuating character in the Arthurian tales because she is woven from so many tributaries.

Morgana (Keltic) – "Dweller by the sea" from Welsh 'mor' – sea.
Morgan la Fee was the sister of King Arthur and from her is derived the old Sicilian theory that the palaces and watch-towers on their shores should be dedicated to La Fata Morgana – "the Lady of the Sea."
***Every Woman's Encyclopaedia* Vol IV (1800)**

This adds to the many things Morgan has been in myth. Alongside her guises as healer, goddess, fairy, priestess, shape-shifter, sorceress and witch, we also have her connected to sea legends: mermaids, sirens and the phenomenon of the fata morgana mirage, named in her honour. In stories, she uses illusions to lure souls to their deaths, embodying the mystical and 'other' in a patriarchal world and vast swathes of literature that can never quite settle on how to describe and portray her. She is untameable, you might say, something of an 'other' – a wild woman.

It is said that because of Morgain's interest in enchantment, she left human society and passed day and night in the forests by the fountains, so that people foolishly said that she was not a woman, but they called her "Morgain la déesse" (Morgain the Goddess).
Lucy Allen Paton, *Studies in the Fairy Mythology of Arthurian Romance* (1903)

On her island of Avalon, like Circe on Aeaea, she is a woman apart from society. Maybe that's why she seems so closely connected to the witch, like the image of the witch that dwells in the wildwoods. In some stories, her realm is the place people find only when they are lost; Morgan has a castle of her own deep in the forests and mist-bound valleys laid under spells.* And

* *Lancelot and the Ring*, Dr Lucy Allen Patton (1929).

in classic imagery of evil women and of witches, clouding minds of men, trapping a lover or seeking revenge and perhaps most feared to all knights and men "[she] rejoiced that he is at last in her power…and reducing him to utter weakness…"[†] Her power made her a fearsome, untameable force. A witch woman, a flighted fairy, a tricksy sorceress. But the modern priestesses of Glastonbury (and many before them) took her image and made her part of the fabric of the Glastonbury landscape: dwelling all at once under the Tor, flying over it and growing from it. Like Cerridwen, the Welsh sorceress, and Rhiannon[‡], the noble lady of the fairy realm in the *Mabinogion*, the figures of women have been raised up as goddesses over time, or, returned to goddess figures that came first. Perhaps because such figures were so lacking in Judeo-Christian religions. Female figures were found and in time, they were raised up to goddess status.

In many of the Arthurian texts I have explored this month, Morgan's character holds a duality that is not always afforded to, for example, the witches in the Middle Ages and early modern era who were painted as purely evil entities. Figures such as Morgan remind us that it was much more complicated than that…we are much more complicated than that. These female figures – the witch, the mermaid, the goddess, the fairy – have swirled around our storytelling consciousness for a thousand years or more as we rummage with ideas of powerful women, their kindnesses and their wrath. How may this apply to both ourselves and the world around us: what heals us…and what harms us? What mysteries are held in earth and water? What is the balance between healing and harming? How do these stories influence our understanding of the natural world and its mysteries? What do they teach us about balance, respect and the interconnectedness of all things? Magic in stories symbolizes the extraordinary possibilities that lie within and around us. It challenges the boundaries of the mundane, encouraging belief in the miraculous and the transformative. Whether we see these Morgan figures as heroes or villains, their enduring presence as figures of female power speaks to their profound impact on our collective consciousness, conduits for exploring themes that resonate through generations of power, healing, mystery and how we can see magic in the natural world.

The spirit of Morgan le Fay is alive here in Glastonbury, in the mists, be-

† *Sir Lancelot of the Lake*, Dr Lucy Allen Patton (1929).

‡ Cerridwen and Rhiannon are two other goddess figures that enjoy their own dedicated priestesses in Glastonbury.

neath the Tor, in its healing waters. And for me getting as close to the underland of the Tor and the waters of the springs as possible, was part of trying to get closer to who and what Morgan le Fay is, in all her complexity.

Glastonbury is a crucible of neopagans, Druids and priestesses, all echoing the roles that Morgan once played in this landscape, as magic makers and healers, if there is any truth in the myths. Glastonbury today still draws vast numbers of people seeking mystical experiences and healing. The blend of myth, ancient traditions and modern spiritual practices makes Glastonbury a unique focal point for those pursuing contemporary magical and pagan paths. The landscape still holds the magic to be experienced, gathered and embodied by those who seek it.

*

Once dried and dressed, Trish and I say farewell to our group to walk up the Tor. From the shade of the well, we emerge to be bathed in the golden light of a late afternoon, all mists now long departed for a gloriously sunny day. The path meanders, gentle at first, and we soon leave the soothing sound of the wells behind. With each step, the grassy Tor unfurls in ridges like an old map's topographical lines: undulating shelves and ledges of grass, buttercups nod in the breeze.

The incline steepens and our breath deepens in tandem with the climb; this is a pilgrimage route that sees the Tor populated at almost every sunrise and sunset through the year. The wind picks up and clouds drift, casting shadows upon the gentle undulations of soft felt fields of the Somerset Levels below. Hundreds of patchwork squares stitched together with bubbling seams of trees and hedgerows, buttons of houses cast in clustering ranks. You can see for miles around, afloat on the scenery.

We reach the peak and the tor's distinctive tower; the partly restored remains of St Michael's Church. It stands vigil over the landscape and admires the views of Somerset below us. It is smart and angular in grey stone dappled with lichen. Two pointed archways show the interior of a shining flagstone floor worn smooth by feet and straight through to the countryside beyond. A neat skirt of cobbles and concrete surrounds this watchtower of the Summer Lands. We sit on the grass and watch the world go by; tourists walk up and down, birds circle and sheep graze. I eat an apple from my bag and a couple of crumbled oat cakes.

Birdsong drifts in faint calls carried on the wind. The air smells of earth and sun-warmed grass. Here, time feels ancient and fluid, as if the land holds memories of the thousands of rituals and reveries that have happened here. Nearby, someone is drumming and chanting. Everywhere we have been has had music somewhere in the background, which has been lovely and *very Glastonbury*. Stories and music hang in the air (and every hedgerow) around here. No great epic happenings today. Just a little time above and below – underground springs and beautiful countryside on a sunny May day and a background hum of the magical and the mystical.

I don't know if I am any closer to Morgan and her myriad forms, she is as hard to grasp as the mists of Avalon. But as always, I have enjoyed my time in Glastonbury, a truly wonder-full place to see the season of summer on the horizon.

SUMMER

June • July • August

Graves • Shadows • Fairy Bells •
Green Teeth • Mother Stones

FIELD NOTES:
A-CONJURING SUMMER IN!

Oak, Ash and Thorn
Of all the trees that grow so fair,
Old England to adorn,
Greater are none beneath the Sun,
Than Oak and Ash and Thorn.
Sing Oak and Ash and Thorn, good sirs,
(All of a Midsummer morn!)
Surely we sing no little thing,
In Oak and Ash and Thorn!
...
Ellum she hateth mankind and waiteth
Till every gust be laid,
To drop a limb on the head of him
That anyway trusts her shade:
But whether a lad be sober or sad,
Or mellow with ale from the horn,
He will take no wrong when he lieth along
'Neath Oak and Ash and Thorn!
Oh, do not tell the Priest our plight,
Or he would call it a sin;
But – we have been out in the woods all night,
A-conjuring Summer in!
And we bring you news by word of mouth-
Good news for cattle and corn-
Now is the Sun come up from the South,
With Oak and Ash and Thorn!

Rudyard Kipling, "A Tree Song" (1906)

The greenwood dazzles in summer. Trees shine with green life and growth this season, becoming the golden gates through which midsummer sunbeams gleam. Some consider that the oak, ash and thorn made up a sacred trio with powers to heal, or with connection to the fairies and magic. As such they feature together in poems, (like Kipling's above) ballads and texts. And to swear an oath by oak, ash and thorn seems to be particularly powerful, perhaps with the respected trees acting as a witness to the words.

The Oak King and Holly King, so the Wiccan story goes, do battle under the bright skies of the summer solstice, to take claim of the throne of seasonal rule. The battle is so fearsome and crowded with hot tempers that lightning crashes around the warring kings and the veil between our world and the fairy world is cracked open. The fairy folk are delighted to slip through and cause mischief. So those who wish to speak with the midsummer fairies or meet them during their revels, need only to leave gifts on doorsteps in invitation or sleep out in auspicious places of magic, but be warned: trouble often follows in fairy footsteps!

Glasgerryon swore a full great othe, By oake and ashe and thorne.

Francis James Child, *The English and Scottish Popular Ballads*, Vol. 2 (1885)

The oak tree *(Quercus robur)* is native to Europe (as well as parts of Asia and Africa) and is a long-lived tree – symbolic of strength and nobility. Sacred throughout Europe, including to the Norse and Celts, Druids were thought to practise their rites in sacred oak groves. Acorns were used as amulets, often kept in a pocket, acorns were also thought to protect the house from lightning (you may see a whisper of this old talisman charm still: light pulls and blind cord toggles shaped as acorns are still widely found in homes in the British Isles and parts of Scandinavia and Europe).

Ash *(Fraxinus excelsior)* was also regarded by the ancient Greeks, Romans and Scandinavians as a sacred tree and as one of good omen. The Norse World-Tree is a giant ash tree known as *Yggdrasill*, that linked and sheltered all the realms of gods, humans, creatures and underworlds.

Both ash and oak may be used in folk magic and ritual for healing, offering their own *a'conjuring*. Scottish trial records suggest that in 1644, Margaret Reid was accused of working with fairies and demons and practising folk healing, midwifery and unorthodox religious practice, seeking healing by walking with candles and chants around child beds and passing a sick child "three times round an oak tree." The ash was also considered healing:

The Shrew Ash was a very ancient gnarled tree near Sheen Gate, which, not uncommonly for ash trees, had a reputation for curing sick infants and animals. Mothers would bring children with whooping cough and other ailments to the tree to take part in a secret dawn ritual led by a "shrew mother", or "priestess", or "witch". The ritual involved passing the child over and under a "witch-bar", a wooden bar wedged into the tree, while the "shrew mother" muttered or sang verses, timing her recitation so that a particular word coincided with the first of the sun's rays.*

Margaret C. Ffennell, "The Shrew Ash in Richmond Park", *Folklore Journal* (1898)

If oak and ash are considered healing trees, how could I not mention the deliciously menacing opposite: elm – *Ellum* from Rudyard Kipling's poem "Ellum she hateth mankind and waiteth…" In Celtic mythology, elms guard the underworld and are connected to elves and burial mounds. There's at least one practical reason why it's connected to death, as Kipling also mentions – elms are prone to drop large branches with no warning.

We have the common field/or smooth leaved elm *(Ulmus Minor)* in Britain and the wych elm *(Ulmus glabra)* which obviously sounds 'witchy' especially to those who only know and speak the name orally. But the wych is not a variant spelling of witch – it is thought to mean a trunk or chest. But told amongst the rural peoples of the British Isles I have no doubt rumours of 'witch elms' existed. In fact, the wych elm was planted as protection against witchcraft. So certainly, those connections were made.

Why is it called the wych elm, do you ask? Has it anything to do with witches? Some people must think it has magic power, for in some parts of England the dairy-maids will not begin to churn till they have put a twig of wych elm in a hole in the churn. Without that, they say, the butter would not come. Wych is the Anglo-Saxon word for box. An early English writer calls the Jewish ark of the covenant a wych, or box; and some suppose that the elm was so called because its wood was used for making boxes and coffins.

Mrs Dyson, *The Stories of the Trees* (1896)

* A hurricane felled the Shrew Ash tree in the Great Storm of 1987.

JUNE

UNQUIET GRAVES

TORRYBURN, SCOTLAND

There is a poem about graves and grief, you may well know it, it begins:

Do not stand by my grave and weep.
I am not there, I do not sleep.

The rest of the poem, is equally affecting.

I am the thousand winds that blow
I am the diamond glints in snow
I am the sunlight on ripened grain,
I am the gentle, autumn rain.
As you awake with morning's hush,
I am the swift, up-flinging rush
Of quiet birds in circling flight,
I am the day transcending night.
Do not stand by my grave and cry –
I am not there, I did not die.

Clare Harner, "Immortality" (1934)*

June and solstice season are here. In this month of longest days, the skies seem often, as they are today a clouded low roof above me. It's been raining on and off this morning. I think of this poem, here in this moment. It's ten in the morning and I am sat on a large stone at the shores of Torryburn, Fife. Before me on the murky silty tideline is a stone slab, slick with water and seaweed. It was never meant to be a witch's memorial, but I think it has become so because it is something even rarer: a witch's grave.

Counter to the poem's words, Lilias Adie did indeed die, this is her grave, but also, she is not here. In final insult after the dubious honour of getting a gravesite (something wildly rare for any accused witch), only afforded to her for dying before sentencing, something that was not so wildly rare in long and tortuous incarcerations. (It was sometimes called *jail fever,* as if distancing the role of jailers, witch prickers, watchers and interrogators.) I am on the Fife Witches Trail that runs along the shores of the east coast of Scotland, a journey that has bought me to a three-mile stretch of coastal path from Culross to where I now sit in Torryburn.

* The authorship of this well-loved poem is widely contested and several variations exist. This is the version published by Clare Harner.

Lilias and her grave represent something powerful in my journey around the country. They are both here and not here, remembered and forgotten, respected and disrespected. And I come, on my own, to sit with that on this *dreich* Tuesday morning. And for whatever it may mean.

*

I flew from Bristol to Edinburgh yesterday and took the train to Dunfermline. Today, Tuesday, June 4th, is a special day: the very first official National Day of Remembrance for the Accused Witches of Scotland. And this evening, at Dunfermline Abbey, people are gathering for a ceremony of commemoration. Almost four thousand names will be read aloud – all those who were accused of and executed for witchcraft in Scotland. These names have left a shadowy mark in history: a history that is currently experiencing a movement of reconciliation by squarely facing the reality of these past atrocities.

The last time I was in Edinburgh, I explored some of the witch tourist haunts in the Old Town, wandering the cobbled streets that lead up to Castle Hill and Edinburgh Castle on a particularly icy St Andrew's Day (St Andrew is the patron saint of Scotland and celebrated on November 30). In Scotland, women and men were burned at the stake as witches from the 1500s all the way into the 1700s: that is centuries of trauma to deal with. The modest, poignant Witches' Well memorial sits near the top of Castle Hill, and is adorned with an image of foxgloves.

The Foxtree

In Old Scots, foxglove leaves were called foxter or foxtree leaves, which are deadly, but were used as medicine in the hands of Scottish wise women and healers. This dichotomy of death and healing is spoken to at The Witches' Well, in a cast iron fountain and plaque, that honours those killed during the Scottish witch trials. The small plaque features a bronze relief of two women's heads: one the archetypal angry crone, the other young and beautiful, entangled by a snake (associated with healing, the goddess and the fallen first woman of Christianity, Eve) and a foxglove plant. It reads:

This fountain, designed by John Duncan, R.S.A. is near the site on which many witches were burned at the stake. The wicked head and serene head signify that some used their exceptional knowledge for evil purposes while others were misunderstood and wished their kind nothing but good. The serpent has the dual significance of evil and wisdom. The foxglove spray further emphasises the dual purpose of many common objects.

In two examples from the Scottish witch trials, Jonet Miller was accused of being a 'witch-woman' and recognised healer and of using foxtree leaves to cure sickness. She advised one woman to wash her ailing mother using foxtree leaves, so that they may leave the sickness behind. And for a man whose tongue had been seized, she thought, by fairies; she recommended a remedy of foxtree leaves and water. Bessie Stevenson was also accused of folk healing, for washing clothes in a sacred well as a curative, an act that would either "end them or mend them". She also attempted cures by laying foxtree leaves under the bodies of the afflicted and leading people around oak trees. Despite both pleading not guilty, both were found guilty of witchcraft in 1658 and 1659 respectively. Stevenson was executed, but whilst Miller was scheduled for execution, there is no record of it taking place, making her one more accused witch whose fate becomes 'unknown'.*

* From the Survey of Scottish Witchcraft Database and *A Source Book of Scottish Witchcraft,* Christina Larner (1977).

Scottish 'witches' tended to be strangled and then burnt to ashes: a small mercy to be dead before they were burnt. The burning to ashes was meant to ensure, depending on who you ask, that their sins were cleansed and/or that they could not ascend to heaven. The Scottish witch hunts burned at a particularly feverish pace. But today, the elements of my journey are less of fire and more of stone and water.

Memorials of accused witches have something of the 'tomb of the unknown warrior' about them for those who wish to remember, honour and celebrate the witches and accused and their history. Sites such as Lilias' grave are places where one can, if so desired, come and reflect. For every named accused like

Lilias, there are unknown dead, unknown thousands who suffered (and some in countries that still suffer). This is a sobering reflection on this journey. I am all too aware that I have used words like *enchantment* and *wonder* to describe what I am seeking on these journeys, but *horror, sadness, grief* are just as much part of the reality of the word that is witch. So, it is important that I am here. And that I tell this story and stories like it. This is a chronicle of both of grief and of hope, of sadness and of enchantment.

We, as a nation, are in the midst of exploring how to honour these people with little knowledge of what happened to their remains, left on their own sites of personal battles. Over the last seventy years or so, we have seen the creation of Wicca – creating a religion from folk magic and practices that were once called witchcraft. Authors, podcasters and researchers have explored their stories and books, sharing and listing their names. People accused of witchcraft have been memorialised in Scotland and many other places through art, sculpture, community events like today's in Dunfermline and the seeking of pardons or recognition. This is part of a journey of exploring the uncomfortable sticky parts of our history. In doing so, perhaps we feel we can in some way atone and in some way let the one we called *witch*, now rest. Today's national recognition is part of this seeking.

The natural landforms that we have travelled to so far, like Vixen Tor and Wookey Hole, have been given folkloric witching tales, in part, for their huge and captivating structures. The real accused women and men that suffered in the witch trials often have far subtler affairs. Tasteful plaques and monuments, nowhere close to huge elaborate memorials to, for example, those lost to war. There is no doubt, some sense of shame of how these people were treated, and I think we as a society are still figuring out how to face that in the creation of memorials. Because it shows us who we were once and, to be honest, how we can still be – judgemental of age, disability and other differences, biased, prejudiced, seeking to scapegoat a single group of people for all our troubles. The witch is a bright mirror, confronting us with how we have, both in the past and in the present day reacted to a notion that women can be more powerful than men; a jarring concept in a place that is largely built on patriarchal ideals. And it is amazing (and awful) to see it still happening in many realms.

There is nothing an accused witch has ever been accused of, even in the farthest realms of fantasy, that can hold a candle to what was done by the very real witchfinders, witch prickers, torturers, jailers, hangmen and burners. As can be seen in the stories of the Fife witches.

So, memorials may be tricky, but they are necessary. And certainly, they stand as a powerful reminder of the true devils we can become when pushed by adversity, prejudice and fear.

*

There is an online interactive map showing the witchcraft trials of Scotland, drawn from information from the national database. It suggests that around ninety people were killed as witches in Dunfermline, Torryburn and Culross. Many more dot the surrounding areas. Travel five miles south, for example, to areas such as Inverkeithing, Aberdour, North Queensferry and Dalgety Bay and you can quickly add eighty-five more. The numbers are truly horrifying.

Dunfermline

Yesterday I walked through Dunfermline, in the glorious sunshine to Townhill Road, a road that once led to the gallows on the edge of the city's boundaries, where witches were executed at a hill called 'Witch Knowe' or 'Witch Loan', far enough from the centre of the city to hopefully prevent the vengeful spirits of those executed from wreaking retribution. Around this place was also a 'Witch Dub', which was a pool of water some ten feet deep seemingly used for an equivalent of swimming accused witches. I visit a street named 'Witchbrae' (*brae* meaning hill) just off the steeply ascending Townhill Road, it is a small reminder and the only remaining physical sign of its history. I take a few pictures in the sunshine, sweating a bit from my walk up through the public park – I came straight from the station, so I am still carrying my rucksack. I am relieved the Witchbrae road is near the bottom of the hill that veers up more steeply. So, I take my pictures and I head for the town centre to check into my hotel. I peel off my jeans and change into fresh clothes for a walk in the evening sun around Dunfermline Abbey.

As is my habit now, I check the doorways of the Abbey for witch marks – I found two faint ones at the south-west door and I am sure there are more inside. I was expecting to find as least some witch marks, as parts of the Abbey, founded in the eleventh century, also served as a royal palace and residence to King James VI and Queen Anne of Denmark after their marriage in 1590.

The journey back to Scotland after this marriage was so marred by storms that witches were blamed and King James' obsession with witches carried into his book *Daemonologie* (1597), a book that would heavily influence witch hunts throughout the country.

The Abbey was closed when I visited, but I took a slow walk around the grounds, taking in the gravestones and saw more than one decorated with the vivid symbol of a skull and a sand timer. An ominous symbol, presumably as reminder that death finds us all, in time, but when considering many of those accused of witchcraft, it came all too early.

"Six Witches Burnt at The Witch-Loan and Two Others Die in Prison" – 1643 was a great witch-catching and witch-burning year in Dunfermline. A staff of officials called, "witch-watchers" and "witch-catchers," had been appointed early in 1643 to seize and put in ward (prison) all reputed witches, in order that they might be tried for their "horrid and abominable crime of witchcraft." Accordingly, "a great many old shriveled-up women, with woe-begone countenances, were warded and if any of them used the long staff in walking, so much the better for the catchers."

... During the month of May, July and August, it seems no less than six poor women were burnt for being reputed witches! Their names were Grissel Morris, Margaret Brand, Katherine Elder, Agnes Kirk, Margaret Donaldson and Isobel Millar.

These victims, having been tried and condemned to be burnt, were accordingly carted east to the loan (witch-loan) near where the railway bridge crosses the road, there was the institution of "the witches' dub." Sometimes and old frail woman was thrown into it. If she sank and was drowned, then it was supposed that "judgment had found her out;" if she swam on the surface... then it was judged that there was something "no cannieaboot her," and on some pretence the victim got to the flames at last. Determined not to lose their victim, they appear to have acted on the principle of "Head, I win; tails, you lose!" Ascending the loan (the witch-loan) and about 100 yards from "the witch-dub" and on the east side of the loan road, there was a small knowe on which the witches suffered and still further up the loan stood "the gallows" where execution was done.

The names of the victims who died "in ward" were Jonett Fentoun and Isobell Marr. In the same Register of Deaths their fate is thus recorded: "The 20th day, June 1643, Jonett Fentoun the witch, died miserably in ward [in prison] and wes bro to the witch knowe, being trailed and cared yrto and castin into a hole withot a kist" (a coffin)... Let those who sound the praises of "the good old times" take such doings as these into their "earnest consideration."

This extract of the *Annals of Dunfermline and Vicinity* by Ebeneser Henderson (1879) paints a very vivid picture of the fervour of the witch hunts of the time.

*

Back to today, and the National Day of Remembrance. I start my walk at the furthest point of the Fife Witches Trail at Culross (pronounced *curr-us* – I tried my best to say it correctly to the poor bus driver; she was patient as I tried to pronounce it several times). I caught the bus from Dunfermline. Rain dots the bus windows and I follow our route on my phone as we head downhill towards the coast; we'll pass through Torryburn and then I'll walk the route back. The tide is out as I planned with the tide times, and I see the grey morning light glinting just a little on the mudflats of Torry Bay. And as the bus trundles along the shoreside road, I catch a fleeting glimpse of Lilias' grave and feel little leap in my chest. I've travelled a long way to arrive at this place. And she's here. I'm comforted and rather excited to know I'll be able to spot her again when I come back this way.

It's still quite early, just after 8am in Culross where I disembark. Nothing is open. I spot the Culross palace, an orange-toned house and the grey stone townhouse, where it's thought many local witches were held. Both have signs outside ready for visitors when they open later (including several signs about it being a set for the TV series *Outlander*).

Records differ in their thoughts about where Lilias was held. According to Parish Records, she died in Dunfermline prison. Others say the tollbooth at Torryburn, others say here in Culross (there were enough people accused for records to be muddled in such matters).

I am sure the first marker of the trail – the first of three memorial plaques – is supposed to be opposite the townhouse on the village green next to the bus stop. I look carefully, but there are no signs to indicate the start or end of the trail; there is, however, an ominous empty circle of crumbled concrete next to the bus stop, like a crushed biscuit. There is an old woman at the bus stop sheltering from the rain with her three dogs. I become terribly English and apologise for bothering her, but ask *does she possibly, perhaps, know anything about the witch plaque that is supposed to be in this area?* "Oh yes, it's gone. That's where it was," she nods to the now empty circle by the bus stop, "I don't know who nicked it," she adds. I thank her and say I'm reassured that I was at least looking at the right spot, but this is obviously not a fantastic start. I do a loop around the little village green to see if there is anything connected to the Witches Trail or its plaques, but I find nothing. There are signs for the Pilgrim's Way and Fife Coastal Trail – the Witch's Trail is technically part of the Fife Coastal Trail, but there is no additional information about this special witchy route. I do find a nice quote on a sign for Culross and the Fife Pilgrim Way that runs to St Andrews:

> *It is good to have an end to journey towards, but it is the journey that matters, in the end.*
>
> **Ursula K. Le Guin (1929-2018)**

Le Guin is a famed and fabulous American author of folkloric and fantasy books. I am happy to see her name, but I am unable to find any connection to Scotland, I think it may have just been a good quote for pilgrims.

I know the direction I'm headed, so when it seems I'll find no trace of the start of the witch trail here in Culross, I strike out towards Valleyfield, the site of the next marker. Let's hope that one is still in situ. On the path, a deer jumps out from hedgerows of gorse, birch and oak in front of me and then skips away into the trees. At first, I assume it's a red deer because of its bright orange-red coat, very auspicious I think; red deer are a national symbol of Scotland. But on checking later, I don't think it was big enough for a red deer, so I'm guessing a roe deer with its russet spring-summer pelt. I think that still counts as auspicious. The roe deer is a native of the British Isles since at least the Mesolithic Era, once close to extinction due to hunting, they are now reasonably widespread in the UK.

Reformation

The Reformation in Scotland, if I can describe something very complex as simply as possible, was led by the establishment of the Presbyterian Church, which rejected the authority of the Pope and Catholic practices. It was driven by a mix of factors, as these things always are. The result was that in 1560, the Scottish Parliament adopted Protestantism as the national faith, in the form of Prebyterianism, transforming the religious landscape and influencing

Scottish society, politics and culture. And, most importantly to our journey, was highly influential on the fervour of the Scottish witch hunts. Just three years later, the 1563 Scottish Witchcraft Act was passed that made witchcraft, sorcery and consulting with witches capital offences punishable by death. Seeking to eradicate what were seen as diabolical practices and protect the community from supposed malevolent influences (this law marked the beginning of an intense period of witch hunts in Scotland). The Reformation was a quest, a Presbyterian vision to create a 'perfect' godly society. But what that vision fuelled were fierce and harsh punishments that left people terrified: terrified of punishment, terrified of demons, terrified of being in any way connected to an accused witch, their perceived heresies or moral impurities. Religious leaders of the newly established Presbyterian Church often supported and participated in the persecution of suspected witches. Thirty years after the burial of Lilias, the Witchcraft Act of 1735 brought the witch hunts largely (but not completely) to a close throughout the UK. It became a crime to accuse someone of witchcraft or claim to be a witch, because in the eyes of the law, witches and witchcraft now, simply, didn't exist.

*

The Fife Witches Trail is, or should I say is supposed to be, a series of three plaques, along a three-mile-ish walking route from Culross to Torryburn. Commemorating the women executed as witches, in the villages of Culross, Valleyfield and Torryburn. The plaques – illustrated discs cast in bronze like giant coins – are the breadcrumbs of my trail. "We chose to be a little bit playful with the subjects, in part to portray how ludicrous the notion of dancing with the devil was. The discs contain some decorative elements that relate to herbalism and the story behind each of the discs summarise the tragedy and plight of the victims," says the design team behind the creation of the plaques. The trail was officially opened in 2020. I have done quite a bit of research before coming out here, printed maps with scribbles on them and gathered descriptions I found in blogs and videos of exactly where the markers are. I would have just one chance to find them on this Tuesday morning, so I really didn't want to miss them or get lost.

I cross over a railway bridge just before Valleyfield and meet another friendly dog walker in his sixties. His caramel-coloured spaniel sprints back and forth around us as he tells me a little of his childhood. He grew up here and remembers the mudflats being covered in ash from the collieries and factories and as a teenager he would wade out with his friends in the mud to reach little islands that would eventually be built up to make the Preston Island Nature Reserve. He asks if I am walking the coastal trail and I am relieved and heartened that when I reply, "Sort of, I'm actually looking for the witches," he knows exactly what I mean. He says that at school they were never taught about the local witches but that his grandmother told him that in her day they lit bonfires for the witches at Torryburn, at the spot where a playpark now sits (which is very close to Lilias' stone). He helps me figure out where the second plaque will most likely be; I share the description I have printed out that reads: *under an information sign for the entrance to Valleyfield's woodland and car park*. I thank him for his help and journey on and am pleased to locate the second plaque. This second plaque is for Lilias Adie, the third plaque is for Lilias as well. The Fife Coastal Trail and Pilgrim Way are both very well signposted, which guide me near to the right places. I hope in years to come signs may appear for the Witches Trail as its own special journey.

The missing plaque from Culross, I know from photos, would have illustrated the figure of a woman holding herbal plants with reputed healing properties, notable buildings in the village and thirty-two crosses to represent the accused, it reads: "32 innocent women were accused of being witches. So many ordinary women were accused of being witches in Culross. Innocent victims of unenlightened times." The second plaque is at the entrance to Valleyfield Wood, a slight detour off the coastal path. It is located under an information board and is illustrated with the figure of a woman dancing with a devil figure, who with his hands holds her at the soles of her feet and the top of her head, an image drawn from Lilias' 'confessions'. The plaque reads: "Lilias Adie 1640-1704, an innocent woman accused of 'lying with the devil.' An innocent victim of unenlightened times." I gather some buttercups and lay them on this plaque.

Here at Valleyfield, it was at the house of a man named Patrick Sands that Lilias said she met the devil and the night party that was lit by a mysterious blue light. There is a grey house in front of me as I sit by the plaque. There is a smell of tar and ash in the air, perhaps thrown up by the rain in sooty petrichor. I doubt very much it could be the same house. But I take pause all the same. I walk past the house to continue my journey, following signs to rejoin the pilgrim and coastal path. I walk through some trees, past a fenced-off derelict building and car park in which I see two rabbits who swiftly scurry into the undergrowth when they spot me. From here, the path brings me back to the sea, past some coastal cottages that, along with cars out front, seem to have been half consumed by trees and brambles. I pass through Newmills, another place mentioned by Lilias as where she met with the devil, and I see a small railway bridge and know that the Torryburn plaque and Lilias' grave stone is just past it, overlooking the beach.

*

Torryburn, is a small cluster of houses looking out onto Torry Bay, the Forth Estuary, and out into the North Sea. In the 1600s, it was predominantly a mining village but also had outlying salt pans; coal and salt were exported through its busy port. There are areas I walk past called the 'ash lagoons' created by landscaping ash slurry generated by a huge coal-fired power station, producing in the present day. This is an important natural habitat for wildlife as well as access to the old industrial buildings on Preston Island, which my dog walking friend waded out to explore with his teen pals (which I found a bit horrifying as he said sometimes they got stuck in the mud up to their waists). Back along the coast, work with iron, salt and coal made Culross similarly prosperous. So, this area has a history of mines, coal, power stations and collieries. Some are still here. I won't pretend to understand the technicalities of mining and collieries but there is certainly a sense of that for centuries this place, even though prosperous, has been under clouds of ash – making the beach sand black, blocking out the sun, and this strange connection rolls around in my mind of the women that were also made into ashes. By the grinding engines and machinery of misogyny and reformation.

An accused witch was burnt to ashes, but when either before or after conviction they died in prison, they may be "carted yrto and castin into a hole yr withot a kist" (a coffin) as we saw earlier in *The Annals of Dunfermline and Vicinity.* Lilias got her *kist*, but a century after her death, grave robbers dug up her body – her skull was put on show and the wood from the box was made into walking sticks that were gifted to rich men. At the end of her life the very little Lilias had – a final resting place – even that was taken from her.

*

The tidal mudflats of Torry Bay are exposed at low tide, which was at 6.30am this morning. It's 9am now, high tide is not until almost 2pm. From here, the stone slab under which Adie was buried is visible. I start at the third plaque just after the railway bridge, by a low stone wall that lines up closely with Lilias' grave stone – it is illustrated with her face surrounded by herbal plants, notable buildings of Torryburn, a crescent moon and another devil figure. It reads: "Lilias Adie, 1640-1704 – they feared she would rise from the dead – how could she as she was an ordinary woman accused? 'Oh keep me. There she is coming'".

From the plaque I see her stone once more, flat amongst larger stones. I see part of the low stone wall is crumbling away and flattened grass suggests people have climbed over this point in the wall to go see Lilias (again, not a single sign: you could easily miss the stone, it is one of many on the tideline). I walk along to find a less disruptive path to the beach and walk up to see what remains of what was intended to be Lilias Adie's final resting place – the stone slab placed there specifically to ensure she didn't rise up as a revenant or evil spirit. I do a little beachcombing on the short walk and find a shell with a hole through it. Not quite a hag stone, but I decide it will serve as an offering.

I am wary of the mudflats, guides advise not to walk out to the grave and as you'll remember from the New Forest, I have form of getting stuck on my own in marshy ground. But she's just at the foreshore, so I walk out to place my hand on her stone for a moment and place my shell to stay there until the tide rises and carries it away. I stand there for some time watching the tide draw in.

*

But how did Lilias end up under this stone slab? On June the 13th 1704, a woman called Jean Bizet from Torryburn was at Helen Anderson's house of an evening, a woman we may assume was her friend, and she was seemingly drunk. She had spent the evening drinking, going from house to house, stopping by Mary Wilson's for a "choppin of ale"* or two. There was much drinking of ale and people coming and going, it's hard to keep up with it all. But at some point before this night of drinking, a woman named Janet Whyte suggested Jean Bizet had not paid her for two barrels of ale, which

* All trial notes drawn from Minutes and Proceedings of the Kirk-Session of Torryburn and the *Confession of Lilias Adie in a collection of rare and curious tracts on witchcraft and the second sight,* with an original essay on witchcraft by David Webster (1820).

certainly suggests Jean was having troubles with both money and alcohol. As Helen Anderson told it, when Jean Bizet was in her house, she seemed to be strangely distempered and she cried out, "Beware lest Lilias Adie come upon you and your child."* After some time sleeping, Jean Bizet awoke, perhaps with something of a hangover she was heard to say, "O keep me! Keep me! There she is coming, Lilly Adie with her blew doublet!"

This outburst from Jean Bizet that she was "under certain Bewitchment", along with an accusation from a Jean Neilson who was "dreadfully tormented", but of whom little else is said in records, and certain variables that were detrimental to her reputation – she was old, single, and tall – at over six feet – sent out ripples of allegation. Lilias was arrested about a month later, in July and imprisoned for a month, deprived of sleep and interrogated by the minister and church elders four times. During 'confessions', Lilias spoke of gatherings of witches and meeting with the devil. Maybe these were fantasies or scraps of happy memories stitched together. Told by a tired, scared and ordinary woman; meeting with friends, dancing at sunset in golden fields and at harvest time. When Lilias was instructed to declare the truth and nothing but, she replied what she said would be "as true as the sun is in the firmament." This is not the only time she mentions the sun and all it may have meant to her – light, warmth, truth and perhaps dying hope that it would prevail. In contrast when she confessed that she had a covenant with the devil, she said he came "like a shadow and went away like a shadow." She met with the devil in a tryst at the harvest, before the sun set. She saw him at Martinmas, summoned by Grissel Anderson (Lilias is very clever, even in her addled state, when she mentions other women, as she would have been strongly encouraged to do more than once, she chooses women who have already been accused and killed as witches, so as to not incriminate any more women she knows: Grissel Anderson was executed as a witch in Torryburn in 1703). In her account of the Martinmas gathering Lilias says their number was about twenty or thirty, of which none are now living but herself. It was a moon-lit night and the group danced with the devil. The next time was at a meeting at the back of a house, in Valleyfield. They had no moonlight but she

* This a story we have seen echoed before in Wales, that of William Griffith, Dorothy Griffith and the corpse candles – in both cases, there is certainly a suggestion that alcohol may well have played a part, but Griffith and Bizet may also have been suffering with their own demons that may have caused them the great fear, distress and possibly visions that they would attribute to witches.

said they "got light from darkness"; a blue light "not so bright as a candle." Here is where the devil places a hand at Lilias head and at the soles of her feet as portrayed in the Valleyfield plaque – and she had to say all that was between her feet and crown were his. But ultimately, Lilias said, of the many good things the devil promised, all she ever had were misery and poverty.

It's unclear how Lilias died, her words suggest her eyes were dimming, but she still could see the summer sun shining. Maybe that's why her tired mind spoke so strongly of light and shadows, that's what her world had become in that final month. Lilias even said she would have met with the devil more often, but could not attend for age and sickness, so clearly, she was not in strong health, though perhaps she also wanted to stress her ill health to her interrogators to seek compassion. Hours before her death, her confession included, "It is as true as the sun shines on that floor and dim as my eyes are, I see that." And incarcerated and exhausted, Lilias died.

Left with a confessed, but not convicted, witch, the authorities took the decision to bury Lilias at the shoreline, within the seamark at Torryburn, with a rectangular stone slab placed on top of her simple coffin. This was to keep her body from rising; either physically floating out to sea or as a vengeful spirit, both undesirable outcomes and when witches were concerned – like the Handsel sisters of Wiltshire, who had trees as their funerary guardians, Lilias has stone and sea. It's possible that the motion of the tide was considered another restraint, the common lore being that witches cannot cross running water (but they can set sail and raise storms in other Scottish water lore, so who knows). But after such care was taken to prevent her from rising from her grave, she did rise in the end, though not from her own doing. During the nineteenth century, her remains, including her skull, were dug up and sold to antiquarians and their whereabouts are now unknown. The stone slab marking her grave was located and cleared in 2014, the only physical remnant of Lilias story.

Women other than Lilias died before their formal trial in the Fife area, so was Lilias' burial a warning? Something for women and men to see lurking on the shore as they went around town, a cautionary tale and haunting presence to strike fear and encourage good behaviours? Or did she just fall through the cracks between confession and trial? I imagine a bit of both.

*

If you are looking for a witch, you are looking for a woman, and it could be any woman.

Christina Larner, *Witchcraft and Religion: The Politics of Popular Belief* (1986)

Many more names swirl around the accusations of 1704, in and around Torryburn, tangled up in this summer of drinking and distemper. Mary Wilson was another name declared by Jean Bizet and Janet Whyte (who was aggrieved by Bizet not paying for her ale) were both also accused of witchcraft. I turned to the always useful *Source Book of Scottish Witchcraft* by Christina Larner, to double-check the fates of these women and to my surprise a 'Jean Bizet' is listed too in the 1704 trials: she also ended up accused as a witch then. Jean, Janet Whyte and Mary Wilson's fate are all marked as 'not known' as often happens with these incomplete records. My 1820 Webster text similarly didn't note their fate. One assumes it was not favourable. But Lilias' fate is noted as 'Miscellaneous', which I rather like; technically, it was used to denote outcomes of escape or death in prison. But her remains have risen from the grave she was put in (Lilias' skull, was as far as we know, sold to St Andrews University in 1852 and disappeared after being put on exhibition in Glasgow in 1938). Nationwide campaigns have been launched to find Lilias' remains over the last few years so that she may be laid to rest. So, her fate is not yet sealed; the end of her story is not yet told…

Grave expectations

There is going to be some debate about what constitutes a witch's grave and there are a few other contenders for the title of grave of a witch, all of them however, like Lilias' somewhat imperfect memorials. Alice Nutter at Pendle is thought perhaps to have been snuck, unnamed, into a family grave, due to her wealth and status. Also, in Lancashire a stone sits in a churchyard with a plaque beside it that reads, "The Witch's Grave – Beneath this stone lie the remains of Meg Shelton, alleged Witch of Woodplumpton, buried in 1705." In St Osyth in Essex, bones found in a man's garden were said to be those of 'witch' Ursula Kemp. He charged people to see them in the 1920s, however eventually the bones were found not to be Ursula's, and were re-buried respectfully. And seven women who were executed for alleged witchcraft are said to be buried in unmarked graves at the back of St Nicholas' Church in Great Yarmouth, Norfolk. (I am sure you have a few more suggestions to add to these.)

The only grave that holds a skeleton for sure and which has a properly marked headstone I am aware of, is far, far south of where I am now, in Boscastle, Cornwall. That of Joan Wytte – the fighting fairy woman of Bodmin. A Cornish witch with a reputation, as her nickname suggests, of brawling and speaking to fairies. In fact, Cornwall gives us some of the most truly memorable women/witches (or the stereotypes of what was written of them): Anne Piers – the pirate witch of Padstow, Joan Wytte – the fighting fairy woman of Bodmin and Ann Jeffries – fairy healer, rumoured to have been sustained by fairy foods and magic whilst imprisoned as a witch.

People may well have called on Joan Wytte for her skills in divination and healing and in communicating with fairies and spirits. She used clooties for healing: strips of cloth were taken from a sick person and tied to a tree and in sympathetic magic – when the cloth deteriorated, so did the disease. We've seen contemporary clooties in Grovely Woods, at the very beginning of this adventure, used more as a general prayer or blessing nowadays. Joan was known to be frequently ill-tempered and was often involved in fights (her great strength was allegedly too great to be wholly natural). When she was held in Bodmin Jail, it was for public brawling, rather than witchcraft. But in the damp, desperate conditions of this jail, Joan died of pneumonia at the age of just thirty-eight. It's not clear where her bones were first buried, but the story goes that her bones were disinterred and displayed as curios and at some point later hung up on display at the Museum of Witchcraft and Magic in Boscastle. It was decided that Wytte should have a proper burial and she was finally laid to rest in a peaceful wooded glen nearby; her gravestone reads: "Joan Wytte. Born 1775. Died 1813 in Bodmin Jail. Buried 1998. No longer abused."

"…Joan Wytte of Bodmin, Cornwall. This skeleton has been submitted to inspection by a Home Office forensic expert, the report states: "In stature she was a small, short person, undernourished and very slim… the bones are exceptional in that they show two things. One that the water supply source used by the Wytte household was exceptionally rich in natural fluoride, the other that the bones show that she was in long contact with kaolin or china clay." The report concluded by pointing to the huge abscess cavity in the right wisdom tooth… As the expert said, "anyone with a thing like that would certainly be bad tempered and aggressive." As to the unusual fact of natural

fluoride found in above average quantity in her bones, this pin-pointed the location of the Wytte family home in Bodmin town where she was born and brought up... "There was a holy well called Scarlett's Well, long famous among the population for its reputed healing powers... Scarlett's Well was rich in natural fluoride. It is interesting to note that back street where the Wytte family lived is close to this source of drinking water..."

Cecil Williamson for the Museum of Witchcraft and Magic at Boscastle

I walked there once pre-pandemic, which feels like another age. It was late October, and I was visiting for the event known as the Dark Gathering, held at Halloween in Boscastle, a fabulous pagan festivity of fire, dancing and merriment. The grounds of Minster Church are a steeply sloping fern-padded valley; Joan is, of course, not in church grounds, but just outside, nestled amongst moss and fern fronds of Minster Wood, with a small, smart slate gravestone, topped with a triple moon symbol. It seems tradition to not be too specific about the location of Joan's grave, in perhaps another act of respect. I will follow suit. But Boscastle is a beautiful place to visit if you wish to find the magic there for yourself and pay your respects in the fairy glen.

So, Lilias was buried and then pulled up from the earth. A skeleton said to be Joan was hung up as a curiosity and then finally buried and given her rest. And in this journey in my mind of various ways witches may hope to be laid to rest I think of another Cornish witch, this one is mythical: Madgy Figgy* and in her stories we find images of the witches' light – a way by which witches may recognise each other and the rarity and value of graves: we all need a place to grieve.

* You'll also find spellings of Maggy and Maggie.

The Tale of Madgy Figgy and the Witches' Light

At the most western point of Cornwall, the very tip of the toe of England, is the promontory of granite stone known as Gwennap's Head, also called Madgy Figgy's Chair. Here, it is said, Madgy was wont to seat herself when calling up the spirits of the storms, tumbling in from the Atlantic.

Many versions of this story are told, this is one drawn from Popular Romances of the West of England; or, the drolls, traditions and superstitions of Old Cornwall, *collected and edited by Robert Hunt (1865).*

Madgy Figgy, who sat upon her stone seat of storms on an evening of mist and winds, saw an ill-fated Portuguese galleon wreck into the cove below. All passengers drowned and were washed ashore. Their bodies were stripped of valuables and with respect, buried by Figgy and her helpers in a green dell with rough stone markers. The spoils on this occasion must have been large; for a long time, gems and gold continued to be found on the sands of the cove. But amongst the bodies thrown ashore was one of a lady particularly richly dressed, with chains of gold and gems about her. Figgy would not allow any of her golden chains or gems to be divided. A dreadful quarrel ensued, but Figgy stood her ground. These treasures were to be hers, and she gathered them carefully and placed them into a chest in her cottage. All the lost souls were buried that same evening and at midnight, a light was seen to rise from the grave of the golden lady, pass along the cliffs and seat itself in Madgy Figgy's chair. Then, after some hours, it descended, entering the cottage, resting upon the chest. This occurred nightly, but Figgy was not concerned; she said it would all be right in time.

One day a Portuguese man arrived at the cottage, and he was led to the graves. At the grave of the golden lady, he sat and wept, remaining there until nightfall, when the light arose from the grave more brightly than ever before, moving to the cottage and resting as usual on the chest, now held in Madgy's arms, ready to hand over to the man. He selected a ruby ring that belonged to the golden lady, refusing to take any more. Leaving the rest to the wreckers in thanks, before taking his leave into the night.

Madgy Figgy was satisfied, for she had known the golden lady was a witch and was bound to honour her. "A witch always knows another," said she, "be they living or be they lost."

She who Remains

Some of my favourite books on witches have taken tours of Scotland's witch monuments and its unique witch trial history – *Ashes and Stones: A Scottish Journey in Search of Witches and Witness* by Allyson Shaw and *Witchcraft: A History in Thirteen Trials* by Marion Gibson explores the story of the famed North Berwick witch trials that prompted King James to write his book *Daemonologie* on witchcraft. And *The Visions of Isobel Gowdie: Magic, Witchcraft and Dark Shamanism In Seventeenth Century Scotland* by Emma Wilby, where Wilby actually rediscovered the original documents, thought lost for centuries amongst seas of archives, from Gowdie's trial in her journey of writing the book.

It is because of amazing and passionate authors and researchers such as these that we learn more all the time about the witches and their history. I know that the seaweed surrounding Lilias' stone is bladderwrack because Allyson Shaw told me so in her beautiful book. And I think of all the women that went before and have come to this spot, to these lands, for curiosity, to pay their respects, to pause and reflect and this is something of what this whole book, this journey, is all about: the women who went before and the land we walk today, and the connections between the two, so often omitted from history.

Women and a few men who worked with charms or herbs, some devout Christians, some foul-mouthed drunkards and maybe a few who really did poison their husbands, neighbours or landlords' livestock – they're all dead now, so they don't care, but their stories continue to inspire us. Maybe they don't need an apology. But hell, they deserve it. Perhaps remembering the lost can help sustain the living, as a source of strength, comfort, or as a catalyst to live better ourselves.

Of the almost four thousand people accused as witches, around two thousand five hundred were executed. But those who escaped with their lives did not necessarily return to a happy life of freedom. They may well have been ostracised, their neighbours still suspicious, fearful and harbouring resentments.

> *Margaret Smaill, 66, declares she desyres not to live, because nobody will converse with her, seeing she is under the reputation of a witch." Another, on seizure, implored permission to escape, otherwise she would run into the sea and drown herself.**

* Details of the trials of Margaret Smaill, 1678 and Annie Tailzeour, 1624. Found in *The Darker Superstitions of Scotland*, John Graham Dalyell (1834).

To be accused was, for many, to be damned forever. The lost have certainly left their mark in our consciousness, our stories and our land. Lilias, is, was just one of thousands accused: a drop in the ocean.

*

In the evening, I head to Dunfermline Abbey and join with at least fifty people, honouring and remembering Scotland's accused witches.

The event begins with a lament on the bagpipes, a piece written for the occasion. The names of all the people in Scotland who stood trial, accused as witches, are read aloud simultaneously by eight women, hosts of this evening's event. We listen to the names read out…and listen and listen. And as a group we realise just how many people four thousand is – it takes twenty minutes for these women to read out their portion of names, various well-known ones catching the attention, like Lilias Adie and Isobel Gowdie. But also, ominous records simply of 'many witches'. And also, so many *unknowns; unknown wife, unknown husband, unknown daughter, unknown, unknown, unknown.* Even though it's June, there is a roar of cold wind, whipping around us on the Abbey grounds, as names are put out into the air and ride the winds. There are too many to remember; perhaps that's why Lilias and her gravestone represent them all in a way. Poems and songs are offered up and the ceremony ends as it began, with bagpipes. Along with the fifty attendees, a vicar in his dog collar is present and next to him is a woman in a lavish fur coat. We are invited to sing together in simple call and response. They do not join in.

The Earth, the Air, the Fire, the Water
Return, return, return, return
The Earth, the Air, the Fire, the Water
Return, return, return, return
Heya, heya, heya, heya
Heyo, heyo, heyo, heyo

The theme of bodies under the ground, returning to the ground, under the surface of things, comes up a lot in myth as well as in our *Witch Country* journey – as inevitably tied up with exploring ideas of death; something the art of storytelling was used to explore and still is, to help us get our heads around such vast themes as death and loss. But also, of realms of the occult, hidden under our day-to-day dealings of life. The Wookey witch, Morgan and her sisters under Glastonbury Tor and Lilias at the tidemark. They are all not quite *here nor there*, each witch figure has one foot in this world and another in myth.

Connecting these women of both myth and history, are threads of light and shadow, stone and tide. From the furthest south-western tip of Cornwall, up to this north-eastern Scottish coast, there is a certain connection, *"I am the day transcending night"*, drawn from that poem about grief and the few words Lilias was able to say that, by whatever magics, she drew *"light from darkness"* on moonless nights.

The new moon is on June the 6th, so on my journey back down south by train on the 5th, the very last sliver of moon is visible in the night sky. And in two weeks from this journey, I step into the lightness of the Midsummer solstice. As always, some kind of light returns for those of us who remain, if we can pause to see it. And events like that of Dunfermline offer us a chance to bring light to dark histories, to see more clearly and to step out from dark pasts into lighter, brighter futures.

Summer Solstice

I want to close the chapter with words to honour this time of year, fittingly by another Lilias:

"The spell of midsummer lies on the land. Down by the river in the shadow of the pale moon-flowered elders the shimmering heats hold the world in thrall. Time is sunk in the green dimness of the wood. The only sound from its depths is the low croon of the turtle dove and the fledgling tits' thin, fleeting cries, as in little companies of eight and ten they slip through the oak trees in ceaseless search for grub and caterpillar. An hour filched from a fairy-tale, when fantasy seems fact and one stands on the threshold of that secret lotus land of purple glooms one knew as a child.

For at midsummer the old gods walk the world again, seeking their ruined altars..."

Lilias Rider Haggard, *Norfolk Life* (1943)

JULY

Water Witches

Shropshire

The sun is blasting out after a full day of rain. The air is thick, heavy with moisture that hangs in the air as I close my eyes for a moment. I can hear the wind in the trees, sultry susurrations. A moorhen mother sputters across the water toward the reeds. I saw one of her tiny chicks as I walked around the edge of the pond, like a little ball of soot rolling on the water. I am sat on a mossy bench. I open my eyes and before me now, a variety of white ruffled flower heads, sprays of tiny white flowers in star-domed crowns and a few bowed green stems dipping their heads as if to cool them in the water. Later, a kindly green witch will tell me that the star crown flowers are hemlock water dropwort, one of the most poisonous of all British plants. Like the very best of charmers, its sweet scent gives no indication of how deadly it truly is.

The perfumed plumage of meadowsweet nestles alongside nettles that frill the banks of the pond, so you can't quite see where the solid ground falls away into dark water. Within that water, hundreds of water weed spires rise in reaching fingers, and a tide of tadpoles* wiggle through them. Bubbles rise to break the surface from the tannic depths. Lapis lines of damselflies with clear glass wings fly in trembles above a gently rippling film of water. A white butterfly rests upon my bag. Trees leer above the waters and create blurred mirrored edges of exactly where water and leaf meet. I'm hot now, I wish I could swim in the water, but there is a 'No Swimming' sign, which is almost certainly for the best. I walk to a shadowed corner and admire a beautiful spread of water lilies – golf ball white buds beginning to emerge. And there are tree roots dropping into the water with the elegance of long-fingered hands plucking a flower or the chicken claws of Baba Yaga's hut.

I'm in Shropshire on a writing retreat, trying my best to go against almost a lifetime of seeking to be unnoticed and unchallenged in a space. To share with other writers about my journey. The retreat tutors are two nature writers that I admire greatly and I'm keen to give a decent account of myself. Shropshire was not on my original list for places to travel for this year of witching journeys, so this month is something of a wildcard. One I am very grateful for and because every county has its witches, I knew I would find them here too.

This is my first visit to the county of Shropshire, in the western heart of England. I've admired sunny, tree-lined fields and cosy villages—but a climb through moorland and hills could lead somewhere older, stranger. To the ancient rock ridges of the Stiperstones, for example, where mists coiling over the

* My editor tells me that this is wildly late for tadpoles, so I cannot account for their presence!

stone peaks is believed to signal the devil and his witches gathering, brewing magic and bad deeds.

I was thrilled to find that in the grounds of the retreat house, there is a pond. In Shropshire, generations of parents warned children to stay away from ponds. For this is where the silted spirit Jenny Greenteeth watches and waits. Hungry, she is ready to drag you from the water's edge, into the water, rippling as she pulls you under into the dark. Down to meet sharp teeth and clawing nails.

Her long hair matches her long limbs, dripping wet and wrapped in weeds. They slip and slide around her as she moves, slowly, slowly. This malevolent water spirit, a bitter river witch. Long and pointed of tooth and grasping fingertip. Her teeth, of course, are green, as is her hair and her skin takes on the sickly hue of turned milk. She lurks in pools and rivers, her bulging froggy eyes peeping from dark and covered corners, her hair rising around her in a dark corona. She lies ready for one who walks too close, who sits too long, who throws something in and disturbs peaceful waters.

The tricksy growth of duckweed in a pond is a sure indicator that Jenny haunts the area and some call the duckweed plant itself: Jenny Greenteeth.

What does this story reflect of us, those who create it and tell it? Is Jenny simply a river hag in search of blood? Or is she a ragged revenant of our great water goddesses: Sabrina, Sulis, Coventina and Danu? Half-forgotten idols, fallen from the sacred altars. What happens to deities when they are no longer revered and petitioned with offerings and tributes? Must they go feral like Jenny to drag their unfortunate prey into the murky, muddy depths?

Jenny reflects the health of our fraying waterways. Growing ever more forlorn, reminders of our neglect. Or do pollution and rot feed Jenny, nourishing her rage, provoking an ominous encroaching presence, a creeping desolation in poisoned streams and rivers?

Whichever it is, elemental power remains. For all our technological wonders and luxuries of living, the unassuming elements of earth, air, fire and water might still pull the legs out from under us and drag us to dark.

I slip away quietly, unnoticed, I hope. Leaving the waters undisturbed.

*

I've met Jenny before. Briefly, I wrote of Jenny Greenteeth in *The Witch and the Wildwood*.

Around the Midlands and Northern England there is Jenny Greenteeth and un-named female river hags whose long green hair resembles the water-weed that drags their prey down toward sharp teeth and claws.

And many have mentioned her in fabulous descriptions:

One finds a female bogy-figure used by parents to scare children away from deep pools and wells; she is a cannibal witch called Jenny Greenteeth, known chiefly in Lancashire and Cheshire and she is associated or even identified with a type of small weed which forms a carpet over stagnant water.

Jacqueline Simpson, *European Mythology* (1987)

Of still more sinister import is the colour in the case of "Jenny Greenteeth" the evil water-spirit (appearing as the green scum on stagnant water) "what cromes [claws] you in," as country children say, if you go too near or in the obscure and horrible English folk-tale of "Green Lady" – who appears to be a sort of Lamia or vampire – living on or delighting in, blood and perhaps deriving her name and hue from a classic serpent-ancestry. But Jenny Greenteeth and perhaps Green Lady also, is allied to the German water-nicks with green hats – the hat appearing to be a tuft of beautiful vegetation growing in the water – who drag down the unwary to the depths – their horrible fate being visible in a fountain of blood which sprouts up through the surface of the water.

***Folk Song Society Journal*, (England Folk Song and Dance Society): Vol 6 Iss 22 (1919)**

And my favourite…

"Jenny Greenteeth" is the name of a water-witch who has none of the outward charms of the mermaid. She is an old woman who lurks beneath the green weeds which cover stagnant ponds and Eliesmere children are warned that if they venture too near the edge of such places, she will stretch out her long arms and drag them in to her.

Georgina Jackson and Charlotte Burne, *Shropshire Folk-Lore: A Sheaf of Gleanings* (1883)*

* It happened on more than one occasion that in my research of folkloric books I was drawn into the interesting lives of the authors as much as the folklore they collected – co-authors of *A Sheaf of Gleanings*, Georgina Jackson and Charlotte Burne were just such a distraction. Georgina Jackson (1824-1895), a schoolmistress, started gathering folklore, sayings and dialects of Shropshire in the interest of preservation, but in the 1870s, she fell terminally ill and passed the project onto her friend Charlotte Burne and the book *A Sheaf of Gleanings* was published in 1883. Burne joined the Folklore Society in the same year and in 1909, became the first female president of the Folklore Society.

The water forest & foxgloves

I must still have water on my mind as we head on our next adventure in the hills and vales of Shropshire. As a group, we clamber into cars for an excursion to a patch of woodlands known as Clunton Coppice. We weave through narrow country roads, before parking in a hot, dry car park and tumbling out with water bottles, sunhats and notebooks. We walk up a gently sloping path to read information signs that tell us of the resident flora and fauna, including dormice and pine martins and a little spired plant of tiny white flowers, enchanters' nightshade *(Circaea lutetiana)*, named for the witch goddess of Greek myth, Circe, known for her knowledge of herbs, lines the path, luring us into the woodland. The tiny flowers are like miniature pink-winged fairies.

> *Inchanters Night-shade… groweth in obscure and darke places, about dunghills and untoiled grounds, by path-waies and such like… It flourisheth from June to the end of September.*
>
> **John Gerard, *Herball*, or *Generall Historie of Plantes* (1597)**

My thoughts are still lingering on the watery lore of Jenny Greenteeth. As I envisage a tide of trees to wade through, feeling somewhat submersed in thick and humid air, a swim through fractured light. The canopy high above serves as the imagined waterline, placing me in shadowy, fathomed depths. The lazy morning breeze flows through young oaks and rowans, creating the sound of the rolling waves. At the edge lands of this woodland sea lies a birch and hazel coral reef; past them, the wind ripples through a golden field, revealing the shipwreck of a sheep carcass. Deeper into the forest, the banks transform. Ferns stand as seaweed fronds and anemones while the shifting sands of leaf litter crumble underfoot. Fallen trunks, split and torqued, writhe like sea serpents in their final rest. And coppiced trees split into twos and threes, their trunks becoming hydra heads of growth. Above, clouds drift like ocean liners in a deep blue expanse, sailing towards hidden horizons. Moss drapes over rocks as algae and the sunlight is now the play of flecked light on a sea floor. A tranquil realm of slow time. An ancient, forgotten sea. This underwater world of the forest carries an undertow of peace as I seek the sway of foxgloves in flower. They start blooming in late spring and are still brightening the woods and hills. In the West Country, we say that foxgloves dance and sway even when there is no wind because the plant bows to the fairy folk as they pass by.

The foxgloves I see in the woodland are all purple. I later found out (from the green witch again) that white and pink varieties are cultivated. They are the paler, tamer sister foxgloves then. The purple ones are the wild ones, the witches of the woods. Many plants have dropped flower blooms from lower on their stalks, leaving little seed capsules that will slowly dry and burst. Right now, they are green and remind me of little faces complete with thin tongues protruding, like little aliens jeering out from the stem. Moving up the spired stalks, blooms drop from the bottom once pollinated to draw bees and other pollinators onward to the peak of the plant.

Foxgloves are both beautiful and highly poisonous – an old saying suggests they '*can raise the dead or kill the living*,' because they can be deadly, but they can also save lives. As I mentioned in the last chapter – they were used in healing, and by those called witches.

Documented by William Withering, a doctor practising in Edinburgh who hailed from Shropshire, in 1785 he published the medicinal qualities of foxgloves. Some say Withering's account is the first formal medical documentation of the power of foxgloves. *Culpeper's Complete Herbal* mentions the healing powers of foxglove over a century previously, in 1653, in more general terms, and we've heard of its use by accused witches in Scotland around 1658. Withering admits that it had long been used as a folk medicine before he put it into print, a 'hedgerow cure' brewed into a bitter tea, Drugs derived from foxgloves are now used to treat a variety of ailments.

In the year 1775, my opinion was asked concerning a family receipt for the cure of the dropsy. I was told that it had long been kept a secret by an old woman in Shropshire, who had sometimes made cures after the more regular practitioners had failed...

This medicine was composed of twenty or more different herbs, but it was not very difficult for one conversant in these subjects to perceive that the active herb could be no other than the Foxglove.

William Withering, ***An Account of The Foxglove and Some of Its Medical Uses*** **(1785)**

Old wives and wise women gathered a lifetime of knowledge of such things as herbs and healing, cooking and caring. Over time, men wrote down this knowledge, sometimes like Withering acknowledging their sources, others publishing it as their own personally 'discovered' wisdom. The wisdom spoken by the old women became more likely to be dismissed as gossip and 'old wives' tales' or worse – used as evidence of witchcraft; in both cases, stories got somewhat lost. But, as brilliantly put by someone I recently spoke to in a pub: *"We say old wives tales as a derogatory, but what do you think those old wives were doing? Just dicking about?"* As if any woman running a household/family/homestead had the time and energy to do things that weren't of use. No, they were doing what they could with what they had – often with ingenuity and centuries of learned knowledge, such as of trees and plants. Technology has moved on, but these old methods aren't without merit, including seeing the many uses, good and bad, of the foxglove.

> *There were however White Witches in the county who could effect amazing herbal cures. Their brews were the fore-runners of many modern drugs. They used deadly nightshade, the berries of which contain belladonna and rye fungus, which developed into ergot. One of the effects of belladonna, which is absorbed by the skin, is hallucination.*
>
> *Witches used to anoint their patients with a mixture of grease, soot and deadly nightshade. Sometimes, the patients had hallucinations and 'saw' witches riding by on their broomsticks. Mandrake was used by the witches for hypnosis and one of our latest hypnotics is, in fact, called mandrax.*
>
> *In addition, the witches extracted opium from the poppy and the herbs they used were called "medicine from the meadows", for they contained healing properties and were nature's most efficacious source of health. The witches used a number of soporific and narcotic herbs which they found growing wild in the Shropshire woods…*
>
> **Jean Hughes and Christina Elliot, *Shropshire Folklore: Ghosts and Witchcraft*** (1977)

*

One of our retreat tutors is a poet and we read a poem in a morning workshop about the origin of so many words having far more wild, tangled roots than the dictionary may suggest. Ideas of where the common name for *Digitalis purpurea* is one such tangle. A popular suggestion is the English name foxglove is a corruption of 'folks' gloves' as in the fairy folk, who delight in nestling in the bell-shaped flowers and hiding from humans or ringing them to create music by which to dance. When you admire closely the softly furred bell-shaped blooms you will see little dark specks haloed in white – these are surely the footprints of fairies tottering in and out of the flowers, or further by some portal to another realm.

My personal favourite origin story is of the literal foxes' gloves, with foxes slipping a flower on each paw as little mittens and booties so that they can tread more softly in order to capture unsuspecting prey, but also to keep the wet dew off their furry paws.

In Norway, both foxes and fairies are involved in foxglove lore. The plant is known there as the *rev-bielde* (fox-bell) and *reveleika* (fox-music) and the connecting folk story is that the fairies taught foxes the secret to ringing the bell-shaped flowers to warn their kin of approaching hunters. Or the foxes wear the bell-shaped foxglove blossoms around their necks, the ringing of bells offering a spell of protection against hunters and hounds, thus saving the fox from extinction. In Wales, the bells of the foxglove are *menyg gllyllon* (goblins' gloves) for the hobgoblins who wore the long bells on their fingers as gloves that imparted magical properties.

We are taught in the same workshop of tangled root words, of 'goblin words' as poet Ted Hughes called them – each word holding a spirit, a life, a certain mischief, and they can sneak into our writing to bring it alive, if we are lucky. Goblin words evoke to me the play between language and creativity that is part of the essence of folklore. We can think of words and the spells they can weave as imbued with unique qualities and energies, evoking great magic. I suggest that like goblins if we want magical words we must first give something in offering, something of ourselves perhaps: a little time, respect, humility…

Other folk names include witches' gloves, fairy caps, witches' thimbles and fairy's petticoat. Picking foxgloves is generally considered unlucky. They are often forbidden inside a house as, according to folk superstition, this gave witches, devils and fairies access to the house via the flowers. This is useful practical advice due to foxglove's fierce toxicity.

Finally, as trees give way to open fields, I emerge from my imagined underwater realm and land of tolling foxglove bells into the bright sun of the shoreline and parched solid ground. It's time to go back to the house for lunch.

*

A housewife of Shropshire may once have made the sign of the cross in flour or malt before baking and brewing to prevent the mixture from being bewitched, for meddling in matters of brewing and dairy was the very worst of malevolent magic. A silver coin or silver spoon might be placed into a butter churn for similar protection. Food is much cherished in Shropshire and poor luck comes to those who take more than their fair share…

The Milk Witch of Mitchell's Fold

This story can be found in Shropshire Folk-Lore: A Sheaf of Gleanings *by Georgina Jackson and Charlotte Burne (1883).*

On the moorlands of west Shropshire, stands a half-ruined stone circle called 'Mitchell's Fold', upon which a tale hangs. A dreadful famine was sweeping through the country. But luck would have it that a pure white fairy cow settled at a certain green hill, and no matter how many came to milk her, there was always enough for all. So long as everyone that came only took just one pailful, she would always fill it. Well, there came along a spiteful old witch whose name was Mitchell. And she brought a sieve and milked the cow into that, and of course, the poor fairy cow couldn't fill it. The old woman milked her and milked her and at last, she milked her dry. The fairy cow was never seen again and was sadly missed. But the old witch got her punishment. She was turned into stone, and the other stones around her were positioned to keep her in check and that's how the place came to be called Mitchell's Fold.

AUGUST

Mothers and Daughters

Pendle & Penrith

Lammas and Lughnasadh pass on August 1st, as attention draws from forest to field and harvests are gathered in. Harvest loaves, corn dollies and poppets are made, by those who partake in such rural crafts.

The county of Lancashire, located in the north-west of England, is known for its rich industrial heritage; the county comprises a contrast of bustling cities alongside charming towns and scenic countryside, including the Ribble Valley and the Forest of Bowland, which hold wild folklore of witches. At the village of Pendle, below the imposing Pendle Hill, you'll find the story of the so-called "Pendle Witches". Nearby Lancaster Castle is where they would be imprisoned. The shadow of this history still looms over the county in many ways.

> *Superstition still clings to the hoary hill tops and rugged slopes and mossy water sides, along which the old forest stretched its length, and the voices of ancestral tradition are still heard to speak from the depth of its quiet hollows, and along the course of its gurgling streams.**

In both Lancashire and Pendle, you will see signs that will proudly tell you, that you are entering Witch Country… (which inspired the title of this book). There are trails, sculptures, books, documentaries, tours and events all connected to the Pendle Witch Trials, which are among the most famous witch trials in English history.

The summer of 2023 was…sweaty, muggy, close. Tempers seemed to fray at every edge of the world stage: hate, fury, anger. War still raging between Russia and Ukraine. I, in my tiny part of the world, had been invited to speak at the inaugural Witches Revival conference, organised in part because it has been over 400 years since the execution of some of Britain's most famous 'witches'. I'm excited to attend – a mini adventure away from my desk to meet witchcraft in the modern day as well as exploring the famed tales of those known as the Pendle Witches. It is a busy conference. I'm here with Lucy H. Pearce, the founder of the publishing house that publishes my books.

> *It was in the lonely forest of Pendle among the wild hills of eastern Lancashire that there lived two hostile families headed by Elizabeth Southerns, or "Old Demdike," and by Anne Chattox. The latter was a wool carder, "a very old, withered, spent and decreped creature," "her lippes ever chattering"; the former a blind beggar of four-score years, "a generall agent for the Devell in all these partes," and a "wicked fire-brand of mischiefe," who had brought*

* "Remains Historical & Literary Connected with the Palatine Counties of Lancaster and Chester", published by The Chetham Society. Vol VI (1745)

up her children and grandchildren to be witches. Both families professed supernatural practices. Both families no doubt traded on the fear they inspired. Indeed Dame Chattox was said to have sold her guarantee to do no harm in return for a fixed annual payment of "one aghen-dole of meale."

Wallace Notestein, *A History of Witchcraft in England from 1558 to 1718* (1909)

August is when, many centuries ago, the Pendle witches, whose names many of us in England know in passing – Old Chattox, Old Demdike and the Device family – were hanged, except poor Demdike, who died in the cell. And a tiny little cell it is. When you pass through the grand gate of Lancaster Castle, opposite the venue where the conference is being held, all the signs are still in place from when it was a modern HM Prison: this imposing building, towering over the town has been a place of incarceration for a very long time. A small sign for the Pendle witches sits on the right as you enter through the main entrance to the Well Tower (some, it says on signage, were held in a dungeon underneath the tower where tourists step, others elsewhere in the castle) and a modest display of the story.

Away from castle, jury, judge, huge crowd, rough rope, short drop, no grave:
Only future tourists who might grieve.

So read the lines of the poem "The Lancashire Witches" by former poet laureate, Carol Anne Duffy, which are displayed as you enter the Well Tower.

The Pendle Witches are not confined to history. Under an image of "The Wonderfull Discoverie of Witches in The County Of Lancaster" pamphlet printed in 1613, is a paragraph that says in 1998 a petition was presented to the UK Home Secretary for the Pendle witches to be pardoned. It was decided their convictions should stand. Ten years later another petition was organised in an attempt to obtain pardons for Chattox and Demdike. At the time of writing, no official pardon has been issued. Many witch trial records are bought to mind, where names are not fully recorded, no one cared quite enough to record the details properly. And it seems that no one – with the official powers to do so, cares quite enough to pardon the Pendle witches – it is a messy topic. Fascinating and infuriating, is a term used a lot over my week in Lancaster, with every new snippet of history and story I learnt.

Thomas Potts' account is all we have in terms of evidence of what happened in and around Pendle, so whilst we must be trusting he's telling a truthful account, it is through an obvious bias. His telling of the story is a second-hand account, the 'confessions' drawn out by magistrate Roger Nowel and then passed onto the clerk, Potts, to make sense of and write down.

Roger Nowell lived on the edge of Pendle Forest. The Pendle Witch trials started when he investigated a complaint made to him by the family of a pedlar, John Law, regarding his mysterious run-in with Alizon Device. It was Nowell who committed Demdike, Chattox, Anne Redferne and Alizon Device to Lancaster to be tried for maleficium: causing harm by witchcraft.

In 1633 we find that Pendle Forest was still of bad repute and that traditions of old Demdike and her rival Mother Chattox yet floated round the Malkin Tower and hid, spectre-like, in the rough and desert places of the barren waste…

Court clerk Thomas Potts' account of the proceedings, from *The Wonderfull Discoverie of Witches in the Countie of Lancaster* (1613)

In March 1612, a young, very poor woman was walking through woodland from Pendle Hill. Her name was Alizon Device. The Device family were well known in the area for offering traditional herbal remedies and good luck charms and so, of course, they were also known as witches. When she passed by a pedlar named John Law, one version of the story is that she asked him for some pins and he refused (one imagines not particularly politely). Alizon became angry and responded with a curse. We don't know her exact words, but the man took just a few steps further on his journey before falling down, seemingly bewitched. His arms went limp, his speech faltered and his face drooped (it is generally agreed in hindsight that Law suffered a stroke). Alizon was convinced that her words had directly resulted in the injury to John; she later confessed that her curse had caused the injury and begged forgiveness.

This was the beginning of the Pendle witch trials and a complex web of family feuds. Alizon Device confessed her guilt and also accused her grandmother, Elizabeth Southerns (known as Old Demdike) and members of another family, of witchcraft. She accused Anne Whittle, known as Old Chattox, of murdering men by witchcraft, including Alizon's own father. In turn Anne Whittle accused her own daughter, Anne Redferne, of making clay figures which she used to practice witchcraft.

So, Alizon and Demdike were arrested along with Chattox and Anne Redferne. Both Demdike and Chattox were in their eighties at this time, with failing sight. They both admitted to selling their souls to the devil. With three admittances of guilt, all four women – Elizabeth Southerns, Alizon Device, Anne Whittle and Anne Redferne – were taken to Lancaster Castle and held in the dungeon to await an official trial at the next Assizes, Elizabeth Southerns did not survive the cold, damp cells and died awaiting her trial.

In her 'confession', Elizabeth Southerns told of an experience she had twenty years previously. As she was coming home from begging, she encountered a spirit in the shape of a boy. He told her that if she would give him her soul, she should have anything she desired, including skills in magic. He gave his name as Tibb and became her familiar. He would reappear several times, often years apart, during Elizabeth's life, in various forms including that of a brown dog, hare and black cat.

But this was not the end of the story. The following month, in April 1612 on Good Friday, Elizabeth Device (mother of Alizon and daughter of Elizabeth Southerns AKA Demdike both currently incarcerated) gathered a meeting at Malkin Tower.* This could have been a family gathering to commiserate, pray or even to make plans to hire lawyers or seek some manner of help. We don't know why they met, but we know the outcome of this meeting which would see more souls arrested and executed for the crime of witchcraft. Malkin Tower was the home to Demdike, her daughter Elizabeth Device and her children, Alizon, James and Jennet. Those who heard of the meeting, possibly primed by the history of the magical reputation of the family and the fact that some members were already in prison, envisaged a coven of witches gathering, which, of course, in the minds of locals meant they were plotting evil. And so this Malkin Tower gathering became whispered of as one to plan the destruction of Lancaster Castle and murder of the jailer with witchcraft, in an attempt to free the incarcerated women. Word of this infamous meeting spread and shortly after, many of those who attended, or even those simply suspected of attending, were accused of crimes of witchcraft and sent to join the others in Lancaster Castle. This included the remainder of the Device family, all apart from the nine-year-old Jennet, as well as other poor folks from nearby towns and villages.

The trials took place from August 18th to 19th, 1612. The accused were denied witnesses to plead their innocence and on August 20th, 1612 ten were hanged on Gallows Hill in Lancaster, including Elizabeth Device (accused by

---

* Mentions of Malkin Tower suggest it was within the Forest of Pendle and by Pendle Hill, within the ancient Forest of Bowland. But it has long since been reclaimed by the land and probably the decay was assisted by locals still fearful of the place.

Jennet, her daughter, who would be the only surviving member of the Device family) and her children James and Alizon Device; Anne Whittle and Anne Redferne. The others that would hang that day were Jane Bulcocke and her son John Bulcocke, Alice Nutter, Katherine Hewytte and Isabell Robey, in what is considered the first mass execution for witchcraft in England. (I actually searched online for how many victims it takes in a day to be called a mass execution; it turns out no agreed number exists. I imagine no one is clawing to step forward and define such a term.)

*

Gallows Hill, an area of moorland that looks over the city, is much smaller and less known perhaps than Pendle Hill. The walk over Pendle Hill to Lancaster is one I would like to walk at some point in the future. But the final journey of our Pendle Witches was from Lancaster Castle to Gallows Hill. So I retrace their steps on a hot and muggy day; grey clouds hung low on an oppressive heat. On a break from selling books at the Witches Revival, I walk from where the accused were held in squalid conditions in the dark, damp stone cells in Lancaster Castle. Their last walk was most likely the first time they had seen sky, trees or grass in months.

I walk steadily uphill through a busy city, through the hustle and bustle of people and traffic, past grand monuments to Queen Victoria and the men of Lancaster who died in the war. I walk under long rows of rowan trees growing and leaning over long stone walls; fallen berries smear the pavement. I wonder if any were picked up when the group walked to the gallows. I pass a ghost door in the wall, its pale stone lintel still visible but bricked up. Behind these walls is the Royal Grammar School. The site of Gallows Hill is now just a green space between pavilions and picnic benches for students. The city is still just visible below. A black cat waits for me, and I say hello and stroke its back before I cross into woodland at the bottom of what is now called Williamson Park. Steep banks create a held, quiet space that cradles scents of damp mosses and ferns. I am immersed in this peaceful fern-embraced path, wandering slowly against the incline, when with unexpected speed, the trees fall away and I arrive at a playpark, children running, families chatting. Busy, noisy, laughter fills the air. A stunning building tops this park hill. It is a memorial for a woman, but not the witches. A wife of a rich man. I don't go inside; I wouldn't find my witches here.

*

From the accounts of the Pendle Witches written by Potts, the myth of the witches of Pendle took flight: a belief that great seams of witches – family groups skilled in witchcraft – terrorised the land. As a result of these wild stories of witches from the forests of Pendle, history intertwines with superstitions and folk tales.

Fear of the covens of Pendle would endure for centuries to come, and the true sad history of the witch hunts that were fuelled by squabbles, fear and superstition turned, in time, into enduring folklore. This history produced various regional protective rituals to guard oneself from the witches that were rumoured to still roam Lancashire. The stories told that great gatherings of witches assembled on Halloween in the Forest of Pendle and the infamous Malkin Tower where the Devices had lived (the actual gathering many were arrested for took place on Good Friday, but clearly Halloween makes for a better superstition). It is said that one must carry a lighted candle about the hills between eleven and twelve o'clock on Halloween night, without it being extinguished, in order to be safe from witchcraft during the coming year (witches would, of course, employ their utmost efforts to snuff the light). This was called "lating the witches."

Lammas again

The story of the Pendle Witches is a tangled web of feuds, and a cautionary tale on the catastrophic results of challenging relationships between mothers and daughters certainly seem part of that. This leads us in a twisting sort of way, to today. I am heading to meet a stone circle called Long Meg and her Daughters.

We've passed Lammas once again. Last August, it was Pendle; this August, it's Penrith in the Lake District and another strange story of mothers and daughters. Ambiguous as it may be, the stone Long Meg and her daughters and the unfortunate souls named the Pendle Witches, both became more with the power of story – a stone circle became a woman and her kin punished for imagined sins, and the Pendle folks became devilish witches, accursed creatures and ghosts that some think still haunt the hills of Pendle.

The circle of Long Meg and her Daughters can be found near Penrith on the edges of the Lake District National Park. It is one of the larger stone circles in England, after a few others such as Avebury and Stanton Drew. The Lake District, located in north-west England, is famous, as you might imagine, for its beautiful lakes, such as Windermere, Coniston Water and Ullswater, the pretty stone houses and villages that nestle at their banks and patchwork parcels of farms divided by miles of stone walls. It also holds some of the country's highest peaks, including Scafell Pike, the tallest mountain in England. The landscape has inspired many poets and writers, including William Wordsworth, Samuel Taylor Coleridge and Beatrix Potter, who found inspiration in the landscape and its wildlife.

My train arrives just after noon at Penrith Station, and I am met in the car park by David of Blue Bird Tours, who kindly agreed to help me seek out Meg and other Magics in the area before I have to catch my train home at 5pm. The stone circle of Long Meg and her Daughters dates back to the Bronze Age. The monument is elliptical in shape and consists of, depending on who you ask, up to seventy large granite stones plus the stone known as Meg, standing a little apart from the granite stones that are her daughters.

The most common story of how these stones came to be suggests that the witch Meg and her daughters (all witches), who were dancing the night away on the Sabbath, were turned to stone as a punishment by a wizard from Scotland. As at many sites, these stones are said to be uncountable; if you manage to count them twice and get the same result, perhaps the spell will be broken and the women may dance again, or alternatively, you will be lucky enough to hear Long Meg whisper words of wisdom.

MEG OF MELDON

Some connect Long Meg with Meg of Meldon, but this Meg's ghostly myth rests in Northumberland some seventy miles away, and her story seems unrelated to that of dancing standing stones. Many version of this story exist, this one is drawn from one in The Lore of the Lands *by Jennifer Westwood and Jacqueline Simpson (2005). To me it holds little connection to our Long Meg stones. But it is a fun tale in its own right, so I'm sneaking it in!*

A woman named Margaret Fenwick lived in Meldon, Northumberland, in the 17th century; she was known as Meg of Meldon. During her life, rumours were whispered of her work with witchcraft, but this came to nought when she died, for she was buried at Newminster Abbey, an honour that would not have been afforded to any witch. But if stories are to be believed, she did not rest easily… Soon after her burial, people began to see a beautiful woman gliding around the graveyard in a burial shroud or walking with phantom black dogs on Meldon Bridge, surrounded by lights and colours that flickered on the water. They claimed that these visions must surely be Meg, back from the grave. Meg was also seen sitting on a stone coffin at the abbey. The sightings continued for seven years and then appeared to cease.

Hurrah! Thought the locals. Meg has finally gone. Only she came back seven years later. The locals believed that her practice of witchcraft condemned her to wander the earth for seven years and rest for seven, forevermore.

One additional story saw a sceptic decide to dress in white and sit on Meldon Bridge to scare passersby, having heard this was a favoured occupation of Meg's. But after making himself comfortable, who should appear but the ghost of Meg herself, who sat gently beside him and said, "You've come to fley [frighten] and I've come to fley, let's baith fley together" but the sceptic was already off running…

Long Meg is a nickname for tall women, so it's more likely to my mind, to be a nickname rather than a specific person called Meg. In looking back on these stories, I realise how many nicknames are involved; another similarity between these two cases of witches both real and mythic: Anne Whittle was Chattox, Elizabeth Southerns was Demdike, Elizabeth Device was Squinting Lizzie and in Penrith we meet Long Meg. What these nicknames meant is up for debate, some theories include that Chattox may have been a term for one who chatters or mutters and Demdike a term for demon and dams/dykes/ditches being places between realms, or more derogatorily, muddy, grimy places. This was a time when folks were rarely kind to witches, so I find it hard to believe they were names used fondly.

We arrive and David parks up. I take my time walking the circle, through long damp grass and around the granite daughter stones nestled softly amongst plants, clasped by foxgloves. Heavy clouds hang around us, threatening rain, but we have a dry moment. Long Meg herself stands away from the south-western edge of the circle. She is almost twelve feet tall – a red sandstone pillar with rock art, including grooves, spirals and rings, carved into her side. I also spotted some terribly neatly carved names, presumably graffiti, which was brave as another legend suggests that if this stone is ever broken, it will run with blood. Also, trying to move the stones would raise a great storm – a good warning to eras such as the Victorian, when standing stones were sometimes pinched for private collections. Today, all the stones are moist and gritty to the touch, they have been doused with heavy rains, but it is very 'four seasons in one day' weather and we are lucky that the heaviest rain falls when we are in the van and when we head to walk around the circles, we get treated to some sunshine and dramatic dark clouds over mountains.

> *"Up and down the country, whether they have been set up by men, isolated by weathering or by melting ice, conspicuous stones are commonly identified with human beings. Most of our Bronze Age circles and menhirs have been thought by the country people living round them to be men or women turned to stone. The names often help to express this identification and its implied sense of kinship; Long Meg and her Daughters, the Nine Maidens, the Bridestone and the Merry Maidens. It is right that they should most often be seen as women, for somewhere in the mind of everyone is an awareness of woman as earth, as rock, as matrix. In all these legends human beings have seen themselves melting back into rock, in their imaginations must have pictured the body, limbs and hair melting into smoke and solidifying into these blocks of sandstone, limestone and granite."*
>
> **Jacquetta Hawkes, *A Land* (1951)**

Romantics

The Romantic poets William Wordsworth and Samuel Taylor Coleridge, along with several other poets and writers, including William's sister Dorothy Wordsworth, were deeply passionate about the Lake District. They became known as the "Lake Poets." Their work inspired Percy Bysshe Shelley and John Keats, both of whom stayed there for short periods. In the late eighteenth and early nineteenth centuries, the lakes served as a catalyst for creativity, with the vast landscapes, tranquil lakes and rugged mountains providing inspiration. Artistic and literary movements such as the Picturesque and Romanticism mark something of a turning point in appreciating the wild as a place for contemplation and retreat, creatively seeking a certain myth and magic within the wilds and can be linked to a renewed interest in nature and wild spaces as an escape from urban life and industrialisation.

A weight of Awe not easy to be borne
Fell suddenly upon my spirit, cast
From the dread bosom of the unknown past,
When first I saw that family forlorn;
Speak Thou, whose massy strength and stature scorn
The power of years – pre-eminent and placed
Apart, to overlook the circle vast.
Speak Giant-mother! tell it to the Morn,
While she dispels the cumbrous shades of night;
Let the Moon hear, emerging from a cloud,
At whose behest uprose on British ground
That Sisterhood in hieroglyphic round
Forth-shadowing, some have deemed the infinite
The inviolable God that tames the proud.

William Wordsworth "The Monument" or "The monument commonly called Long Meg and her daughters, near the River Eden" (1822)

Coffin roads

In my excitement at seeing the stones, I completely forgot to ask David about the coffin roads, also known as corpse roads, burial roads and lych ways of this area. I know from preparatory research that until about 1700s, outlying communities carried their dead along one such coffin road to Shap's burial ground, which is close to Long Meg. And Shap is the source of the granite that made her daughters. Coffin roads, just as they sound, are paths used to carry coffins for burial in consecrated ground. It, of course, was not the fate of any accused witches to be given such honours. But it was that idea of people going to what was known as their *Mother Church* that created a tiny spark of connection in my mind, another use of the word mother in this chapter of mothers and daughters. In days gone by, remote communities often had nowhere nearby to put their dead. Only the churches held burial rights, but they could be miles away from the smaller villages. Corpse roads connected the graveyards to the small communities, granting access to consecrated ground. As you can imagine, they've become associated with tales of hauntings, wraiths and ghosts. But through the mountain lands of the Lake Districts, people may well have sought comfort in the imagery of a Mother Church, mothers and of finding one's way home.

*

Christianity no doubt contributed to the notion of such standing stones once being sinners, transfixed by a curse or divine judgement. The petrifaction of Long Meg and her Daughters is similar to stories countrywide – the motif of revellers turned to stone for sabbath-breaking or some other misdemeanours is ancient. But I imagine Christian religions may have fostered such stories to encourage leaving older ways behind.

It's reasonable to assume this circle, as so many stone circles are, was built to be associated with seasonal rituals. A celebration of the landscape and astronomical alignments that signpost seasonal rhythms. At winter solstice, if you stand in the centre of the circle, the sun sets behind Long Meg.

Long Meg is still able to celebrate the solstices, it seems seasonal acquaintance is built into monuments and this rhythm pulses through us too. Or at least it did once. Prehistoric societies built monuments across Britain and Ireland to align with yearly celestial events. The most famous, Stonehenge, Newgrange and Maeshowe, all aligned with the sunrise and sunset of solstices at midsummer and midwinter; these monuments are an intertwining of skyscapes and landscapes, entanglements of places and natural features – of stone, light and earth, as well as the movements of the sun and moon. The modern world is a buffer to any major effects of changing seasons on our day-to-day lives, but monuments such as this offer a whisper of a time when people's lives were built around them, a tempo of seasonal beats and rhythms, land and the sky.

From Long Meg who sits between the north Pennines and the Lake District National Park, we travel deeper into the National Park to Castlerigg, perhaps a more well-known stone circle and one with the most amazing views I think, of any stone circle in the country, certainly of the ones I have seen. Standing in the circle and taking in the 360 degree views, I can see some of Cumbria's highest peaks, Blencathra and Skiddaw veiled behind mists that soften the colours into soft greys and blues. The views of such peaks were so impressive that Coleridge once said, "the mountains stand one behind the other, in orderly array as if evoked by and attentive to the assembly of white-vested wizards." More wizards! We have time to see a few more sites so David takes me to Mayburgh henge, the earthworks known as King Arthur's Round Table (see, I told you he was everywhere). And finishing with the medieval Brougham (pronounced broom) Castle, a medieval fortress located in the Eden Valley, near Penrith. Surrounded by sheep grazing in fields and the odd wild swath of ragwort rippling in bouquets of yellow. I spot a few faint witch marks in steepled doorways.

While we do not use coffin roads for their original purposes anymore. They are precious because they are kind of ancient monuments of their own, humble and mundane, but equally special as the stone circles, where we can only guess at the activities that took place. They are both artefacts we have to accept we will never know fully in present day. Though all these places can be offered some respect.

I thank David and catch my train in the afternoon, making my way home, my last train journey for this year's travels of *Witch Country*. But perhaps there's time yet for one last wander…

GATHER IN

One Last Wander at the Equinox

Witchcraft was hung, in History
But History and I
Find all the Witchcraft that we need
Around us, every Day.

Emily Dickinson (1830-1886)

Autumn seems to have been impatient to descend this year. Already in August, the maples outside our house were blushed with red. Now, in September, the birches in the garden are dropping their leaves when the winds gust in, carrying spots of rain and low clouds. Within the sparser branches of birch trees now can be seen, the nest-like clusters of twigs called *witches' knots,* appearing, so they say, after witches have flown over the trees (but that are in fact the work of a fungus which prompts this growth). The harvest full moon shone beautifully bright a few nights ago; now, it is just beginning to wane, as is the year.

It is September again and it is time to close out our book and journey together. The warmth of late summer/early autumn is a shining embered time to finish a journey that has had its fair share of darkness, and an appealing time to walk in the last of the year's warmth. I'm on that hunt for light at golden hour right now; I'm headed for the edges of the valley which runs through my Wiltshire home down to Bath. It is both very beautiful and a little bit mundane: this is the route by which I travel by bus many mornings to head into Bath. But I intend to find a place to sit for the sunset close to the day, the tideline of the autumnal equinox. As I said this time last year, I adore autumn, so it is exciting to be passing once more into this time. The darker half of the year lies ahead. But here September, with the earth still warm and the harvest still being gathered in, feels like a cosy dark of glowing sparks, of burnished gold and lustrous copper hues. There is time yet to journey through the glow of autumnal leaves and Halloween pumpkins before the crisp whites and deep dark blues of cold winter nights descend.

So, it's time for one last wander, and I can take some time to reflect on how far I've travelled.

In each culture, certain rituals and stories are unique (and tied together with common threads: fear of loss, for example), so when I explore the folklore of a place, I look to the witches. Those who hold a unique quality to exist in realms of history, folklore, superstition, fiction and the material world all at once.

Sarah Robinson, *The Witch and the Wildwood* (2024)

I walk along a busy road away from my house – a pavement that is scattered with leaves, twigs and the odd white flash of the velvety pale interiors of spiked conker cases. I'll start with myself. What have I learned about myself on this quest of seeking? That I am capable of making journeys and creating my own little adventures to seek witch trails, trees and lost graves. That's reassuring, as when I set out, for the last few years at least, I had done precious little of either. Have I changed? What has my research reflected? I've learnt that my walking was equally important to this journey as all the writing and research. Walking the words and the stories, walking with the weight of all this history. I have gone deeper into what it means to write of witches and follow their stories. I enjoy an idea that comes to my mind that I am doing my part to craft the greatest fear of many a puritan or witchfinder of the Middle Ages and early modern era; I'm helping witches rise again. What a delicious thought. Are they becoming now the revenant, the reminder, the rebellion of those accused and tortured? I feel honoured to be doing my own tiny part of preserving or sharing stories of women good and bad (because they had elements of both, as we all do, Morgen le Fay taught us that in May). We can't raise their bodies, of course; we can't even find their remains for the most part. To give them any kind of thoughtful burial. So, stories will have to do.

Thousands have died under the weight of fear and superstition of witches; their stories have been carried onwards within those same superstitions, alongside folktales, magic, rituals and a few precious texts. Many communities that created feted celebrations and eerie rituals, creating portals into other realms to understand the natural world in new ways, have been lost and disbanded. To love the natural world, to love rural folklore that was once embedded within it, is to feel its losses. Just as to care for nature is to care for what suffers and is damaged through carelessness. To cherish the earth and its stories on our tongues will always hold a taste of wonder laced with grief. Both cheering carols and mournful keening – but all the more reason to cherish what is here, to celebrate ways of being and doing. To act with respect and gratitude, to protect what you love, and to find your own powers to create change, enjoying the freedom and privilege to step into them.

*

During the journey of creating this book and following these stories, I attended my first wassail and visited many places that were always well within my reach, for the first time, as well as revisiting places I've been many times, delighting at newfound magic within familiar spaces. I have also been led astray by witch hares (if you'll forgive me the wild romanticisation of getting lost and engrumpened in a muddy field). And for the first time I've read the names of the accused witches of Wales and stood beside a robbed intertidal grave and was honoured to be present for the first national day of remembrance for Scotland's accused witches and a historical milestone. In writing this book, I have discovered so much and I am privileged I could bring you along with me for the journey. I don't think I could have done it without you, certainly not without the witches, that's for sure.

I turn off a busy roundabout and onto a narrower road flanked by open fields. I know there are no particular standing stones or mythical trees nearby. But just as at the beginning of this story when I also started out from home, there is more than enough magic to go around in the rowan, ash and birch, swooping in the wings and claws of crows. I see white clouds softly scribbled across the blue sky in the evening light, alongside plane trails. And I watch a herd of dark brown cows moo and gently stampede over to the field edge for their supper. The sun is shining low in the sky, there is a nip growing in the air, and I'm wearing my favourite navy turtleneck jumper; autumn has definitely arrived.

It can be a certain bewitchment that makes a year go by so fast. If you don't stop and pause whenever you can, you may get whisked away through the seasons at quite a terrifying pace. There were many more mini journeys I took that didn't make the book: the Devil's Cauldron, Whitelady waterfall, ancient oaks, forest bathing events and many seasonal chance findings of magic in the landscape. In ways big and small, mundane and magnificent, I have found a multitude of magical moments and places. As the spiralling wheel of the year has turned, I have spiralled out to the far edges of the land and spiralled back home, ending, for now, where I started. At the beginning of this book, I walked south to walk around a park, now I'm heading west to see the sun set.

I reach the viewpoint of two benches placed side by side looking over the valley. I arrive with a few minutes to spare until the sun starts setting in earnest. A woman sits on one bench at almost the same time that I arrive and I sit on the other. She has a glass of wine in her hand. *Now that is a brilliant idea,* I say. "I've got a fish pie in the oven" she says, "I just popped out to see if I could spot any bats." She tells me that the nearby caves of Box Hill Woods hold one of the largest colonies of horseshoe bats in the country, but that there had not been many sightings of late. I replied that I had heard similar things about insects this year. There are alarmingly reduced numbers of many flying creatures, this year it seems. But we sit in companionable silence to watch the beauty of the moment all the same. A white glow rises at the edges of the circling horizon, milky-edged and soft evening blue above us.

Somewhere behind me the sound of crow caws seems to bristle and grow. I can smell grass, woodsmoke and the sweet tang of silage in the chilling air. The hum and grumble of traffic. Over the valley a plume of smoke rises from a fire. The dimming light turns the whisps of cloud dark grey, like smears of charcoal on canvas alongside silhouetted birds. The sky drops through softer colours of peach and yellow, and then a splash of orange before the halo of colour sinks into deep dark blues.

The last light of the equinox day dips, and the sun disappears behind the far hills. The woman stands and wishes me a good evening, heading back to a nearby house for her supper.

I think about how the many places I have been, have each affected and coloured my stories and my writing: the weight of Lilias' ordeal in Scotland; the whimsy of folk superstitions in Shropshire admiring ponds with relative contentment that I wouldn't be dragged under, but also that I shouldn't mess about at water's edge; the ancient echoing haunt of Wookey Hole. The figure of the witch has walked beside me through it all, conjuring a sense of place.

We've seen how the folk traditions, legends and superstitions of Britain and Europe are inscribed on its landscapes, trees and wildflowers. They lie, still waiting to be read by those who want to unlock the stories shaped by how our ancestors thought about the places where they lived, how they valued them and what they believed – a legacy left to us. These stories are not just entertainment for an evening by the fireside (though that is a wonderful role they can play) but also ways of exploring profound questions, allowing speculation and discussion about life, death, love, fear and anger, the land we live on and its multifaceted history. And these stories found their way so deep into minds, hearts and into the landscape itself and its place names, it is comforting to me that they endure many centuries after they were first told and that they can be remembered and reignited.

Enchanting

A few days ago, I sat down at my desk and saw a scrawled Post-It note message which said, "In enchantment, we may find new wealth in our lives and in the world around us." I have no idea if that is from something I've read or just a reflection I've had, I can find no source for it. The Post-It is stained with a coffee cup ring, so it could have been here some time. I am always losing my coasters and using Post-Its instead. But I wholeheartedly agree with the sentiment. Because rolled up within enchantment, I think, is a wealth of gratitude, invitation and possibility. Invitation to connect and remember that all things pass, which in turn can foster both gratitude and a sense of possibility. I think the practice of reminding ourselves of what is possible can be comforting and exciting.

Is a land more enchanting when you know its stories? Of fairy trees and tree witches, storm raisers and crystal balls in caves? In knowing the stories of a place, we may find some of its magic; maybe we learn the history of an area and see things a little differently. To embrace wonder, place and community that can be nurtured and nourished by meaning, myths and folklore and traditional skills that can read the wings of the wild things. And in journeys through roots and wild edges, we can bring enchantment home, wherever we may dwell.

Each landscape I have journeyed through offered its own magic quite apart from the stories of witches and fairies that adorned it. Parks, moor, tors, bogs, estuary, ocean, river, waterfalls, wishing trees, caves, chalk, stone circles, tide lines, marshes, mountains and hills, valleys, beaches, church boundaries and sacred ground, forests, fields and hedgerows. And what does the witch add to these already beautiful spaces? She is an integral part of the spirit of place. We have explored just a fraction of the land where witches roam in countless forms. I am heartened that the witch continues to both inhabit and offer spaces where the unknown and the *other* can emerge, she provides an invitation to adventure and discovery, a place to play, to think, to breathe deep and a place that offers infinite story.

Rewilding wonder

To rewild is to return a land to how it may once have been. Maybe we can apply this to societies as well, a sprinkle of rewilding for people and stories. We live in a world of more. More cars, more roads, more houses, more people; there is not so much room in there for more trees (although many people are making noble efforts), more plants, more wild. What can I do? Simply this: to share stories, to remember that nature is all around us, we can connect to it even if we are far from wild spaces. Perhaps that is our doorway back to enchantment, towards rebuilding our connections to nature

Myths and folk tales knit us into the rhythms of the seasons, helping us embrace life's necessary cycles. I needed help and still do, on days I lack a sense of awe and connection. Myths, fairy tales, folk tales, whatever we call them, are old and powerful, from those kindled around sacred fires to those gathered and forged in ink. We were born to seek narrative and see story, our legacy as hunters and gatherers, our wild minds shaped by reading of cloud, deer-trod, paw print and branch tip. We need story; we need myth and magic to nourish us, to feed us inspiration, courage and hope and to feed our souls and the parts of us that hunger for wonder, wildness and magic. Folk tales are, perhaps, a spell of their own, shapeshifting, word-magic, antlered messengers from the wilds and ancient magic echoes. This is a winding, roundabout way of looking at things, unfurling inexplicably in the half-light by sharing stories of fairies, witches, hauntings and transformation in forest, glade and grove. But what else can we do with what we have left? But to wander the land and respect its beauty, retell the tales, rewild ourselves and nurture our sense of wonder?

Spirit of place

The spirit of a place is a wondrous and elusive thing, you might even call it magic. There are places that captivate us, possess us and linger in our memories. Or perhaps it's the other way around – as people live and dream and die, they imprint their spirit and energy onto their surroundings, infusing walls and trees with thoughts and ideas. For a fleeting moment, laying a hand upon an ancient tree trunk, running fingertips over a mark carved in stone or looping a ribbon of wishes through your fingers allows you to cross into an otherworld, another century, another life. Lost hopes, ideas, revelries and ferocities become momentarily our own. And then, we lift our heads and blink at the sun. We are once more ourselves, but not quite the same…

Stories, folklore and superstitions all do their part to create and contribute to 'spirit of place' and the unique energy and feeling that can be experienced by many who hold places in reverence. Cherished ideas are connected in folk tales, festivals and beliefs as much as physical elements such as stones, boundaries and pathways. In some cultures, this nebulous sense felt in a place may be described as particular spirit bodies in an attempt to capture something of what one may sense in a special and sacred space. The ancient Romans called it the *Genius Loci,* a protective, guardian spirit, sometimes embodied by a particular deity. So, you have both the spirit of place – its energy, feeling, atmosphere and spirits of a place – figures and guardians, many of whom we have met in this book – fairy folk, water witches, goddesses, guides, watchers – protecting places from trespassers, with varying levels of ferocity or wisdom. One might connect this to ideas of animism and our innate need to create and read symbols and patterns, finding sparks of divinity, spirituality and connection in all corners of our lands. So many stories and myths are profoundly rooted in a place – how places came to be named or how a feature of the landscape came to be there. When we know a place's stories – it becomes more personal to us and more real. We hold affection for places that can hold and nurture our imagination, we feel a personal sense of belonging: we care for and protect that which we belong to.

Spirit of place can include both the tangible and intangible elements of an area; together, they can give meaning and mystery to the place. Allowing me to seek witches in ancient barns and graves, as well as woods and moorlands. When we peer under the surface of the commonplaces of contemporary life, we can discover a passion for a wild place and seek to reclaim its hallowed nature. In revisiting stories, we can also create a way of looking, of rediscovering what we do still have and what we may yet find. Perhaps we listen out for ghosts to give a voice to a land that cannot speak for itself. And to remember the people that became stories, and the stories that settled on ancient places. Long after trees are felled and stones toppled, what remains is story.

We might consider those who share stories of a place as custodians of the landscape's memory and its ancient customs. Each story helps us understand the landscape and its traditions. Stories can help us in finding our roots and anchors in a place, wherever we might happen to live. Stories can be our anchors. The stories of a place change over time, as do the people that live there. This body of lore is continuously reconstructing itself, just as the world around us is in a constant process of transformation. Places and their stories are in a continuous process of becoming. And we too, when we live in a place, become a small part of its story as well. We bring new possibilities to it, forging – if we are prepared to countenance the possibility of such enchantments – unique relationships with it and with the plant and animal life around us. And so, familiarity with the old stories of a place is an integral part of coming to truly know a place. We become portals of the history (both material and mythic) of human life in it and ongoing natural and cultural history, we'll go on to make our own stories and our own ways of experiencing places. Humans have always been myth-makers; in that myth-making, we may find power and the spirits and stories we want to live by.

Stories and spirits decorate the land, documenting our attempts over millennia to try and explain it. Humans have always found webs of enchantment and stories hanging in the trees and the many stories of the witch are just part of that library of wonders held within the land. We can all find magical stories, both old and new, of the witch and magic in Britain (and beyond) every day. Perhaps we can do our own part to preserve or revive local myths for hedgerows, meadows, little corners of green and great wild spaces – gently rekindling our connection with nature and our own sense of the special and the sacred. Perhaps this may launch us into the action of caring and stewarding this land that we do not own; it is here for us to walk upon and take joy in for just our short lifetime and then we return to it, leaving a few tales of our own behind us, to live on after us.

We can see nature in new ways and walk the old ways all at the same time – new ways and old ways, magical and mundane ways. Stories and names that stay with us, natural wonders we cherish, that we carry onwards, those we can create and connect to – holding as precious cargo to share out in segments like an orange eaten around a fire on a dark night.

All of our stories are a culmination of everything and everyone who has gone before us – all gathered in, a golden harvest. We are a creation of all that comes before us. We add to that with every day and everything we create and we have the power to create what comes next – a new day, taking us somewhere new.

To be a writer is to pass on what you know. And so I pass on what I have discovered from myth, witches and words. To feel as best I can, the spirit of place and convey it to you. And embrace my own ability, simply to walk somewhere and then tell you about it.

I have been to places that were lost lands and been lost myself and found new corners I never knew existed. I've walked to relics of history. I've walked with old and wild wisdom. I've walked to meet with enchantment, and I've done my best to listen. I've also sworn at crappy weather, had a little cry, cursed my expensive hiking trousers that are always just a little too tight around my belly, been frightened by tree shadows, eaten chips and ordered caramel coffees to console myself, had blisters and missed trains. So, you know, it's not all magical romantic whimsy around here, but it has been damn good fun.

Lights sparkle on in homes through the valley, leading to a warm glow of the city and I think I'll wait just a little longer for the first stars to appear. And tomorrow, it starts again: the sun will rise, and with it the potential of a fresh start and new adventures, with the delightful prospect that a hint of magic may be waiting somewhere just past the edges of the horizon.

Myths and lore allow us to walk through both enchantment and history for accused witches and just maybe for these shadowy souls to rest and for their stories to fly. I am grateful for the adventures, big and small, that have taken me around the British Isles in search of all things wonderful and witchy. This land is magic, I think as I ready myself to head for home. How lucky we are to walk upon it, even if it is just for a short spell.

ACKNOWLEDGEMENTS

A huge part of the magic in these journeys, to rival that of the witches themselves – was the kindness and generosity of time and knowledge of many people who helped me on my research journey.

A huge thank you to:

- Chris Binding, Chris Goodchild and the marvellously magical Sarah Mooney of Wookey Hole Caves.
- Shaun Cooper and the Sussex Dialect & Folklore Group for help with the Sussex phenomenon of hag-tracks.
- The wonderfully warm and welcoming Essex Writing Group at the Red Lion, Manningtree held by Lelia Ferro.
- David from Bluebird Tours for helping me meet Meg and see the beauty of Cumbria in both sunshine and rain.
- Creative Coven Scotland and the charity Remembering the Accused Witches of Scotland who welcomed me at Dunfermline for the first National Day of Remembrance for Scotland's witches.
- To the awesome and inspiring writers Miriam Darlington, Patrick Barkham and Noreen Masud, who shared their wisdom with such generosity at the Arvon Writing Week at The Hurst. To all the wonderful students who learned alongside me and to the Arvon Charity, who helped get me there.
- To listeners, patrons and supporters of my 'Witch Country' podcast documenting the journeys of this book.
- The fabulous team of Womancraft Publishing that is Lucy, Patrick and Leigh. It is an honour and a joy to work with you!
- To my magical friends Trish and Katie for allowing me to steer our adventures to my own magical designs.
- As always, to my beloved Dan for ferrying me around in the car to pootle about in search of witches.

SELECTED BIBLIOGRAPHY

I have grouped these books as best I can, but please bear in mind that many of the UK site guides and folklore books contain both.

Folklore of the British Isles

Counties

The Stone Circles of Cumbria – John Waterhouse

Ghosts and Witches of the Cotswolds – John Attwood Brooks

Norfolk Life – Lilias Rider Haggard

Wiltshire Folklore – Kathleen Wiltshire

The Spirit of the Downs: Witchcraft and Magic in Sussex – Martin Duffy

Folk-lore & Legend of the Surrey Hills and of the Sussex Downs Forests – Edward Lovett

The Folklore of Sussex – Jacqueline Simpson

Shropshire Folk-Lore: A Sheaf of Gleanings – Georgina Jackson & Charlotte Burne

Shropshire Folklore: Ghosts and Witchcraft – Jean Hughes and Christina Elliot

Myths, Scenes & Worthies of Somerset – Mrs E. Boger

Somerset Folklore – Ruth L. Tongue

Magical Animals: Folklore and Legends from a Yorkshire Wisewoman – Claire Nahmad

Silent as the Trees: Devonshire Witchcraft, Folklore & Magic – Gemma Gary

Devonshire Characters and Strange Events – Sabine Baring-Gould

Walking the Stories & Legends of Dartmoor: A Guide to 20 Walks Retracing the Stories and Legends of Dartmoor – Michael Bennie

Witchcraft and Folklore of Dartmoor – Ruth St. Leger-Gordon

The Windy Post and Other Dartmoor Poems – V. Phillips

Popular Romances of the West of England or, The Drolls, Traditions and Superstitions of Old Cornwall – Robert Hunt

Wales

Folk-lore and Folk-stories of Wales – Marie Trevelyan

The Vale of Glamorgan: Scenes and Tales Among the Welsh – Charles Redwood

British Goblins: Welsh Folklore, Fairy Mythology, Legends and Traditions – Wirt Sikes

Mysterious Wales – Chris Barber

The Mabinogion – Lady Charlotte Guest

Folk-lore of West and mid-Wales – Jonathan Ceredig Davies

Welsh Fairy Tales – William Elliot Griffis

Folk-lore and folk stories of Wales – Marie Trevelyan

Witchcraft and Magic in Wales – Richard Suggett

Ireland

The Irish Fairy Book by Various

Ancient Legends, Mystic Charms and Superstitions of Ireland – Lady Wilde

The Poem-Book of the Gael – Eleanor Hull

Fairy Legends and Traditions of the South of Ireland – Thomas Crofton Croker

Brittany

Le Foyer Breton (The Breton Fireside) – Émile Souvestre

British Isles

Folklore and literature of the British Isles – Florence E Baer

Myths and Legends of the British Isles – Richard Barber

England

Folk-lore and Legends: English – Charles John Tibbits

More English Fairy Tales – Joseph Jacobs

Round About and Long ago: Tales from the English Counties – Eileen Colwell

The Book of English Folk Tales – Sybil Marshall

British Folk Tales and Legends: a sampler – Katharine Briggs

A Dictionary of British folk-tales in the English language – Katharine Briggs

English Fairy and Other Folk Tales – Edwin Sidney Hartland

Folklore of the British Isles – Eleanor Hull

The Lore of the Land – Jennifer Westwood and Jacqueline Simpson

Arthurian Mythology

Le Morte D'Arthur – Thomas Malory

De Instructione Principis – Gerald of Wales

Otia Imperialia – Gervase of Tilbury

Studies in the Fairy Mythology of Arthurian Romance – Lucy Allen Paton

Book of Taliesin

Vita Merlini – Geoffrey of Monmouth

Lancelot and the Ring – Dr Lucy Allen Patton

Sir Lancelot of the Lake – Dr Lucy Allen Patton

Folklore, Fairy Tale and Mythology: General

Grimms' Fairy Tales

Goblins and Ghosties: stories of darkness from around the world – Maggie Pearson

Midsummer Magic: A Garland of Stories, Charms and Recipes – Ellin Greene

De Temporum Ratione – Venerable Bede

Complete Folk Tales – Alan Garner

Encyclopaedia of Superstitions – Edwin Radford

Lore of the Land – Dr Jacqueline Westwood and Jennifer Simpson

The Fairy-Faith in Celtic Countrie – W.Y. Evans-Wentz

Fairy Mythology – Thomas Keightley

The Queer, the Quaint and the Quizzical: A Cabinet for the Curious – Frank H. Stauffer

Stranger than Fiction, being tales from the byways of ghosts and folk-lore – Mary L. Lewes

The Queer Side of Things – Mary L. Lewes

Complete Folk Tales – Alan Garner

Every Woman's Encyclopaedia Vol IV

European Mythology – Jacqueline Simpson

Dictionary of Folklore Mythology and Legend – Maria Leach

The English and Scottish Popular Ballads – Francis James Child

Metamorphoses – Ovid

A Land – Jacquetta Hawkes

"Poly-Olbion" – Michael Drayton

UK Site Guides

Magical Britain: 650 Enchanted and Mystical Sites – Rob Wildwood

The Secret Country: an interpretation of the folklore of ancient sites in the British Isles – Janet Bord and Colin Bord

Atlas of Magical Britain – Janet Bord

A Guide to Occult Britain: the quest for magic in pagan Britain – John Wilcock

A Land – Jacquetta Hawkes

History in Earth and Stone: Prehistoric and Roman Monuments in England and Wales – Jacquetta Hawkes

Legend Land VOL.3+4 – G. Basil Barham, commissioned by Great Western Railway

English Medieval Graffiti – Violet Pritchard

Nature

Where the Forest Murmurs: Nature essays – Fiona Macleod

Long, Long Life of Trees – Fiona Stafford

An Account of The Foxglove and Some of Its Medical Uses –William Withering

The Forest in Folklore and Mythology – Alexander Porteous

The Old Ways – Robert Macfarlane

The Wild Place – Robert Macfarlane

Plant Lore, Legends and Lyrics – Richard Folkard

The Stories of the Trees – Mrs Dyson

Witchcraft

Witch: A History of Fear, from Ancient Times to the Present – Ronald Hutton

A Mirror of Witchcraft – Christina Hole

The Rebirth of Witchcraft – Doreen Valiente

Witch's Garden: Plants in Folklore, Magic and Traditional Medicine – Sandra Lawrence

The Witch and the Wildwood – Sarah Robinson

Kitchen Witch: Food, Folklore and Fairy Tale – Sarah Robinson

The Jackdaw and the Witch – Sybil Leek

Diary of a Witch – Sybil Leek

The Ash Tree – M. R James

Witch Trials

Witchfinders: A Seventeenth-Century English Tragedy – Malcolm Gaskill

Select Cases of Conscience towards Witches and Witchcraft – John Gaule

Daemonologie – King James

The Discovery of Witches – Matthew Hopkins

Godly Zeal and Furious Rage: The Witch in Early Modern Europe – Geoffrey Quaife

Witch Hunt: the persecution of witches in England – Andrew Pickering

Witchcraft: A History in Thirteen Trials – Marion Gibson

Saducismus Triumphatus – Joseph Glanvill

A Guide to Grand-Jury Men, Divided into Two Bookes – Richard Bernard

A History of Witchcraft in England from 1558 to 1718 – Wallace Notestein

Regional Witchcraft

Witches of Dorset – Olive Knott

Witches Of Wessex – Olive Knott

Essex Witches – Peter Brown

A Source Book of Scottish Witchcraft – Christina Larner

A true and exact relation of the severall informations, examinations and confessions of the late witches, arraigned and executed in the county of Essex – Charles Clarke

Witchfinders: a seventeenth-century English tragedy – Malcolm Gaskill

Ashes and Stones: A Scottish Journey in Search of Witches and Witness – Allyson Shaw

The Visions of Isobel Gowdie: Magic, Witchcraft and Dark Shamanism in Seventeenth Century Scotland – Emma Wilby

Witchcraft and Hysteria in Elizabethan London – Michael MacDonald

Annals of Dunfermline and Vicinity – Ebeneser Henderson

Confession of Lilias Adie in a collection of rare and curious tracts on witchcraft and the second sight, with an original essay on witchcraft – David Webster

The Darker Superstitions of Scotland – John Graham Dalyell

Websites

Mysteriousbritain.co.uk

Britishfolklore.com

Folklorethursday.com

Survey of Scottish Witchcraft Database – witches.shca.ed.ac.uk

Pamphlets, Articles, Papers

"The tryal, condemnation and execution of three witches; viz. Temperance Floyd, Mary Floyd, & Susanna Edwards." (1682)

"A Most Certain, Strange and True Discovery of a Witch: Being taken by some of the Parliament forces, as she was standing on a small planck-board and sayling on it over the river of Newbury: together with the strange and true manner of her death, with the propheticall words and speeches she used at the same time."

"West Country Magic", Elizabeth Goudge, *The Horn Book* magazine (1947)

"A relation of the diabolical practices of above twenty wizards and witches of the sheriffdom of Renfrew in the kingdom of Scotland, contain'd in their tryalls, examinations and confessions and for which several of them have been executed this present year" (1697)

Notes and Queries: A Medium of Inter-Communication for Literary Men, Artists, *Antiquaries, Genealogists, Etc.* Issue 61 (1850)

"The Wonderfull Discoverie of Witches in the Countie of Lancaster"
– Thomas Potts (1613)

"Folk-lore of the Wye Valley", Margaret Eyre. Folk-lore
– *A Quarterly Review.* Volume 16, (1905)

"A True and Exact Relation of the severall Informations, Examinations and Confessions of the late Witches, arraigned and executed in the County of Essex" (1645)

ABOUT THE AUTHOR

Sarah Robinson is a yoga teacher and author. She lives on the green edges of Wiltshire, just a few miles from Bath, UK. With a background in science, she holds an MSc in Psychology & Neuroscience and has studied at the universities of Bath, Exeter, and Harvard. Her work weaves together a love of myth, magic, and story, exploring how they can guide, ground, and inspire.

Find Sarah online:

Website: sentiayoga.com
Instagram: @Yogaforwitches

ABOUT WOMANCRAFT

Womancraft Publishing was founded on the revolutionary vision that women and words can change the world. We act as midwife to transformational women's words that have the power to challenge, inspire, heal and speak to the silenced aspects of ourselves.

We believe that:

- ☾ books are a fabulous way of transmitting powerful transformation,
- ☾ values should be juicy actions, lived out,
- ☾ ethical business is a key way to contribute to conscious change.

At the heart of our Womancraft philosophy is fairness and integrity. Creatives and women have always been underpaid. Not on our watch! We split royalties 50:50 with our authors. We work on a full circle model of giving and receiving: reaching backwards, supporting TreeSisters' reforestation projects, and forwards via Worldreader, providing books at no cost to education projects for girls and women.

We are proud that Womancraft is walking its talk and engaging so many women each year via our books and online. Join the revolution! Sign up to the mailing list at womancraftpublishing.com and find us on social media for exclusive offers:

womancraftpublishing

womancraftbooks

womancraft_publishing

Signed copies of all titles available from shop.womancraftpublishing.com

ABOUT THE ARTIST

Sarah took an Honours Degree in Education in 1975, with art and craft as the main subjects, and followed the craft avenue professionally after college. She set up a craft business in 1976, and for over ten years she was a handloom weaver in a craft centre in Devon. She moved to her own textile gallery in 1988 and produced a wide range of items in printed fabrics, painted silks, batik, embroidery and patchwork. The gallery also sold the work of 150 craftspeople and held exhibitions. From 1982 to 1990 Sarah was a council member of the Devon Guild of Craftsmen, and also served on various Craft Committees, and the local Chamber of Commerce. She moved to West Penwith in 1996 and started painting full time.

"My painting expresses my love of the land, especially south-west Cornwall, and is a connection with the beauty and power of the landscape. The paintings are realistic and representational, but not in a solely photographic way; they are hyper-real, or more than real. I paint with heightened and intensified detail to give the paintings a strong impact. I look for the symmetries and similarities of patterns, the inherent fractals of growth and movement, and emphasise these to try to show the magic or earth energy, the resonance, of a place, a stone, a tree.

"I love the qualities of oil paint, which enable me to build up complex layers of colour, combining classic technical methods of "thin to fat and dark to light" with Pre Raphaelite techniques of layers of translucent glazes on a brilliant white ground. As the paintings are left to dry for a week or so between stages in different areas, I have several in progress at a time, and they can take up to nine months. They are then left for six months or more before varnishing. My studio is perfect, as it is white and light, with velux roof windows and a large window facing west with a view out to the sea and a glimpse of the Isles of Scilly."

KITCHEN WITCH: FOOD, FOLKLORE & FAIRYTALE

Sarah Robinson

Welcome to a place of great magic – the kitchen!

Magic, superstition, cooking, and food rituals have been intertwined since the beginning of humankind. *Kitchen Witch: Food, Folklore & Fairy Tale* is an exploration of the history and culture of food, folklore and magic and those skilled in healing and nourishing – herbalists, wise women, cooks, cunning folk and the name many of them would come to bear: witch.

Kitchen Witch is an invitation to see the magic in every corner of your kitchen. With the Kitchen Witch as our guide, we'll explore food, nature, magic, and transformation. We'll discover what the name of Kitchen Witch could mean to us in modern interpretations of ancient practices. May this book of stories and ideas show that there's magic in the mundane, witchcraft within your walls and the Goddess really is in the details.

THE KITCHEN WITCH COMPANION: RECIPES, RITUALS & REFLECTIONS

Sarah Robinson and Lucy H. Pearce

The Kitchen Witch returns in this beautifully illustrated companion book to Sarah Robinson's bestseller *Kitchen Witch: Food, Folklore & Fairy Tale*…

This is a book to be read curled up in a comfy chair, before being covered in earth as you gather in seasonal goodness and splattered with sauce as you cook! The first half of *The Kitchen Witch Companion* is a reflection on the fantasy and reality of making magic in the kitchen. The second half is a seasonal collection of recipes and crafts, foraging and ferments, spells and simmer pots, meditations and blessings to inspire you to create, celebrate and gather throughout the Wheel of the Year.

THE WITCH AND THE WILDWOOD: FOLK WISDOM, FAIRY TALE & FANTASTIC LORE

Sarah Robinson

Welcome to the wildwood, where magic hides in ancient roots. In the hidden shadows amongst the trees, tales of witches are whispered. What is it about the wild that draws us in and has captured our imaginations for so long? *The Witch and The Wildwood* delves into stories of the woods as told through some of its most enchanting inhabitants: witches, fairy folk and magical creatures.

This is an invitation to find enchantment. And why not? Surely, we can all bear a little more magic, and a little more wild in our days. This book is an ode to the untamed spirit that resides within all of us – a reminder that there is magic in the air, ancient wisdom and beauty in the wild.

Let's journey through the wildwood and her spells together…

Prepare to:

- Fall under the spell of the witch maidens, deer-women, she-wolves, 'wild-alones' and women of wild waters who sit in willow trees plotting delicious revenge.
- Meet the real witches of the wildwood, and those who were tried for witchcraft.
- Unearth the common threads that bind the wild woman archetype across time and its explosion of popularity in recent times.
- Explore the fairy and folk tales of the witch that lives in the woods, beckoning you into a world where magic and reality intertwine.